Alien Soil

Ceres: Rutgers Studies in History

Lucia McMahon and Christopher T. Fisher, Series Editors

New Jersey holds a unique place in the American story. One of the thirteen colonies in British North America and one of the original states of the United States, New Jersey plays a central, yet underappreciated, place in America's economic, political, and social development. New Jersey's axial position as the nation's financial, intellectual, and political corridor has become something of a signature, evident in quips about the Turnpike and punch lines that end with its many exits. Yet New Jersey is more than a crossroad or an interstitial "elsewhere." Far from being ancillary to the nation, New Jersey is an axis around which America's story has turned, and within its borders gather a rich collection of ideas, innovations, people, and politics. The region's historical development makes it a microcosm of the challenges and possibilities of the nation, and it also reflects the complexities of the modern, cosmopolitan world. Yet far too little of the literature recognizes New Jersey's significance to the national story, and despite promising scholarship done at the local level, New Jersey history often remains hidden in plain sight.

Ceres books represent new, rigorously peer-reviewed scholarship on New Jersey and the surrounding region. Named for the Roman goddess of prosperity portrayed on the New Jersey State Seal, Ceres provides a platform for cultivating and disseminating the next generation of scholarship. It features the work of both established historians and a new generation of scholars across disciplines. Ceres aims to be field-shaping, providing a home for the newest and best empirical, archival, and theoretical work on the region's past. We are also dedicated to fostering diverse and inclusive scholarship and hope to feature works addressing issues of social justice and activism.

For a complete list of titles in the series, please see the last page of the book.

Alien Soil

Oral Histories of Great Migration Newark

KATIE SINGER

RUTGERS UNIVERSITY PRESS
NEW BRUNSWICK, CAMDEN, AND NEWARK, NEW JERSEY
LONDON AND OXFORD

Rutgers University Press is a department of Rutgers, The State University of New Jersey, one of the leading public research universities in the nation. By publishing worldwide, it furthers the University's mission of dedication to excellence in teaching, scholarship, research, and clinical care.

Library of Congress Cataloging-in-Publication Data

Names: Singer, Katie, 1961– author.
Title: Alien soil : oral histories of Great Migration Newark / Katie Singer.
Other titles: Oral histories of Great Migration Newark
Description: New Brunswick : Rutgers University Press, [2024] | Includes bibliographical references and index.
Identifiers: LCCN 2023047807 | ISBN 9781978833531 (paperback) | ISBN 9781978833548 (hardcover) | ISBN 9781978833555 (epub) | ISBN 9781978833579 (pdf)
Subjects: LCSH: African Americans—New Jersey—Newark—Interviews. | African Americans—New Jersey—Newark—History—20th century. | Newark (N.J.)—Race relations. | Newark (N.J.)—Social conditions—20th century. | Great Migration, ca. 1914–ca. 1970. | Krueger-Scott African-American Cultural Center (Project) | Krueger-Scott Oral History Collection (Rutgers University) | Krueger Scott Mansion (Newark, N.J.)
Classification: LCC F144.N69 B537 2024 | DDC 974.9/32—dc23/eng/20240228
LC record available at https://lccn.loc.gov/2023047807

A British Cataloging-in-Publication record for this book is available from the British Library.

Copyright © 2024 by Katie Singer

All rights reserved

No part of this book may be reproduced or utilized in any form or by any means, electronic or mechanical, or by any information storage and retrieval system, without written permission from the publisher. Please contact Rutgers University Press, 106 Somerset Street, New Brunswick, NJ 08901. The only exception to this prohibition is "fair use" as defined by U.S. copyright law.

References to internet websites (URLs) were accurate at the time of writing. Neither the author nor Rutgers University Press is responsible for URLs that may have expired or changed since the manuscript was prepared.

∞ The paper used in this publication meets the requirements of the American National Standard for Information Sciences—Permanence of Paper for Printed Library Materials, ANSI Z39.48-1992.

rutgersuniversitypress.org

So, in leaving, I was taking a part of the South to transplant in alien soil, to see if it could grow differently, if it could drink of new and cool rains, bend in strange winds, respond to the warmth of other suns, and, perhaps, to bloom.
 —Richard Wright *in* Black Boy: A Record of Childhood and Youth

The black culture's story and the white culture's story are as different as night and day. We share the same sky, the same county and the same air. But our human experience has been as different from one another as you can get.
 —Actor-Director Charles S. Dutton

Contents

Prologue ix

1 The Krueger-Scott Mansion Project 1
  The Mansion 1
  The Oral Histories 37

2 Sundays 39
  Church 39
  Not Just Church 62

3 Workdays 85
  Paid Work 85
  Sociopolitical Work 112

4 Hot Days 129
  The Setup 129
  Rebellion 146

Afterword 169

Appendix 171
Acknowledgments 183
Notes 185
Bibliography 205
Index 209

Prologue

One of the best storytellers of the Great Migration was the painter Jacob Lawrence. In 1941 Lawrence finished a series of sixty paintings, along with simple captions for each one. It would later be called *The Migration Series*. The images he painted, and the captions that he wrote, were based upon stories he learned from family, friends, and people in his neighborhood. It was important to Lawrence to document this historical era, not only to add to the historiography, but because he believed the story was one that would resonate with African Americans for generations to come.

In 1993, in preparation for an upcoming show, Lawrence rewrote his 1941 captions. These new captions, juxtaposed alongside the old, along with his powerful images, taught anyone who wanted to know just what the Great Migration was—and how it transformed the United States in the twentieth century. To provide an overview of the Great Migration here, as foundation for the oral histories to come, I utilize Lawrence's 1993 captions (in quotes, with corresponding panel numbers). I encourage the reader to view the paintings as they read.[1]

"During World War I there was a great migration north by Southern African Americans (1)." There are many explanations as to why African Americans were leaving the South. Most generally, it was for jobs that were becoming ever more available in the industrialized North. But there were also natural disasters contributing to the migration. "Some left because of promises of work in the North. Others left because their farms had been devastated by floods (8)." Or "They left because the boll weevil had ravaged the cotton crop (9)." Prices for basic goods were rising due to these calamities, while "Food had doubled in price because of the war (11)."

African American parents also wanted their children to have better lives. "Their children were forced to work in the fields. They could not go to school (24)." It was also the case that African Americans departed the South for matters of life and death. "There were lynchings (15)," and "After a lynching the migration quickened (16)." The fact that "In the North they had the freedom to vote (59)" was also a draw for many Black Southerners. All in all, there was an urgency to this migration. "Families arrived at the station very early. They did not wish to miss their trains north (21)."

Racist violence was a constant threat in the South, and "For African Americans there was no justice in the southern courts (14)." One facet of Southern injustice was the sharecropping industry, typically keeping families in debt through illicit means. "Tenant farmers received harsh treatment at the hands of planters (17)."

At the same time, police were arresting Black men arbitrarily, building what would become the prison industrial complex, a substitute for the free slave labor the South had lost after emancipation. "Migrants left. They did not feel safe. It was not wise to be found on the streets late at night. They were arrested on the slightest provocation (22)." Thus, "The railroad stations in the South were crowded with northbound travelers (32)."

"The war had caused a labor shortage in northern industry. Citizens of foreign countries were returning to their native lands (2)." Some immigrants chose to fight in their home country's army at the same time that scores of American men were going off to war. With this, African Americans—as well as women—finally enjoyed access to well-paying factory jobs. "All other sources of labor having been exhausted, the migrants were the last resource (4)."

News concerning life in the North was communicated through newspapers such as the *Chicago Defender*. "In many of the communities the Black press was read with great interest (20)." "The black press urged the people to leave the South (34)." Southern whites attempted to mute this call by banning the reading of newspapers and restricting Black press publication. While there was rarely acknowledgment of the foundational reasons behind the African American desire to flee, "In a few sections of the South leaders of both Black and White communities met to discuss ways of making the South a good place to live (43)."

The Great Migration is generally defined as having lasted the first three-quarters of the twentieth century; not everyone left at the same time, or for the same reason. Sometimes "The African American professionals were forced to follow their clients in order to make a living (56)," even as they were already typically well established in their communities. "In every southern home people met to decide whether or not to go north (30)." They heard continuing reports from multiple sources, "And people all over the South continued to discuss this great movement (26)." Some of this information came from written correspondence by those who had already relocated. "Letters from relatives in the North told of the better life there (33)." At other times these tales were exaggerated in order to encourage family and friends to join; yet practical information regarding pay scales and job availability was typically provided. These letters would be passed around the same way that newspapers were shared, creating communication networks throughout the South.

"From every southern town migrants left by the hundreds to travel north (3)." This was not always an easy decision. In the first place, money was usually limited; choices had to be made as to who would go first and who might follow later. "The female workers were the last to arrive north (57)," quite often continuing to take in laundry, do domestic work, or keep up the farm while they waited. "They were very poor (10)." Sometimes families refused to be separated. After all, due to slavery, many had only recently enjoyed the opportunity to reunite. So, "many men stayed behind until they could take their families north with them (27)."

Whites resisted this exodus for myriad reasons. "To make it difficult for the migrants to leave, they were arrested en masse. They often missed their trains (42)," which had typically been paid for ahead of time, such that aspiring travelers would have to start saving all over again. More violence and trickery ensued in the face of what scholars now refer to as the largest protest movement ever. Southern whites began to realize just how much they had relied on African American labor. "The crops were left to dry and rot. There was no one to tend them (13)." In states like South Carolina and Mississippi, neighborhoods turned to ghost towns. "They left their homes. Soon some communities were left almost empty (25)."

Occasionally, "Migrants were advanced passage on the railroads, paid for by northern industry. Northern industry was to be repaid by the migrants out of their future wages (5)." To some this practice echoed the sharecropping system, but for many it was the only way they were able to leave. "The labor agent sent south by northern industry was a familiar presence in Black communities (28)." At times these agents faced the same violence the migrants endured. "The South was desperate to keep its cheap labor. Northern labor agents were jailed or forced to operate in secrecy (41)." This did not mean they were all there on altruistic missions. "The labor agent recruited unsuspecting laborers as strike breakers for northern industries (29)." Some African Americans found themselves used as pawns in Northern labor-management conflicts, and once the war had ended those jobs were reclaimed by returning soldiers.

"The trains were crowded with migrants (6)." And sometimes, simply wherever the train stopped is where they got off: Chicago, Pittsburgh, Detroit, Newark.[2] "The migration spread (23)." The journey was often treacherous. "The railroad stations were at times so crowded with people leaving that special guards had to be called to keep order (12)." Racist transportation policies of the South resulted in African American travelers herded into cramped Jim Crow cars, banned from moving about the train. Southern "Railroad platforms were piled high with luggage (39)," luggage that was often stored in the same cars where the Black passengers rode. Thus, standing room only was often the case until the trains crossed into the North, where segregation was less prevalent and some freedom of movement became available.

"There had always been discrimination (19)," so no matter these hardships, "The migration gained in momentum (18)." According to James N. Gregory in his book *The Southern Diaspora: How the Great Migration of Black and White Southerners Transformed America*, by the end of the 1920s more than 1.2 million African Americans had migrated.[3] "They left the South in great numbers. They arrived in the North in great numbers (35)."

"The migrant, whose life had been rural and nurtured by the earth, was now moving to urban life dependent on industrial machinery (7)." Even those who simply moved from the country to the city within their own Southern state experienced culture shock. But for migrants making the long trip east, north, and sometimes west, they were met with a landscape of stark contrasts. Initially, "The migrants found improved housing when they arrived north (31)." However, this did not remain the case as the decades ensued.

"The migrants arrived in great numbers (40)," and as this mass movement continued, the areas of the cities relegated to African Americans became overcrowded. "As the migrant population grew, good housing became scarce. Workers were forced to live in overcrowded and dilapidated tenement houses (47)." Employers had promised Southern migrants housing along with work, but often "Industries boarded their workers in unhealthy quarters. Labor camps were numerous (46)." So "Housing was a serious problem (48)," and throughout the cities tenement neighborhoods appeared. "The migrants, having moved suddenly into a crowded and unhealthy environment soon contracted tuberculosis. The death rate rose (55)." "But living conditions were better in the North (44)," and flourishing Black communities coalesced among the city blocks. Eventually, some "African Americans seeking to find better housing attempted to move into new areas. This resulted in the bombing of their new homes (51)." The growth of the Ku Klux Klan soared in the North. But, as Jacob Lawrence writes in the caption for his last painting in the series, "And the migrants kept coming (60)."

Some "Migrants arrived in Chicago, the gateway to the West (36)." The Windy City was thoroughly transformed by the migration, becoming a renowned cultural mecca of Black life. Davarian Baldwin's *Chicago's New Negroes: Modernity, the Great Migration, and Black Urban Life* paints a picture of what this historical era looked like in the city; the Black Renaissance, he argues, did not take place only in Harlem.[4] Still, "They found discrimination in the North. It was a different kind (49)." And "Race riots were numerous. White workers were hostile toward the migrant who had been hired to break strikes (50)," for example. The summer of 1919, often called Red Summer because of the many violent uprisings, profoundly affected Chicago and other industrialized cities. "One of the most violent race riots occurred in East St. Louis (52)."

"Many migrants found work in the steel industry (37)" for the first time during World War I. "The migrants arrived in Pittsburgh, one of the great industrial centers of the North (45)." The work was hard, and African Americans were typically assigned the most difficult and dangerous jobs. "They also worked on the railroads (38)," first on the tracks and later, famously, as porters. One of the many contributions of the Great Migration was the growth of union activity for African Americans. In 1935, A. Philip Randolph helped organize the first official Black union, representing the mostly male Black employees of the Pullman Company, which operated the sleeping cars on trains.

This self-determination in the Northern migrant sometimes resulted in a disregard for their Southern counterparts. "African Americans, long-time residents of northern cities, met the migrants with aloofness and disdain (53)." In part because "in the North the African American had more educational opportunities (58)," there was a way in which some Northern transplants characterized the newly arrived Southerners as ignorant and unrefined. This rift is highlighted in Davarian Baldwin's book within the paradigm of "old and new settlers."[5] And Amiri Baraka, in his book *Blues People: Negro Music in White America*, also speaks to the differences between those who had arrived first to the Northeast and the migrants who came up later, still unfamiliar with the ways of their new world.[6]

One thing that held consistent during this time was that "For the migrants, the church was the center of life (54)." This would change slightly as the decades passed, but in those beginning years the church was the familiar and comforting community center within alien urban spaces for most everybody. The church provided many required services, from job placement to funerals.

Another way in to really understanding the Great Migration is through the voices of those who lived it. Newark, New Jersey, is fortunate enough to have its own Great Migration history, recorded in the Krueger-Scott African-American Oral History Collection. This is a set of 107 interviews of Newarkers, most conducted in 1997. This project was meant to be a part of a larger mission to create an African American cultural center in Newark. Oftentimes the interviewers referenced the fact that the interviews—and assorted collected memorabilia—would be archived in this center. Unfortunately, the center never came to fruition. More on that tale will follow.

This oral history project, facilitated by peers, and directed by fellow Newarkers, was an invaluable labor of love for the city, and for the country more generally. It was also a very intentional statement of representation. African Americans have been the majority demographic in Newark for a very long time, yet the efforts to preserve and highlight their extensive history have been surprisingly limited. This oral history collection contains individual stories, while providing an expansive illustration of the great influence that Black Newarkers had on their city.

One important facet of this collection is its inclusion of people from varied walks of life—with varied experiences and varied opinions. It challenges the sometimes monolithic perspective presented to the public regarding the "Black community." A lot has happened since the time these oral histories were recorded. When I began working with fellow graduate students to digitize these narratives, years had already gone by, and most every one of the interviewees had passed on. Even the historians who launched this valuable project have passed—prematurely and to many people's great sorrow.

My relationship with these interviews began in 2011 when I was just beginning my PhD program at Rutgers University–Newark. A fellow student had uncovered the cassette tapes at the public library and was hoping to get some help in preserving them digitally before they completely disintegrated. I jumped at the chance to help as my focus has always been on foregrounding the voices of African Americans—whether that be in the teaching of a literature class or participating in community activism.

By the time I began writing this book, I had listened to and annotated each interview numerous times. They are central to the history I share here, a story I do not tell but actually present—through the stories of people whose lives are the foundation of this important historical era. Newark is an important city to me, due in large part to these interviews. I became increasingly involved in community activities and local public history inspired by the stories I heard and the people I became familiar with through these recordings. I attended lectures at the Newark Historical Society; showed up at the Abbot Leadership Institute on Saturday mornings; and was a consultant for the 350th Anniversary Fundraising Committee, all while studying and teaching at Rutgers University–Newark. I was trying both to learn from and contribute to Newark. All the way across the country now, without these oral histories I would be bereft of my relationship with the city of Newark. I present them here, in part, so that the reader too might enjoy the depth and breadth of what Newark has to offer, historically as well as presently.

Alien Soil

CHAPTER 1

The Krueger-Scott Mansion Project

The Mansion

In order to introduce the oral histories, I must first introduce you to the place where they were meant to reside: Newark, New Jersey's Krueger-Scott Mansion. In understanding the Mansion, it is necessary to learn something about the city within which it stands. Just as when Confederate monuments and their tall tales are toppled, the greater public is learning the importance of place-making stories that can help unravel confusing history. And this country certainly has its share of confusing history.

The Krueger-Scott Mansion restoration project of the 1980s and 1990s offers a view of Newark—and urban centers more generally—at a transitional moment. Newark was launching one of its "renaissances," as a site of renewed commerce and culture, once again endeavoring to shrug off the mantle of despair placed upon its shoulders by decades past. Yet even as glistening buildings arose and notable awards were received, the Newark experience remained, for many of its people, one of continued poverty and racial inequality.

And Newark was not alone. Many cities were in turmoil by the 1970s. Residents of higher socioeconomic status were making their way out of the cities, and so were some of the better-paying manufacturing jobs. This exodus to suburban and rural areas, and the Sun Belt, led to sharp increases in poverty, particularly in older industrial areas, such as Newark or Detroit. In fact, the most distressed cities became even worse off during the 1970s. Cities like Cleveland and St. Louis began the decade already burdened with a concentration of poverty and unemployment, and then only became increasingly worse off. This trend affected many of the nation's largest urban areas, including Philadelphia and Newark.[1] By 1980 the heightened severity of social and economic problems set these places apart from other cities.

1

It was at this moment in Newark's history that the idea was presented to build a center in the primarily Black Central Ward that would pay homage to the city's African American history. Other wards already had such sites, like that housed in the historic Clark Mansion, dedicated to the primarily Italian American population remaining in Newark's North Ward post-1967. And it was time, many thought, for Black citizens to have a center of their own, one that served the community while also preserving and highlighting their history. What better place than the Krueger-Scott Mansion, last owned by Louise Scott, a Black millionaire entrepreneur and philanthropist? As social chaos, and economic mobility was increasing for African Americans nationwide in the 1980s, the Mansion's most recent history aligned with a growing attention to Black history, culture, and commerce. It was time to publicize the importance of African Americans to Newark's history, and to America's history more broadly.

The proposed Krueger-Scott African-American Cultural Center had as its mission to tell the stories of Newark's Black history through the oral history project, collected memorabilia, and public programming. It was hoped that the Cultural Center would provide a bridge to the yawning gaps in the sociohistorical understanding of Newark, from within the city and without. This trend of historical insertion began nationwide in the 1960s when a boon of "grassroots" African American museums "exclusively devoted to the collection, conservation, and display of black history and culture" began appearing throughout the United States.[2]

Chicago's DuSable Museum of African American History, for example—considered the first Black museum in America—began in 1961 in the basement of the home of Margaret and Charles Burroughs. In Detroit, four years later, Charles H. Wright, a Black physician, helped form the International Afro-American Museum (IAM). The IAM established numerous sites of Black historical commemoration within Detroit, and eventually culminated in the Charles H. Wright Museum of African American History in 1998. The movement continued with institutions such as Charlotte, North Carolina's Harvey B. Gantt Center. In 1978, African American museums passed the one hundred mark, and the African American Museums Association (AAMA) was created. The AAMA includes "educational institutions, research agencies and cultural centers" and works as an "advocate for the interests of institutions and individuals committed to the support of African and African derived cultures."[3]

While Newark may have been a bit behind in the cause, the idea of Black cultural preservation was a guiding force for the Krueger-Scott Cultural Center, at least in the initial proposal. Just as Detroit's Museum of African American History, for example, "became a cultural representation for black political power and black control in the city," the Krueger-Scott Mansion project was intended to do the same.[4] Many Newarkers started working tirelessly in an effort to foreground African American history in their city. But it was not always easy to convince those in power that such representation was actually necessary.

Gertrude Fraser and Reginald Butler argue in their chapter, "Anatomy of Disinterment: The Unmaking of Afro-American History," that because Blacks and whites have had different experiences throughout American history, that the two groups tend toward "contrasting views of history." However, there is one approach common among both races, and that is the practice of "great persons" history-telling. Fraser and Butler observe that social history (also known as lived experience) has had little effect on most of us because we are trained—as students and citizens—to pay attention to and see value in the accounts of "important" people, but not the everyday. With this in mind, the authors looked at an abandoned African American graveyard in Virgina, implicitly rejected as a site of American history, left to decline. Fraser and Butler conclude that an "emphasis on the material poverty of the Afro-American graveyard implied a parallel poverty of historical importance."[5] In other words, if something is falling apart—say, a Victorian mansion in Newark, New Jersey, last owned by a Black millionaire—then it might not be all that important to begin with.

This battle for the documentation of African American life has been a difficult one. Beginning in 1988, the late congressman and longtime civil rights activist John Lewis began lobbying for a national museum of African American history. Twenty-five years later, the Smithsonian's National Museum of African American History and Cultural (NMAAHC) became a reality.[6] And there is a Newark connection there, too. The city's own historian, the late Dr. Clement A. Price, was on the Museum planning board, along with Newark native Lonnie Bunch, who also served as director of the Museum for many years. Mr. Bunch is now the secretary of the Smithsonian Institution—the first African American (and first historian) to serve as head of the institution. What the blazing pioneers of this historical commemoration project shared was an urgency to arrest the erasure of Black history, and to prioritize the storytellers who knew and lived it. But, place-making stories can be histories in themselves, and creating such a space in Newark, New Jersey, proved to be a complicated one.

One of the many complicating factors surrounding Newark's Krueger-Scott African-American Cultural Center project was that the Mansion did not "belong" to any one group. While the house itself may have been owned by the city at that point, by the time the Center was proposed, many folks from disparate groups were invested in the project's outcome. This could be seen either as a boon, or as too many cooks in the proverbial kitchen. In order to chronicle the Krueger-Scott project, and the varied attitudes toward its completion, it helps to know the backstory of the grand "Castle on the Hill."[7]

The Backstory

Gottfried Krueger (1888–1925). The Krueger-Scott story begins with Gottfried Krueger, a German immigrant who came to Newark a poor man. He soon opened his eponymous beer company and soon thereafter became a very rich man. Among the Krueger brewery's claims to fame was its invention of the beer can.[8] With all his newfound wealth, in 1888 Mr. Krueger built himself an opulent Victorian home at 601 High Street.[9] There were forty-three rooms, some with leather-covered walls. The home included a bowling alley, a Bavarian-style tower, a copper roof, the first elevator in a Newark home, and a stable. Krueger subsequently built homes for his two daughters on the same block, the whole family living side by side in stately luxury.

After a long (and at times harrowing) life, in 1925 Herr Krueger, at eighty-eight years old, and his invalid wife decided that the family would leave Newark and move permanently to their summer home in Allenhurst, New Jersey. The magnificent High Street mansion was sold to the Valley of the Scottish Rite Freemasons. Gottfried Krueger died the following year.[10]

The Masons (1925–1958). The Scottish Rite of Freemasonry is one of several rites (series of degrees) conferred by the Freemasons fraternal organization, which began in Charleston, South Carolina, in 1801. The Newark Masons' literature promoted their new castle-like setting as reflective of their significant membership and noble endeavors. In 1929, the Masons added a 580-seat auditorium, located between the Mansion and the stable, probably utilized for some of their traditionally larger gatherings such as the semiannual degree "communications."[11]

As years went on, the heavy foot traffic caused by the Masons' numerous social activities began to compromise the aging Victorian structure. Such a house was in constant need of repair, and it became increasingly challenging for the Masons to keep it up. The Krueger Mansion was no longer receiving the attention it needed. Meanwhile, the Masons' membership was declining, and the organization had begun eyeing property in the suburbs, hopeful that with more acreage and a less urban setting they could revitalize their membership. In 1958, the Masons relocated to Livingston, New Jersey.[12]

The fact was that at this point in time white residents were slowly abandoning the High Street area, as well as its surrounding upscale neighborhoods. Indeed, they had been leaving Newark and other burgeoning urban centers across the country for the past few decades. It was a matter of both push and pull. Many incentives were being offered by banks, realtors, and the federal government to entice certain people to head to the suburbs. Concurrently, warnings were sounded regarding decreasing property values and high crime rates in the cities. The suburbs began to flourish.

THE KRUEGER-SCOTT MANSION PROJECT

Figure 1.1. From Masons' "Newark Consistory," "Castle Newark," Krueger-Scott Mansion Media File. Photo by kind permission from the personal collection of Clarence E. Brunner.

In Newark, in place of the departing white residents, came more African Americans—most a part of the continuing Great Migration. Black Southerners had been rejecting the many restrictions that accompanied their supposed freedom post-emancipation and, as Eric Arnesen writes in *Black Protest and the Great Migration*, "black southerners registered their discontent through geographical migration."[13] Unfair pay, stolen profits, and continuing violence made up the New South (although these circumstances were certainly not limited to the South). The Jim Crow system pervaded the lives of every African American in some way, shape, or form.

Notably, Great Migration participants make up the majority of the people interviewed for the Krueger-Scott African-American Oral History Project, although a few of the families were already residing in Newark, including on High Street. Black High Street residents were doctors, funeral directors, and other professionals who had the means to afford the real estate, and the wherewithal to ignore the attitudes (and worse) by those still not prepared to have a Black person living next door. At this mid-century moment of transition in the city's history, the Krueger Mansion becomes the Krueger-Scott Mansion.

Louise Scott (1958–1983). Enter Louise Scott, beauty culture entrepreneur and millionaire, Newark's own Madam C. J. Walker.[14] Mrs. Scott, born around 1905,

Figure 1.2. Apex Colleges ad, *Crisis*, January 1938.

was a part of the Great Migration. Scott left a small town in South Carolina in 1936 and, along with so many other African American women, began earning money in New York City doing domestic "day's work."[15] By night Scott was attending the Apex Beauty School, from which she graduated in 1938. That same year she moved to Barclay Street in Newark.

Newark at that time was suffering through the Depression along with the rest of the country. In 1938, when Louise Scott arrived, the Works Progress Administration (WPA) was creating jobs for the many disemployed. In Newark, WPA jobs included an extension to Branch Brook Park, the construction of a swimming pool on Boylan Avenue, and the creation of an administration building at Newark Airport.[16] By this time, almost one-half of African Americans nationwide were either "on relief" (i.e. welfare) or working for the WPA. But African Americans were discriminated against even within this initiative, rarely attaining the same level of employment or pay as whites. In addition, the "last hired, first fired" principle remained in effect in factories and other workplaces, an automatic strike against Black laborers who had only recently been able to secure such lucrative work.[17] Newark's now majority African American Third Ward, the location of the Krueger Mansion, would be the last of the wards to recover post-Depression.[18] Fortunately, for the nation's economy at least, a Second World War would soon follow.

Louise Scott opened her first business, the Scott Beauty Salon, in Newark in 1944. She subsequently launched several more salons and then instituted training programs for stylists. She also introduced her own line of beauty products, once again emulating Madam C. J. Walker. Over the next ten years the Scott Hotel at 565 High Street, and the Scott Restaurant were added to her business empire.[19] "Madam Scott," as she was known to many, quickly established herself as a leader in the Black community. She was ultimately feted at a 1957 gathering at the Terrace Ballroom, a downtown establishment frequented by Newark's upwardly mobile African Americans. At the testimonial dinner, community leaders and politicians lauded her as an advocate for the Black community and a groundbreaking entrepreneur.[20] Hers was a Great Migration success story.

Seeking an opportunity to consolidate her many businesses with her community work, Louise Scott purchased the Krueger Mansion from the Scottish Rite Masons in 1958, with cash. Much is made of the fact that a single woman was able to purchase such a large home with cash, but this was not necessarily simply a show of great wealth. It is said by some that the Masons did not want to sell the home to an African American, only acquiescing once the cash was offered.[21] It is also possible that Scott was unable to secure a bank loan, due to commonplace racist—and sexist—lending policies. At any rate, a *Newark Evening News* article in September of 1958 reported that Scott planned to create a "neighborhood house" in the Mansion, "open to all persons, regardless of creed or color." She also had plans "to organize a 200-member choir," according to the article, transferring "the Sunday religious program she now conducts at her hotel to the 700-seat auditorium that adjoins the mansion."[22] The Mansion was returning to life.

Within the Scott Cultural and Civic Center housed in the Mansion on High Street, Madam Scott established a beauty school, a day care facility for her students' children, and a hotel.[23] In the auditorium, live radio shows such as Bernice Bass's political *News and Views* were aired in front of an audience. In 1961, Scott established the Good Neighbor Baptist Church on the Mansion grounds. Louise Scott had established herself as a pillar of her community, an inspiration to Black residents of the city, and an activist for those still in need.

The mid-century trend toward increased opportunity for African Americans in cities nationwide was due in part to the aforementioned departure of white residents. One of those opportunities came in the form of housing. With white urban residents flocking to the new suburbs, urban housing stock

Figure 1.3. Krueger-Scott Mansion, circa 1960. Courtesy Newark Public Library. The sign reads "Scott's College of Beauty Culture."

became more available, and prices decreased. "The share of metropolitan white households living in the suburbs increased from approximately one-third in 1940 to two-thirds in 1980. Over the same period, the rate of homeownership among black households living in central cities more than doubled from 15 percent to 42 percent.... By mid-century, metropolitan areas like Detroit, Cleveland, Pittsburgh, and Chicago had substantial black populations living in their central cores."[24] And so did Newark.

There was a sense of shifting authority in cities that had for so long been run by, and mostly for, whites. Homeownership was a stake in the ground for African Americans, an investment in a community that brought with it increased engagement in local politics and culture. In Newark, Italian American Mayor Hugh Addonizio gave the perception of being open to the needs of his burgeoning Black constituency. Yet while the 1950s brought one of Newark's major renaissances, in large part due to the expansion of downtown's Prudential Insurance Company, this had little to no effect on the preponderance of Black residents of the city. They were still barred from most construction jobs associated with all that new development and continued to meet with numerous obstacles when applying for corporate-level employment. In addition, even as homeownership increased for African Americans, the housing structures were deteriorating in the majority-Black neighborhoods, such as those of the Central Ward (previously the Third Ward).[25] Purchasing a home and then being able to maintain that home are two very different things. Meanwhile, various high-rise housing projects were being hastily constructed in response to the overwhelming need for shelter.

Mary Roberts, a retired Newark Public Schools teacher and onetime district leader of the South Ward, explained in her Krueger-Scott African-American Oral History Project interview that when she arrived in Newark in 1961, "everybody was happy... it was so beautiful you could just go anyplace... everybody seemed so on one accord."[26] While the city was certainly progressing, both economically and in terms of reputation, Mary Roberts's experience was not universal. And the same issues remain today, as downtown Newark's revitalization thrives at the same time that neighborhood schools remain overcrowded, and the water in some parts of the city is deemed unsafe to drink.

Looking Forward

Consciousness Shifts (1960s). In 1966, the city of Newark initiated a tax action against the Krueger-Scott Mansion's Scott Civic and Cultural Center and its owner, Louise Scott. That same year Madam Scott sold the Mansion auditorium to the religious organization Range's Temple for one dollar.[27] This sale does not necessarily indicate that Scott was in financial need; it may have simply been another act of philanthropy for the Black community. At the same time, in selling the auditorium, Scott would no longer be financially responsible for its upkeep. Whatever Scott's motivation, this was the beginning of a path of financial steps that would take the Mansion into the 1990s, consistently on precarious ground.

The city's tax action coincided with the pressure that urban centers nationwide were feeling to build more middle-income housing. A lot of stock could fit on that land occupied by just one big mansion. Newark was a microcosm of the national postindustrial urban experience, mirroring the aggressive development occurring in so many cities, and later reflecting the resulting problems of all that so-called progress.

As Beryl Satter writes in *Family Properties: How the Struggle over Race and Real Estate Transformed Chicago and Urban America*, "conservation" and "community" groups started becoming urban renewal organizations. In Chicago, the Greater Lawndale Conservation Commission (GLCC), on a quest for what was called middle-class housing, sponsored a development group to "acquire vacant land... build middle-class housing... and then market the units interracially." Satter argues that this project was initiated with the intent of reducing the number of Black residents, the idea being that development would reinvigorate neighborhoods that had been all but abandoned over the years, thus making them more attractive to new white residents. And it turned out that quite often those already living in these neighborhoods could not afford to move into the new, purportedly middle-income housing anyway. Yet others who could afford to buy often did not want to live in the kinds of neighborhoods where this new housing was being constructed.[28] Whether Chicago, Detroit, St. Louis, or Newark, changing demographics and an urgent need for housing collided in ways that ultimately disadvantaged urban Black residents.

This complicated time wound up creating some strange urban bedfellows. In Newark, it meant the intermingling of preservationists, politicians, activists, and ordinary people who would spend the next forty years battling over the life of the Krueger-Scott Mansion, over the value of the High Street neighborhood, and over rights to the city itself. Within this scrum were many bent on reclaiming the cultural and historical aspects of Black Newark, and the economic benefits that should have accompanied the city's growth. Somewhere between factions of economics and culture stood Newark's Krueger-Scott Mansion.

The Mansion was the proverbial elephant described very differently by each individual in a group of blind men. The edifice symbolized an outdated Newark for some, a point away from which the city needed to move. Others saw the house as a reflection of the long history of the people who came to Newark and who were in large part responsible for what it had become—a modernized city of culture, trade, and learning. The Mansion's beauty—and value—were in the eye of the beholder. Lou Danzig, Newark Housing Authority (NHA) director, declared it a "monstrosity" in 1966 at one particularly contentious public hearing. At the same meeting, J. Stewart Johnson, curator for the Newark Museum and president of the Victorian Society of America, argued for the protection of the Mansion, out of respect for the city's early history. "We are destroying the 19th century here as fast as we possibly can," he warned.[29]

Longtime Newarkers once again saw the writing on their neighborhood walls, this time regarding the High Street area. The familiar formula was there: first, the city would "blight" the area, then with limited (if any) public discussion it would negotiate a development plan. Only afterward would those in the affected area learn that they would have to relocate. Edna Thomas, secretary of the Scudder Homes Association, a housing project in the High Street area that was ultimately demolished in 1987, attended that November hearing where the fate of the High Street neighborhood was being hotly debated. She had already tried to warn her homeowning neighbors in the area about the city's plans. In her 1996 oral history interview, Mrs. Thomas recalled:

> They tried to steal it from them about thirty years ago.... The Housing Authority. The Mandelbaum Associates wanted to buy it. I went and knocked on the doors to tell them who was going to sell it. They were going to take their property. So I told them don't say anything, come to a meeting tomorrow, and wear old clothes and just don't say anything. So they came. And they sat there at the Housing Authority right with me and listened to what was planned for their house. And they were utterly shocked. And they did not sell their property.[30]

Only because of an insider tip did these particular homeowners not have their property pulled out from under them. They were the exception.

Amid all the debate regarding the Mansion's future—and housing issues more generally—in 1967 Madam Louise Scott became Mrs. Scott-Rountree, marrying the Reverend Malachi Rountree. There were apparently some in Newark who were concerned that the young man married Madam Scott for money as well as love. And later, various distant members of the family would be accused of participating in the selling of valuable items from the Mansion's interior—as well as stealing the rent monies intended for tax payments. No official complaints were ever lodged.

The year 1967 was an important one in national urban political history, and not just because of the spate of infamous summer rebellions. If one had to choose a single unifying issue during this political season, it may well have been that of housing. Looking past the "riots" themselves, to the causes and effects of these rebellions, will provide a more detailed context for understanding these events. Inadequate housing was one such factor. The national uprisings came at a transitional moment when multiple urban community groups were banding together across the country. And whether sporting dashikis or three-piece suits, they were bent on changing the quality of Black life in America. That mission predictably engendered some resistance.

While these 1960s uprisings are often reported as originating from conflicts between law enforcement and the citizenry, there were decades of backstory to each one. Whether in Detroit, Birmingham, Chicago, or Minneapolis, the proverbial powder keg had just been waiting for a light. Milwaukee provides one example of the simmering frustration and utter distrust of local officials that city residents were experiencing across the country. According to the Wisconsin Historical Society: "City laws in Milwaukee had supported segregated neighborhoods for decades when Alderperson Vel Phillips introduced open housing legislation in March 1962. For the next five years, the Common Council voted it down every time she re-introduced it, and black families remained legally confined in a ghetto on the city's north side. When police put down a disturbance there on July 30, 1967, riots broke out that left four people dead and more than 1,500 arrested."[31] It is summer, your living conditions are subpar, complaints have fallen on deaf ears, and you are tired of the constant surveillance by police in your neighborhood. Then comes yet another unprovoked attack by a police officer on an African American. In many places, this was the formula for rebellion.

Since the emancipation of the enslaved on United States soil, citizens of African descent have been tasked with closing gaps created by racist political and social systems. The Black church, as we will read later, was one of the first examples of Black community formally organizing in order to garner that which was not rightfully provided. Due to ongoing systemic racial inequities, throughout history philanthropists like Newark's Louise Scott have felt called to make up for what was missing in their marginalized and underserved communities.[32] There are many examples of this kind of self-determination as portrayed by Scott and other successful Black Newark residents. Whether providing health care or housing, employment or education, African Americans with resources in this country have quite often been the glue holding their communities together. But by the 1960s, this arrangement had become unacceptable to many. And when formal negotiations proved fruitless, people took to the streets.

Baby Steps (1970s–1980s). The urban preservation movement began to take shape in the late 1800s, but it was still not a part of the national dialogue circa the mid-twentieth century. This is due in part to the ongoing tensions between those who wanted to preserve structures for history's sake and those who believed it most important to provide housing for the here and now. In 1973, the Newark Preservation and Landmarks Committee (NPLC) was formed, and the first board of trustees was appointed by Newark's first African American mayor, Ken Gibson—along with the Chamber of Commerce. The board included two African Americans, William Ashby and E. Alma Flagg.[33]

The "New Newark" era of the 1970s was busy emphasizing downtown development, while historic buildings such as the Old Essex County Prison in the Central Ward sat abandoned.[34] Outside the central business district, neighborhoods became landscapes of empty buildings. Vacant synagogues sat on swaths of unkempt land, and stately homes went up for sale, too heavy a burden for the owners due to tax increases and property depreciation. It was a race against time and demolition to preserve even a few of Newark's historical landmarks.

In 1979, the Krueger-Scott Mansion was still in fair condition, although it had suffered a fire on the third floor that "damaged the structure's heating system" and "destroyed the dome's crystal skylight." The following year the City of Newark made its first investment in the Mansion's preservation, approving a $50,000 grant for "emergency repairs." The Mansion had finally made its way into the conversation already surrounding several local historic preservation efforts. "Mrs. Scott is to be admired for holding onto the mansion for so long," said Margaret Mandhart of the Newark Preservation and Landmarks Committee in 1981.[35] The hope was that Scott's hard work would not be in vain.

On April 21, 1983, Madam Louise Scott passed away. Her funeral made the headline of the *New Jersey Afro-American* newspaper, displacing even the death of famed jazz pianist Earl "Fatha" Hines. Scott lay in state in the Great Hall of the Krueger-Scott Mansion, where Gottfried Krueger's body had supposedly been displayed some fifty-seven years before. "Hundreds of citizens" attended the viewing.[36]

The ensuing year became one of logistical and financial chaos for the Krueger-Scott Mansion, as 1984 brought what were initially private negotiations— between the Scott family and the city regarding the Mansion's financial

Figure 1.4. Ulysses Grant Dietz, Elizabeth Del Tufo, and Richard Grossklauss, at Krueger Mansion, Newark, June 7, 1984,. Courtesy Newark Public Library.

liabilities—into the public arena. Newspaper articles and gossip abounded. Occupants remained at the Mansion's Scott Hotel, which the *Star-Ledger* was now calling an "unlicensed boarding home." The boarders' rent was to have defrayed the property taxes, but payments had apparently not reached City Hall for quite some time. In fact, the city had officially foreclosed on the property in 1982 but, citing respect for Madam Scott, delayed the process. Eventually, twenty tenants were evicted from the High Street property and the city took ownership in March of 1984.[37] The Scott-Rountree family temporarily maintained right of possession of the Mansion such that the city allowed them continued access to the home. This decision was based in part on confusion around the terms of jurisdiction, according to some sources.

By this time the Mansion had been relieved of most of its valuable interior possessions. Stained-glass panels, mahogany finials, and whole fireplaces had made their way out of the home. Some items even showed up later at Sotheby's auction house. This pillaging was not to be blamed on the neighborhood folk either, according to those with information on the situation. Many saw it as an inside job.

As squatters began making their homes in the grand structure, the City of Newark was initially unresponsive. Meanwhile, local historians, preservationists, and members of the community continued their outcry to save the structure. That same year, representatives of various interest groups toured the Mansion with a photographer from the *Star-Ledger* newspaper. Photos were published of the visitors stepping over piles of fallen concrete and walking up stairways with missing banisters. At this juncture, teams were beginning to form: the preservationists, the renovators, and the developers. Sometimes they cooperated, other times they competed. Frustration was setting in for those who wanted to save the place, as well as for those who were ready to see it demolished.

One of many issues that reflects the complicated nature of this project was that if any kind of cleanup were going to occur, the electricity would need to be restored. But no one could seem to get the city to reinstate power to the building. Each time community members inquired at City Hall, including to offer their help on the project, they were simply shepherded from one office to another until they got tired and went home. It always seemed to be someone else's responsibility.[38] The City of Newark, like so many struggling urban centers across the U.S., was focused more on development than preservation at the moment. Development projects were what potential investors and prospective businesses wanted to see before handing over their money. The restoration of a Victorian mansion blocks away from the commercial center did not fit into that plan. As a result, private organizations with resources were continually being tapped to take on community preservation projects. Yet not one stepped up to support the Mansion's refurbishment.

It was now Mayor Ken Gibson's fourth term in office, and his honeymoon was most assuredly over. Newark may have elected its first Black mayor, but the

Figure 1.5. Newark Councilman George Branch leads a tour of the Krueger Mansion, Newark, to generate some interest in restoring the landmark, 1989. (A later structural report would warn that the stairs should not be accessed under any condition until rebuilt.) *Star-Ledger*, Newark, NJ. Courtesy Newark Public Library.

city was still far outside the vision set by the Black and Puerto Rican Convention, which had rallied to get Gibson into office in the first place. As Robert Homes and Richard Roper write in their book *A Mayor for All the People: Kenneth Gibson's Newark*, Gibson's reputation became conflated with Newark's reputation, and neither deserved the onslaught of negativity. The authors even suggest a parallel to President Obama's election here: Mayor Gibson's position as "first" came with unreasonable expectations of what could be accomplished by one man. After all, Newark's position as a "rust belt city" had been a long time in the making, and no one administration was going to turn everything around after just a few terms in office.[39]

Meanwhile, back on what was now known as Dr. Martin Luther King Jr. Boulevard, the restoration of the Krueger-Scott Mansion was beginning—if only in word. In February of 1985, the *Star-Ledger* published a brief update on the project, including references to a number of proposals regarding use of the space. This appears to be the first time that the idea of a specifically African American cultural center was introduced. Edna Thomas, the community activist who had warned her neighbors about eminent domain threats in their neighborhood, told the *Ledger* she had submitted "a package" proposing the Mansion be devoted to Black history and culture. However, City Council President Ralph Grant was quoted in the same article as saying he had seen no "hard data" on any proposed project.[40] This was a foreshadowing of the back and forth dis-communications that would come to represent the Mansion's restoration process.

In fact, a plan had been written and the city was in receipt of it. Entitled "A Plan to Restore the Krueger-Scott Mansion into the Newark Library & Museum of Black Culture," it was drafted in August 1984 by the Central Ward Coalition of Youth Agencies, of which Edna Thomas was chair. Thomas would later say, in explaining the need for such a center, "We as black people ... have no place to hang our pictures."[41] This sentiment echoes repeatedly throughout the oral histories. And we need only think of the National Museum of African American History and Culture's long journey to fruition, all so that African Americans would have someplace to hang their pictures—as well as store their artifacts and tell their stories.

In the Central Ward Coalition's proposal, the merits of Black cultural institutions as promoters of self-esteem in Black youth were argued. The proposal contended that through the introduction to young people of the history and culture of African Americans—so often absent in the classroom and mainstream media—that positive behavior and community responsibility would come to the fore. This was the same thesis that many prospective Black history museums were presenting in the 1960s and '70s when soliciting support for their proposed institutions. In a city that was, at this point, 62 percent African American and whose population had a median age of twenty-seven, the coalition contended that a Black cultural institution would make a powerful impact on the city itself.[42]

Many in Newark also saw the Mansion project as a means of preserving a history that illustrated the centrality of Black people to Newark. Throughout the city, statues and monuments of white historical actors were ubiquitous, but some of the few commemorations of Black Newarkers were tied to the 1967 uprising. An entrepreneur and philanthropist, Louise Scott's story was the perfect antidote, it was argued. An air of hopefulness surrounded the project for this moment; for one thing, Sharpe James, an outspoken proponent of Black business and culture, and supporter of the Mansion project, was now South Ward councilman. (And the next year he would become mayor.)

In the spring of 1985, an "emergency" City Council meeting regarding the Mansion was called by George Branch, West Ward councilman. At this "stormy" meeting, business administrators, community leaders, and politicians argued about who was doing what—and when—with regard to the Krueger-Scott Mansion. The council meeting transcripts make it painfully clear as to at least one reason why the Mansion project was moving so slowly: every time an idea was introduced it seemed to meet with a dead end. There was a lot of "I'm waiting to hear back from him" and "we never received that plan" among those who had the power to make the wheels turn.

There was also continued ambiguity as to the mission of the proposed center. City business administrator Elton Hill said during this particular council meeting that "the house could not be repaired until the city decided what community group would eventually use the structure and how it would be used." George Branch responded, "fixing the roof, the windows and securing it—and getting a program in there are two different things."[43]

Much of the correspondence surrounding the Mansion between the city's Engineering Department, City Council, and various architects, is without reference to Black culture or history. In a February 1985 *Star-Ledger* article, Elizabeth Del Tufo, speaking as president of the Newark Preservation and Landmarks Committee, argued that the best use for the Mansion would be as a suite of offices. Del Tufo had been in the preservation business for some time, and it may be that she offered up this idea simply to direct the city's gaze toward the utilitarian potential of the property. Office rentals generate income, while a museum is not typically a great source of revenue. While Del Tufo was suggesting pragmatic approaches, the same news article had Edna Thomas continuing her campaign for a Black museum to be housed within the Mansion.[44]

A 1986 report on the Krueger-Scott Mansion, commissioned by the City of Newark and prepared by the Grad Partnership architectural firm, makes no mention of anything pertaining to the use of the Mansion as a Black cultural center. The report was mostly composed of historical details of Newark, narratives of the High Street area, and descriptions of the past Mansion owners. The firm even went so far as to contact Gottfried Krueger's grandson in Argentina, hoping to gather missing information on the original façade of the Mansion.[45] In

1986, Grad Partnership became officially employed as the project's architectural firm. The City Council voted to initially invest $1 million in the Mansion's restoration and to pay Grad to perform a study of the entire structure. Subsequently, Grad published a full architectural analysis regarding the possibilities of restoration and renovation for the Krueger-Scott Mansion. The cost of that report was $105,600.[46] The estimate for the work and materials required to restore and renovate the Mansion was approximately $5 million, a long distance from the $1 million investment that the city had so far committed to. (There had been previous studies performed that estimated the total costs to be closer to $8 million.)[47]

In May of 1986, a letter written by City Clerk Frank D'Ascensioto, Newark's business administrator and director of engineering, requested a "status report" on the Krueger-Scott project for the municipal council "as soon as possible." The council wanted "to know what work had been performed to date," since approval for "capital improvements" was given in June of the previous year.[48] The fact was that no work had been performed on the Mansion since the city took ownership two years prior.

According to a *Star-Ledger* article from August of 1986, the first year of Sharpe James's mayorship, Edna Thomas's Central Ward Coalition of Youth Agencies proposal was confirmed as reviewed by the City Council. Thomas said in the newspaper interview that she did not want to give any details, but that she "had some pledges as relates to financing." Thomas also expressed concern that Elizabeth Del Tufo and her Landmarks and Preservation Committee were trying to dictate the Mansion's use. Del Tufo's response was quoted in the same article, saying that she was simply concerned that whatever group ended up in the Mansion be able to afford the "financial responsibilities" involved.[49] As often happens when too many ideas are introduced simultaneously, everything came to a standstill. Once again. The city placed wire fencing around the property and the Castle on the Hill appeared destined to remain a crumbling relic.

Two years later, in May of 1988, a new proposal by the Mansion's neighbor, St. James AME Church, was submitted. In a seventy-seven-page application, the St. James Social Development Corporation laid out a plan to convert the Mansion into a "Restaurant, a Historical Black Museum, Senior Citizens Day Care, a Center for Performing Arts, Job Training Center, and Office Space." The corporation proposed to purchase the property with "monies already allocated by the Newark City Council, as well as other public funding sources." Included in the package was a "Letter of Interest" regarding possible subsidy by the Newark-based Whitney Houston Foundation. St. James provided another such letter from one of Newark's largest employers, Prudential Insurance, which was "favorably inclined toward financial support" of the project.[50] There is never another mention of this proposal in subsequent communications.

The following year, Kastl Associates Architects of Jersey City put forward a report, "submitted in response to a request to evaluate the Krueger Mansion and the 1987 report on it and to suggest initial steps to be taken if the building merits saving." The report concluded that the place was indeed worth saving and proposed a $2 million budget to get the project off the ground.[51] More time passed. According to the *Star-Ledger*, Councilman Branch reported in October of 1989 that the council had solicited proposals for the Mansion but that none were deemed acceptable. And by "acceptable" it seems he meant affordable. Elizabeth Del Tufo railed at a council meeting, saying that had the city acted sooner in favor of past proposals, the restoration costs would not be so astronomical.[52]

During this period of negotiations, Newark's urban development was grinding forward, specifically downtown. As with so many urban spaces at the time, renewal was at the top of the city's to-do list, but seemingly only where it would enjoy high visibility—and reap substantial profit. City business administrator Richard Monteilh told a *Star-Ledger* reporter in 1989 that the city had "other priorities" when asked about the $5 to $8 million dollars that the Krueger-Scott Mansion project would require for completion. At that point Newark was simply trying to "contain further deterioration" and "prevent vandalism" of the Mansion, explained Monteilh. The rest would have to wait.[53]

Progress (1990s). Richard Monteilh was hired by Mayor Sharpe James to help transform the landscape of Newark. According to Monteilh, the city was in possession of "decent pieces to build around." He was referring to the Newark Airport, the Prudential Insurance building, and Pennsylvania Station, among several properties. But first on his agenda was retrieving money that the city was owed, including "$30 million in unpaid water bills, $5 million in parking tickets."

Meanwhile, Mayor James was enduring harsh criticism regarding monies being directed to such a relatively small portion of the city. James explained in a *Chicago Tribune* article that it was not always in the administration's control which projects took priority. "You run with what you have, you run where the dollars are," said James. At this time HUD (the Department of Housing and Urban Development) was contending with an intradepartmental scandal that ultimately led to a new law increasing oversight of its affairs. This may have contributed to some of Mayor James's sense of urgency.[54]

By Mayor James's second term in office, it appeared that Newark was committed to building an African American cultural center within the Krueger-Scott Mansion. However, it is also apparent that there remained a lack of consensus, or understanding, regarding just how many dollars it would take to bring such a commitment to fruition. Catherine Lenix-Hooker, hired as executive director for the Krueger-Scott Mansion restoration project, would tell me later that the city most certainly was aware of the costs involved. Alvin Zach, the director of the Department of Engineering, informed City Council right off that it would require approximately $12 million to complete the Mansion restoration plans. But, said Lenix-Hooker, the city "nickel and dimed" the whole way through.[55]

Councilwoman Mildred Crump, who was on the council throughout this time period, said in passing at a Mansion stakeholders meeting in April of 2017 that the people running the Mansion project simply did not know how to spend or use the money they had. "People weren't serious," stated Crump.

In the beginning of 1990, the City Council voted to apply for a New Jersey Historic Trust (NJHT) grant to cover renovation of the Mansion. They also pledged to match the grant for up to $2 million. In June, Kastl Associates published a "supplemental" report on the Mansion, its vision somewhat more pragmatic than the earlier report's. It was noted as feasible, for example, to replace the fireplaces, but cautioned that the exterior stucco could not be removed within a reasonable budget. In the same vein, work on the roof would have to be delayed, as would construction on the auditorium. The Kastl report also recommended pushing aside plans for the neighboring Carrigan Mansion property, something project managers had been hoping to develop in conjunction with the Krueger-Scott project. The estimated cost for the initial work, according to this latest report, would now come closer to $3 million, as opposed to the earlier estimate of $2 million.[56]

In October of 1990, a *New York Times* article waxed dramatic on the near-fall and now potential rise of the Krueger-Scott Mansion project. Describing the historic High Street community as "raw-boned" and claiming that the home had fallen prey to roosting pigeons and "packs of wild dogs," Anthony DePalma reported that the site would indeed be one dedicated to Black culture—made possible by a state grant, monies from the City of Newark, and donations by "private interests." DePalma had attended a rededication ceremony only the month before, receiving a tour of the house by Louise Scott's daughter, the Reverend Louise Scott-Rountree. It was the first time in seven years that "Little Louise" had been inside her childhood home. It was a painful experience for her, she said, to see the house in such shambles.[57]

The biggest news of 1990 was that Catherine Lenix-Hooker had been hired away from New York City's famed Schomburg Center for Research in Black Culture as executive director for the Krueger-Scott Mansion restoration project. According to the announcement in an arts newsletter, Lenix-Hooker's mission in Newark would be to facilitate "the transformation of the mansion into a major African-American educational and cultural facility."[58] The press release from the mayor's office described Lenix-Hooker's duties: "oversee the restoration of the building, as well as its fundraising and development efforts. She will work with the advisory board in planning long-range activities and events."[59] Was she a fundraiser, project director, liaison for the city, event planner, publicist? "I was juggling so much stuff," she explained to me.[60]

Meanwhile, ill feelings were growing between some council members. Ron Rice, the first African American councilman to represent the West Ward, reportedly had a difficult relationship with Mayor James, Rice often "taking him on

Figure 1.6. "Greeting Catherine Lenix-Hooker." Also in photo, George Branch, Alex Boyd, and Sharpe James, 1990. Courtesy Newark Public Library.

over matters including the budget and judicial appointments."[61] Of all the council members, George Branch and Marie Villani were the most supportive of the Mansion project, according to Lenix-Hooker. Branch had been behind it since the beginning, presumably in part because the Mansion was in his Central Ward district. Villani, widow of the late mayor, Ralph Villani, and the last white person to win a municipal election in Newark, may have been a supporter for any number of reasons. Unfortunately for the project, later that year Villani would "resign after pleading guilty to Federal charges that she misused city funds."[62]

There was constant pressure on City Council members from their constituents—many who lived outside the Central Ward and were demanding improvements to their own backyards, far from historic High Street or the burgeoning downtown area. Simply being African American was not necessarily an indication of support for the Krueger-Scott project. Black politicians and citizens were looking to participate in the city's economic improvements, and to garner the jobs regularly promised by the new businesses setting stakes downtown. A museum for Black culture was a nice idea, but low on the priority list for some.

In November of 1990, Mayor James threw a grand party—as he was wont to do—at the lovely Beaux-Arts Newark Public Library, to celebrate Lenix-Hooker's installation as executive director. James took every opportunity to publicly celebrate the "new" Newark; archived photographs of his time in office abound with galas, festivals, and receptions. Lenix-Hooker's family was invited to this party, as were many Newark dignitaries. But one of the guests, esteemed writer and activist Amiri Baraka, began to complain about the number of "outsiders" present (perhaps including Lenix-Hooker herself), and questioned whether they truly had a stake in his hometown. At one point during the evening Baraka became quite demonstrative, according to Lenix-Hooker, and finally had to be escorted out of the reception. She explained to me that later Baraka recognized her as an ally, "a solid person" who was there to truly "make a difference," and the two subsequently became friendly.[63]

Newark has a long history of suspicion of those not native to the city—or not yet established as committed supporters. This is likely an extension of the old settler/new settler rift of the Great Migration era, which will be explained in more detail later. Like hovering parents, Newark residents want to know who their "child's" friends are and if they are truly worthy of keeping company with their progeny. In Newark at this time, so many new faces were appearing; contractors, investors, directors, and lawyers were buzzing around the city promoting plans for constructing buildings and facilitating commerce. But Newark had been there before. Remember the renaissances? As Councilwoman Marie Villani said to Harry Grant, a developer from Englewood Cliffs who was putting forth myriad building proposals in 1986, "Newark has been fooled so many times by people who come here with great plans, Mr. Grant. Please do not fool us again."[64]

Seven years after the city took ownership of the Mansion, Mayor Sharpe James publicly declared, "We're gonna do something with that house."[65] A redevelopment plan for the Mansion was formally approved by the city's planning board on December 17, 1990.[66] In 1991, the New Jersey Historic Trust granted the Krueger-Scott organization over $600,000 toward renovations.[67] Of course, any funding from a historic agency carried with it specific guidelines in terms of materials and workmanship. As Mayor James described, no "artificial or cheap substitute materials" in the reconstruction of the Mansion would be allowed.[68] That was an understatement. Adherence to historical specs proved to be one of the most daunting facets of the Mansion project, and what many point to as a reason for its ultimate demise. But in the meantime, book parties, teas, and grant proposals ensued, in hopes of both raising money and encouraging goodwill toward the renovation project.

Numerous contradictions surrounding the project plans also continued, evidenced by myriad memos, applications, and proposals. For example, a 1991 report issued by the House and Senate committees on appropriations recommended the city receive "special purpose grants," including "$1,500,000 for a senior citizen employment and social services center connected to the Krueger Mansion in Newark, NJ."[69]

In a proposal written by Ms. Lenix-Hooker in February of that year, a space-use plan was laid out that specified a "Gottfried Krueger Memorial Room" and a "Hall of Fame dedicated to Louise Scott and the famous African-Americans from Newark and to include an oral history/video documentary screening facilities [sic]." The rest of the ground floor, according to this particular plan, would be dedicated to restrooms, a coat check, and a kitchen. The proposal for the second and third floors included no references to African American history, art, or culture. Nor did there seem to be any room for the social service offices mentioned by the Committee on Appropriations.[70] So the federal government was willing to hand over some money if the city was going to support senior citizens; and the Krueger-Scott organization was expanding their scope past African American history and culture. The Mansion became a Rorschach test of priorities.

In January of 1991, a contract was submitted by K. Hovnanian Companies, known as "New Jersey's largest home builder," to act as "construction coordinator" (CC) for the project. One clause seemed to be especially troublesome to the city's contract reviewer, presumably Alvin Zach from the Department of Engineering. Item #4 in the contract, under "Miscellaneous," stated that the construction coordinator "shall not be liable to Owner [the city] or any third party for any reason directly or indirectly related to the breach by CC of its duties and obligations under this letter of agreement or for negligence." Handwritten on the document next to this section is the word "CRAZY," in capitals.

Figure 1.7. Krueger-Scott Mansion with trailer circa 2004. Photo by Samantha Boardman.

Apparently, the relationship between the city and Hovnanian soured after that. In April of the same year, Hovnanian's legal counsel wrote Alvin Zach informing him that the city needed to come get its things. In the short time that Hovnanian was apparently involved with the project, the company had secured a trailer in which to store "artifacts removed from the Krueger Mansion building." Noting that it was "no longer involved in the Krueger Mansion project," the company's lawyer insisted that the city "remove the contents of the trailer immediately."[71]

The physical realities of what it would take to reconstruct and repair the Mansion were becoming ever clearer, although, of course, not everyone agreed just what those realities were. A July 1991 report by Glenn Boornazian Architectural Conservators stated that removing the stucco surface (which was probably applied by the Scottish Rite Masons) in a nondestructive manner from the brick was "unfeasible if not impossible." (Handwritten next to that section on the document is the word "shit," circled and with an exclamation mark.)[72] However, an August report by Grad Partnership included a suggestion regarding "careful removal of a portion of the tower stucco."[73]

In 1991, Newark was one of ten winners in the forty-second annual All-American City Award competition in San Antonio. The award, presented by the National Civic League, honors communities that illustrate both a commitment to and success in overcoming obstacles unique to city life. Newark had received the award once before, in 1954. The city was "on a roll," as Sharpe James wrote in his memoir, "now in the national spotlight for its renaissance."[74] Mayor James and his revitalization programs were credited by many for having earned this award. Such projects as the impending New Jersey Performing Arts Center (NJPAC), the return of the Blue Cross/Blue Shield Company to Newark, and the recent construction of over 2,700 housing units were cited as some examples of the city's turnaround. The U.S. Conference of Mayors also selected Newark that year as one of the nation's most livable cities.[75]

Back in 1987, the State of New Jersey had executed a capital needs survey. A report based on that survey was published in 1990, and soon thereafter the chair of the New Jersey Historic Trust, Joan Berkey, announced that $175 million would be dispensed for historic preservation and renovation throughout the state. In the New Jersey Conference of Mayors' publication, *Conference Quarterly*, Berkey listed various projects benefiting from the funding, including the Krueger-Scott Mansion. She explained, "the grant will fund stabilization of the deteriorated exterior envelope, structural repairs, and temporary building security for this seriously endangered structure."[76]

Things were looking up as money came in from preservationists and others on board with building a cultural center in Newark. A *Star-Ledger* article in November of 1991 reported on local radio station WNWK's contribution of $15,000 to the Mansion project for building barrier-free restrooms. The same article provided a brief narrative of the fits and starts of the Krueger-Scott project while explaining that the Mansion would "become a center emphasizing African-American culture." Lenix-Hooker was quoted as saying that the initial renovations—to the exterior and first floor only—would commence in approximately two months and that she foresaw the completion of the project to occur in the summer of 1993. Lenix-Hooker also acknowledged the delays in the project, citing the intense "scrutiny" required when accepting money from HUD.[77]

Because the block grant received from HUD was for historic preservation, much as with the New Jersey Historic Trust grant, there were stipulations. The Krueger-Scott organization would have to offer evidence that it was either benefiting "low and moderate-income persons," preventing or eliminating "slums or blight," or offering a plan to "meet a community development need." And because the initial grant application would have included such things as "data collection" and "archeological surveys," the information initially submitted would need to be resubmitted if anything changed.[78]

The next few years brought continued donations toward the Mansion project, from individuals and private organizations, as well as from the City of Newark itself in the form of $5 million in bonds. As part of the goal to build affordable housing in the area, "efforts to purchase properties on the block site and to relocate the tenants" were "nearly completed" by July of 1993. In the eyes of many, things were moving forward for the project, and for the High Street/ MLK Boulevard community as a whole. Lenix-Hooker would later tell me that most people on the block "relished" the idea of being bought out to make room for the proposed subsidized housing. The payments were more than fair, she assured me. The city even allowed one man to remain an extra year to tend to his garden that spring.[79] Krueger-Scott was positioning itself as a community project, something that ordinary Newarkers could relate and contribute to. The message was that this project was different from those million-dollar buildings sprouting up downtown—it was a project for the people.

This period also had its naysayers. In 1992, as separate plans for the rehabilitation of the Mansion's auditorium were being reviewed, Lenix-Hooker was once again forced to defend the project's timeline. "People ask me, 'Why is this project taking so long?' They don't realize the long process that goes into a project like this," she explained to a *Star-Ledger* reporter. At that point she was estimating that the bulk of the work on the ground floor would be completed in October of 1993.[80]

Lenix-Hooker told me that there were those who assiduously worked against the Mansion project, including a reporter for the *Star-Ledger* who Lenix-Hooker would not name. She claims the reporter even researched Lenix-Hooker's personal background, attempting to discredit her and thus the project. In fact, Lenix-Hooker believes that this hostility was part of why the project was ultimately scrapped; Sharpe James just could not afford to have another "street fight."[81]

In May of 1993, Lenix-Hooker received a memo from the New Jersey Historic Trust requesting an "Application for Major Change," among other materials, before they could "process the reimbursement request." This application was required after the city requested additional money in order to accomplish work not identified in the initial grant application. Next to the request from the NJHT is written the word "Help," presumably by Ms. Lenix-Hooker.[82] She was certainly in need of some assistance. As executive director, Lenix-Hooker had exactly one assistant, Carol DeSenne, who was hired with grant funds. DeSenne at the time was president of a local production and public relations company. According to Lenix-Hooker, DeSenne helped coordinate some of the programs initiated to "expand the cultural awareness aspects of the project." These included several champagne book parties at the Robert Treat Hotel, Sunday concerts at Bethany Baptist Church, and the Cujo Banquante Festival at the Krueger-Scott Mansion site in June 1995. Another project assistant was "on loan" from the library for "a short while" to perform light office duties.[83]

The amount of bureaucracy required to keep the project going is evident. And every time a new application was required, or a deadline was being negotiated, all work would cease on the Mansion. And every time work ceased, the Mansion's fragile state became all the more so. A report that year stated, "The integrity of structural elements of Krueger Mansion has deteriorated due to lack of maintenance, abandonment and the effect of the elements, especially water intrusion. In addition, construction practices, which are no longer utilized, have also contributed to the degradation of the structural elements."[84] Time was of the essence for the Mansion, as it was for downtown development, but for differing reasons. The Mansion's timeline was not dictated so much by money as it was by a historical memory that was rapidly slipping away.

In 1993, the New Jersey Preservation bond program granted the Krueger-Scott project over $400,000 in funds that were to be matched by the City of Newark. Lenix-Hooker announced that due to this funding, the first-floor renovations of the Mansion would now be completed by the end of 1994, approximately a year later than most recently estimated.[85] By July of that year, the project had suffered a nine-month work delay for various reasons, including an extended quest for suitable bricks in keeping with the New Jersey Historic Trust's restoration requirements.

Lenix-Hooker wrote in a memo to the city business administrator on July 22, "Although the initial restoration to the Mansion began on June 4, 1992, since late October 1992 the construction phase of this project has had a nine month hiatus. . . . Key to the work stoppage was locating a brick that met the approval of the New Jersey Historic Trust, the Engineering Department," and all of the architects and contractors as well. "Queries" were made to "105 vendors worldwide." Apparently there were also "unforeseen conditions in the Mansion" that needed City Council approval. She went on to report that "the project resumed on Monday, July 12, 1993," and they had found the 23,000 bricks, which the city agreed to purchase, and which would arrive that October.[86] Yet tension continued between two general viewpoints: one that saw the Mansion as an architectural structure in need of detailed attention, and one that wanted to know how much could get done for how little, and how soon.

Issues of vandalism were also addressed in the July memo. Lenix-Hooker asked the Newark Police Department for increased surveillance of the property. At one point, phones, answering machines, and an air conditioner were stolen from a contractor's on-site trailer. There were also reports of "roaming groups of young men" throwing rocks at the Mansion and harassing the workers. Also, dead animals were showing up on the front porch, and garbage was thrown over the fence, not only hindering the workers but giving an unappealing appearance to passersby.

Another potentially contentious issue was fair hiring; the Equal Employment Opportunity Commission (EEOC) was working with the Mansion project to ensure a diverse labor pool.[87] Equitable hiring practices were a historically thorny issue in Newark; multiple protests had already occurred around construction sites throughout the city as Black and Latino workers demanded equitable access to jobs.[88] In part due to the 1931 Davis-Bacon Act, minority construction workers continued to be blocked from work going on in their own cities. As explained in a 2017 *Washington Post* article, "Davis-Bacon was enacted in 1931 to require construction contractors to pay 'prevailing wages' on federal projects. Generally, this means paying union wage scales. It was enacted as domestic protectionism, largely to protect organized labor from competition by African Americans who often were excluded from union membership but who were successfully competing for jobs by being willing to work for lower wages."[89] This age-old law remains in effect today. In 1987, Clarence Thomas, representing the EEOC, argued for the repeal of the Act. While unions were much less discriminatory by the 1990s, this Act—and other formal and informal rules—continued to make getting a job in construction difficult for Black and brown workers across the country.

Meanwhile, back in downtown Newark, the New Jersey Performing Arts Center (NJPAC) had just reached completion at a cost of $180 million. Amiri Baraka was one of many Newarkers protesting the absorption of funds by so many downtown projects—as well as the accompanying tax exemptions typically offered alongside.[90] The focus was clearly on downtown improvement and refurbishment of the city's image, while at the same time the Krueger-Scott collaborative was requesting $2 million to get the project back on its feet in a Central Ward neighborhood most visitors would never see. At this historic moment in Newark, some in the city were just not as concerned with lifting up their ancestral history as they were with creating jobs and revising the city's tarnished reputation as "stolen-car capital of the country."[91]

The housing situation, in Newark and in cities across the country, remained in a state of flux, and subsidized high-rise projects were finally being destroyed to make room for more "livable" affordable housing. Hill Manor, located next door to the Krueger-Scott Mansion, was one of the properties on this chopping block. The residents had already been relocated, and the plan was to build 800 townhouses in place of the towering buildings.[92] This became one more chapter in the saga of the Krueger-Scott Mansion. Until Hill Manor was imploded, the Mansion contractors could not remove the wooden boards protecting the restored stained-glass windows. The perception given to many by those boarded-up windows was that the Mansion was just one more vacant structure on a failed block. This did not help the project's cause.

The year 1994 had Sharpe James running for mayor once again, promising to continue his work as executive cheerleader of Newark. One of his opponents was Ras Baraka, a high school principal and Amiri Baraka's son. Meanwhile, Councilman-at-Large Donald Tucker was calling on Black Newarkers to begin collecting their memorabilia to be displayed in the "museum." Finally there would be a place to hang Black people's pictures. Lenix-Hooker herself was anticipating the Mansion's completion, and was reportedly already in possession of various mementos from the Krueger and Scott families, as well as "authentic" Victorian furniture from a local merchant. A May 1994 *Star-Ledger* article carried a picture of a contractor working on the Krueger-Scott Mansion. The headline read, "A Home for African-American History."[93]

Trouble (Still the '90s). Five months later, a *Star-Ledger* headline reported, "Mansion Restoration Costs Called into Question." On September 14, local journalist Barry Carter sat in on a City Council meeting where the council apparently expressed concerns regarding the ongoing financial spending on the Mansion project. Lenix-Hooker was present and informed the council it would now take from two to four years for the project to be completed. She also argued that it had never gone over budget and that "every dime was accounted for." Councilman Tucker announced that he would no longer vote for funding the Mansion, that they had spent $4 million on a project that he had believed was going to cost closer to $1 million. (The $1 million reference is regarding the City Council's 1986 vote to initially commit that amount of money to the Mansion's renovation.) There was then a call to form a council committee that would oversee the Mansion project going forward.

Something had changed over the summer of 1994. The intangibles of trust and attention, required to sustain the project, had dissipated. Mayor James's popularity and desire for control were frustrating some fellow municipal leaders—even as he represented a Newark sitting in the most positive light it had enjoyed for quite some time. One issue at hand was that Councilman Tucker and Mayor James had never been good friends, and the tensions were only growing. Since at least 1982, when Tucker denied James the council president's seat, the two had been at odds—especially when it came to James's spending choices. The mayor, in turn, flooded the council with his grievances regarding lack of local political support.[94] The Mansion became caught up in a kind of family feud.

Disagreements among council members specifically regarding the Mansion project escalated at their September 1994 meeting. Councilman Carrino of the North Ward explained that he thought the building was to have been renovated and then "turned over" to a nonprofit organization. "This could wind up being a black hole," said Carrino. Councilman Rice questioned the value of the neighborhood in which they were revitalizing the Mansion, considering its high crime and lack of public transit. And, he added, he would not allow his West Ward to be ignored when it came to redevelopment. The city business manager, Glenn Grant, reminded Rice that it took time to revitalize any neighborhood and that the Mansion could serve as an "anchor" for the restoration of the whole Central Ward—a reference more often used for commerce-generating department stores than historic homes. Councilwoman Crump then spoke up in defense of Ms. Lenix-Hooker and against the criticisms she was receiving, arguing that "she has been doing it herself." Councilman Branch, an early supporter of the project taking place in his ward, reminded the council that the city had some culpability in the dire state of things; they had never secured it properly when it came into their possession.[95] And so it continued.

The 15th and 16th of September 1994 were "scaffolding dismantling" days, according to Lenix-Hooker's desk calendar. Perhaps this was a step toward preparations for the "gala" to be held on the 23rd according to the same calendar. There is no evidence of this event ever taking place. On the 28th, Lenix-Hooker apparently had an appointment with "Giles and Clem," the organizers of the oral history project that will be introduced in detail in the next section. Reviewing the calendar pages of Ms. Lenix-Hooker, one sees an overwhelming number of places, people, numbers, and notes jotted down within the enumerated squares. It seems to confirm what Mildred Crump implied at the council meeting, that the executive director of the Krueger-Scott Mansion project had indeed been asked to perform an unreasonable number and variety of tasks. Had the project been set up to fail?

In March of 1995, the *Star-Ledger* ran an article reporting on the $1.1 million grant that the Mansion project would receive from the New Jersey Historic Trust, "the maximum grant award given to a landmark building." The article also explained that the project was about more than just the Mansion, which would "become a premier African-American facility for the study and interpretation of the visual and performing arts." It reported that "The City of Newark has demonstrated its intent to support the restoration of the mansion and rehabilitation of the entire block through bond initiatives."[96] Portraying the Mansion project as more than just some historical sentimental journey, but as a greater urban renewal project benefiting many, was a talking point directed at those concerned with the amount of energy afforded just some rambling Victorian house. And this is one of only a few moments where there is actual discourse addressing the possibility of the Mansion as both a site of historical memory and a catalyst for economic growth.

The next month the *Star-Ledger* reported on yet another City Council meeting that heard complaints from University Heights residents, "who voiced concern over the method of land acquisition" and the forcing out of residents due to various Central Ward development projects. The Mansion project was not named specifically. Community activist Virginia Morton spoke out at the same meeting regarding the impending displacement of still more residents as a result of the upcoming Science Park. This fifty-acre, $60 million project would eventually house the Public Health Research Institute and the National Tuberculosis Center of the University of Medicine and Dentistry of New Jersey, among other health facilities. To that end, people would need to be relocated. Mostly poor and Black people, to be sure.

As Morton recalled in her Krueger-Scott oral history interview conducted that same year, "Now they're in the second phase of this which is called Science Park and it looks as if the same thing will happen all over again. However, people have learned from that [1967 medical school expansion], and the remaining homeowners have incorporated, and they don't intend to suffer from the same mistakes again."[97] As much as some associated with the Krueger-Scott Mansion project insisted that residents of the neighborhood had been paid fairly and were "happy" to leave, it was probably not quite that simple.

By 1998, the Krueger-Scott project began to relapse once again, even as a sign outside the edifice heralded it as a "Premier African-American Cultural Center."[98] Essentially no construction had taken place during the last year, and the Mansion's infrastructure continued its decline. Not surprisingly, costs turned out to be even greater than anticipated, more than the $7 million already spent by 1995. The New Jersey Historic Trust was forced to withdraw their most recent grant because the city neglected to spend the matching funds as stipulated. While "downtown boosters and officials were reclaiming resurgence," the revenue anticipated from the recent spate of development was not coming in at the rate expected.[99]

Continued political maneuvering and ongoing land development planning were diverting the attention of City Council members away from the Krueger-Scott Mansion project. Meanwhile, newcomer Cory Booker challenged veteran council member George Branch (advocate for the Krueger-Scott project) for his seat and won.[100] Krueger-Scott lost yet another supporter as downtown boosterism flourished. Then, in a June 16, 1998, memo to Mayor Sharpe James, Catherine Lenix-Hooker expressed her disappointment at the imminent departure of Newark Housing Authority Director Harold Lucas. The Mansion had an ally in him, she wrote, and there was a visible lack of progress since the interim director came on board. The Mansion project was now two cheerleaders down.

Lenix-Hooker, in this memo, also alluded to the negative perceptions surrounding the state of the Mansion. Those boarded-up windows continued to cause unease for some; newspaper editorials and talk on the street were detracting from the significance of the preservation project. Lenix-Hooker reminded the mayor that those boards were there to protect the newly installed windows from the continually delayed Hill Manor demolition project, at that point scheduled for the coming fall. As to the perpetual questions about when the Mansion would finally be opened for business, Lenix-Hooker informed the mayor that with another $3 million the site could be open to its first tenants within the next twelve months. This meant the opening would take place in 1999, six years later than initially announced. One ray of sunshine in this otherwise bleak communication was that "over 102" oral history interviews had been conducted for the Krueger-Scott African-American Oral History Project. This collection would ultimately become the sole product of the effort to turn the Mansion into a Black cultural center.[101]

On June 30, two weeks after the memo was written, the City Planning Committee met at the main library. Grad Associates representatives, city officials, and Lenix-Hooker were in attendance. On the agenda was a discussion of the creation of a center within the Mansion that would serve the proposed subsidized development to be built next door in the place of Hill Manor. Strikingly, the Newark Housing Authority (NHA) was now referenced as the official director of the Krueger-Scott project, while Lenix-Hooker was titled project manager, charged with facilitating the "marriage between cultural center and now proposed community center."[102]

On July 9, Lenix-Hooker received a letter from the City of Newark's director of modernization. Listing numerous questions regarding the Mansion renovations, the director's correspondence culminated with "I feel that until a great deal of issues and [sic] are cleared up, the Ordinance for Council Approval should be placed 'on hold' until a number of actions are completed." These apparent issues included the "need to ascertain that $4.0 million" was a "real number," concerns regarding assigning liability due to the variety of contractors, and how selections were made for the present contractor.[103] Either this fresh set of eyes saw inconsistencies and contradictions in the project's plans, or this was the city's way of stepping back from a project that was becoming increasingly unappealing to its citizens. As happens even now throughout cities and towns in this country, the notion of preserving history is typically met with a positive and enthusiastic response; but after the price tag is revealed the enthusiasm often wanes.

About a month after the first memo, Lenix-Hooker wrote another memo to Mayor James stating that the Mansion would "open the doors" the following summer, and the "grand opening" (of the first floor) would take place that fall. She also reported that the Mansion project was finally granted tax-exempt status, which she explained "opens the doors" for corporations to contribute to the cause.[104]

In his 1999 book *American Ruins*, photographer Camilo Jose Vergara catalogued cityscapes, including Newark's, in various forms of deterioration. Alongside photographs of the Krueger-Scott Mansion and a brief history of its last eighteen years, Vergara wrote, "At this point it makes sense to just forget the cultural center, forget historic preservation, and forget the seven million dollars."[105] This is a somewhat swift conclusion after a relatively cursory look into the structure's life, yet it is most likely a conclusion that many Newarkers had come to share. The city had taken ownership of the Mansion twelve years prior, major amounts of money had been awarded and spent, residents and other supporters attended teas and book parties (as much for the free food as anything else, said Lenix-Hooker), and yet the Mansion looked to be in just about the same state as it had been when the tenants were first evicted so many years before. Meanwhile, Newark residents still needed housing, a dramatic mayoral campaign was underway, and abandoned buildings downtown were vying for attention. The metaphorical windows of opportunity for the Krueger-Scott Mansion project became as boarded-up as its stained-glass windows.

According to Lenix-Hooker, in March of 1999 she and James Scott—pastor of Newark's Bethany Baptist Church, and executive board member of the proposed cultural center—appeared before the NHA. There was, the two were told, money available in the form of a Hope VI Grant, an initiative for the revitalization of housing projects and their surrounding areas. A few days later, Lenix-Hooker and Scott met with Harold Lucas, director of the NHA, at the Priory restaurant on West Market Street. There, says Lenix-Hooker, Lucas told them, "We can stretch it and make it happen." He made a commitment to present the proposal at the upcoming board meeting in June. But, as luck would have it, Andrew Cuomo, who was U.S. Secretary of Housing and Urban Development at the time, invited Lucas to come work for him in May. Lucas accepted the invitation. Without Lucas as an advocate, the Krueger-Scott proposal never made it onto the NHA board meeting agenda. It was a difference of one month and $4 million, said Lenix-Hooker.[106]

In August of 1999, a month before the most recently estimated Krueger-Scott opening, Ms. Lenix-Hooker received a note from the New Jersey Historic Trust. The correspondence concerned "easements"—the rights to the use of the Krueger-Scott property. The tone was friendly, and the executive director of the trust signed off with "good luck in your new career." Apparently, by the time of this correspondence it was public knowledge that the Krueger-Scott project had been transferred to the aegis of the Newark Housing Authority. Yet it would not be until the following year that Ms. Lenix-Hooker's "new career" would be made public.[107] In our personal communications, Lenix-Hooker characterizes the termination of the Mansion project—and her position—as "abrupt." This reflects the pattern of decision making throughout this project, wherein the inner circle made decisions that those outside the circle—including most Newark residents—were rarely privy to.

In March of 2000, the new city business administrator, JoAnne Y. Watson, sent a memo to Robert P. Marasco, city clerk, containing a status report on the Krueger-Scott Mansion. After providing a short narrative of the project—including its many obstacles—Watson argued the merits of continuing the project, stating that it could be completed with another $4 million. "The plans for the interior are flexible and can address a variety of adapted reuse needs," Watson writes. She then lays out a plan for the city to secure the funding. At this point the concept of an African-American Cultural Center appears to be completely off the table.[108]

In June of 2000, the *Star-Ledger* headlined, "Newark Trying Anew to Repair 1888 Mansion." In a somber tone, Mary Jo Patterson writes of the demise of the Krueger-Scott project, yet still with a glimmer of hope for its future. Patterson lists numerous difficulties faced by the project (such as the further destruction of the roof by the $80,000 scaffolding erected to give passersby the sense that work was actually being performed). Also noted in the article was the lengthy search for the elusive bricks, as well as the ultimate termination of Lenix-Hooker's position. (Lenix-Hooker did go on to supervise the oral history project, however.) "The money to complete the work just wasn't there," Lenix-Hooker is quoted as saying in the article. The "hopeful" part of the article reported that the Newark Housing Authority was currently entertaining discussion surrounding the Mansion. Several Newark residents interviewed for the article expressed enthusiasm that the "restoration may get back on track."[109]

Newark's population at the 2000 census was 273,546.[110] But the "daytime population" of Newark was estimated at over 330,000, including a workforce of 47,000 people within a half mile of the downtown area.[111] The city's primary goal was to continue developing its center in order to persuade those who might otherwise be unwilling to set foot on the streets of Newark to remain there for a few extra hours each day after work. Maybe those in question would even consider making the city their home after a while. Mayor James was simultaneously heralding the 52 percent drop in crime since 1995, and the *Star-Ledger* was declaring that Newark was "on a roll."[112] In the midst of this amplified downtown development, historic preservation was sent to the back of the city's funding queue. Newark was busy creating what so many postindustrial cities were striving for, a FIRE (finance, insurance, real estate) sector that would stanch economic decline.

The exodus, or just plain absence, of an urban labor force was an ongoing issue for cities in this nation, especially within what people referred to as legacy cities.[113] Suburban workers streamed into city centers each day, only to exit each evening; the repeal of residency laws made it so that civil employees were no longer required to live in the cities in which they worked. Places like Milwaukee, Detroit, and Baltimore, along with Newark, suffered greatly from this labor shift. In turn, this led to housing vacancies, where families who had lived in these cities for generations were no longer necessarily passing down their homes to the next generation.[114] And so these cities would swell during the day, sometimes even causing a slight injection of cash for local shop owners. But once night fell, business districts became all but ghost towns.

Meanwhile, back on MLK Boulevard, the Hill Manor housing project was finally razed in the year 2000, approximately five years after its demolition was originally scheduled. The boards protecting the historic stained-glass windows of the Krueger-Scott Mansion were finally ready for removal, had anyone been around to do so.

Catherine Lenix-Hooker has asserted that the Krueger-Scott African-American Cultural Center project was not a failure, that they "went the distance" with what they had. A dwindling tax base, concerns over struggling schools, and corruption in government are just some of the reasons she gave for the inability to finish what was started.[115] Mayor James has insisted that cost came in as the number one issue surrounding the Mansion project,

THE KRUEGER-SCOTT MANSION PROJECT 35

Figure 1.8. Krueger-Scott Mansion, circa 2004. Photo by Samantha Boardman.

followed closely by just who would control what once it was finally completed. "Cost and control ruled the day!!!" exclaimed James.[116] The simple conclusion is that economics vanquished this historic preservation effort. When asked, both Lenix-Hooker and James were adamant that race played no part in the Mansion's demise. But as the late historian Clement A. Price said many times, including in his documentary, *The Once and Future Newark*, "Race matters in

America. Race matters in Newark."[117] Race matters in the story of the Krueger-Scott project.

This was a complex tale of economics, preservation, and politics that ended in disappointment. But not altogether. During the early 1990s, the oral history project that was to have been housed within the cultural center began its germination. While the intent was to complete the interviews by 1994, in 1997 the last recordings were made, with ultimately 107 African American seniors interviewed. This particular form of preservation succeeded due in large part to the fact that it cost little money and relied heavily on a group of committed volunteers. The project was supported by a community that believed in the importance of their history and was willing to commit their capital, which came mostly in the form of time. It is thanks to a handful of Newark citizens that these stories exist.

With hindsight one might determine that the idea of preserving the battered Krueger-Scott Mansion was frivolous; all that history could have effectively been contained within the oral history interviews. But the history in question is African American, and there is an intense desire among many involved in this work to reconstitute the copious missing stories of Black America—in as many forms as possible. That said, Newark was a struggling city during the period in question, in terms of finances and identity. Struggling cities crave money, so they "run where the dollars are," as Mayor James put it. A few dollars were at 601 High Street for a short amount of time. But throughout the next decade or so, the majority of those dollars would reside downtown.

Conclusion

Update #1 (2018). In the spring of 2018, a meeting was held at Newark's City Hall regarding the restoration of the Krueger-Scott Mansion. I was in attendance, along with the Reverend Louise Scott-Rountree, her father Malachai Rountree, City Council President Mildred Crump, and developer Avi Telyas of Seaview Development Corporation. Mr. Telyas presented a proposed "makerhood" for the property, a campus of both residential and retail buildings. It was an elaborate plan that held echoes of what has unfolded in this chapter. It was exciting and yet haunting to hear so many of the same words and phrases used around the restoration of this great home some twenty-odd years later.

According to a May 2018 news article, the project was estimated to cost $29 million and be completed in approximately twenty-four months.[118] Another article six months later claimed that construction would begin that month.[119] In March of 2019, Rutgers University published an announcement about a digital mapping project centered around the Mansion; while no construction had begun, the team consisting of Rutgers and New Jersey Institute of Technology faculty and students began working in the Mansion to complete the first phase of this public history project. At the time of the Rutgers announcement, the construction project was "being developed."[120]

Update #2 (2021). Some initial work was done on the Mansion. This consisted mostly of debris removal and reinforcement of weak inner structures. Arguments have ensued between the community, the city, and the developer. Community meetings became sites of contention once again, as neighbors and local activists complained about being left out of the latest plans. Even so, the project is ongoing, and I now sit on the board of the Newark-Scott Cultural and Civic Center Foundation. It is the mission of the foundation to provide "tribute to the life of entrepreneur Louise Scott, by delivering services for community empowerment via educational civic programming, events and activities purposed to positively build and transform youth and adult lives."

Update #3 (2024). Today, the Mansion has been transformed into the popular coworking model. Avi Telyas, the developer and founder of Makerhoods, remains the point person for the property which has been thoroughly renovated. The project is said to have cost around $10 million and includes an adjacent building on the property that provides sixteen workspaces for entrepreneurs. The rent, as of 2023, was $2,500.

The Oral Histories

In an April 1995 City Council meeting it was voted unanimously to adopt a resolution entering "into a one-year contract with Giles A. Wright . . . to provide services as a consultant to create an oral historical plan for Krueger Scott Mansion Cultural Center." At that point several oral histories had already been recorded. Councilman Tucker, perhaps indicating the council's concerns about the project's transparency, motioned for an amendment demanding that "reports, memoranda and analysis" be submitted to the council. The amendment was approved.[121] The next project meeting would not take place until March 1998. The project coordinator, retired teacher Mageline Little, as well as Ms. Lenix-Hooker and various volunteer interviewers, were in attendance. Among discussion topics were the continued collection of memorabilia and the procedure for submitting completed interview tapes.[122]

Two days after the March meeting, the oral history project committee convened again. Six people, including the project director, were in attendance. Lenix-Hooker was copied on the minutes. Proposed actions meant to increase the collection of oral histories included setting up interview stations at senior citizen communities and recruiting additional volunteers. As a result of a $5,000 grant from the New Jersey Council for the Humanities, the group was able to begin the transcription phase of the project. In December of that same year a letter of agreement was signed with a professional transcriber identifying a need for seventy hours' worth of transcription. The bulk of transcription work would ultimately be completed in 2000; thirty-two interviews (approximately one-third of the collection) were transcribed at a cost of $4,900.00.[123]

The oral history interviews of the Krueger-Scott African-American Oral History Project are unique in that they were conducted by friends and acquaintances of the interviewees. Most of those interviewed were participants in the Great Migration, but a few had been lifelong residents of Newark. The questionnaire, designed by historians Clement A. Price and Giles Wright, had the community interviewers pursuing conversation on subjects ranging from travel, to food, to racism, to church. Price and Wright, both African Americans, were very familiar with stories of the Great Migration—through research as well as personal knowledge. Pastors, senators, council members, teachers, and factory workers were interviewed, culminating in hours of first-person historical and cultural resources.[124]

The oral history collection has more recently become the center of scholarly research and public programming, but for years the cassette recordings of these interviews remained in shoeboxes on a shelf in Newark's main public library.[125] The Mansion's preservation project lives on in these tape-recorded interviews; they provide their own kind of housing for Newark's Black history and culture. And while these interviews may not offer any space for hanging one's pictures, they do conjure up vivid historical recollections. In the ensuing pages of this book, due in large part to these interviews, you will read about the history of a microcosmic city, the Great Migration, and twentieth-century African American life. The Krueger-Scott African-American Cultural Center won a kind of victory in the end, preserving the all too often erased voices of "ordinary" African Americans while contributing to scholarship on so very many levels. It is my hope that this book will provide, among other things, an increased understanding of America's legacy cities through Newark's own story. And whatever comes next for the Krueger-Scott Mansion, there will always be these stories to reflect the deep history and major contributions of African America.

CHAPTER 2

Sundays

Church

Before the late Joe Clark was famous for shaping up Paterson, New Jersey's troubled East Side High School, and before the movie *Lean on Me* about his tenure there as principal came out, Mr. Clark was attending weekly prayer meetings with his grandmother at Newark's Greater Abyssinian Baptist Church on West Kinney Street.[1] The Reverend Raphus Phillips Means was pastor. Clark's mother was president of the usher board and Clark's father was a deacon.

> We went to church in the morning—Sunday school—and didn't get back until seven, eight o'clock at night.... I'll never forget the number, 224-6 West Kinney Street. That was the hub of activity... my grandmother... would have me in prayer meeting every Wednesday.... That was the avenue that kept me from going to jail.... I was indoctrinated with the ideology that God was in the sky looking down on me and I dare not do anything that would violate the principles of Christendom.[2]

Reams of interviews and articles have been published about Mr. Clark since his famous stint at East Side High from 1982 to 1991. But only in his own words do we hear of his "indoctrination," and in doing so are able to better understand the principles so clearly integral to his pedagogical and administrative ideologies.

The church played a powerful role in Joe Clark's life, as it did in the lives of so many of the Krueger-Scott interviewees. Church molded Black Newarkers—their lives, their families, their rituals. And church was typically a common bond between the interviewers and narrators in this oral history collection.

The Black church, in one form or another, has been central to Black American history since before the country claimed its independence. For the generation interviewed in the Krueger-Scott collection, the church remained the epicenter of the community. Yet there were those who ultimately rejected organized religion, quite often because they had been forced to attend services as children. Others experienced negative events within their churches and became alienated. There were also those who desired to attend church but were unable to because they had to work on Sundays—or did not even own what they believed was suitable dress for a house of God. These oral histories provide a multitude of illustrations of African American relationships with the church and remind us that the "Black community" is not at all a monolith.

L. H. Whelchel writes in his introduction to *The History and Heritage of African American Churches* that the Black church is more than an edifice or a religion or a set of beliefs, it "is an evolving, dynamic, collective historical presence of a people and their patterns of expressing their beliefs and spirituality." Enslaved Africans, he writes, "took the hybrid Christianity offered them by their oppressors and made it relevant and meaningful to their needs."[3]

Historian Davarian Baldwin adds, "It is precisely in these . . . traditional intellectual spheres of church . . . where class struggles were waged, theoretical insights were produced historically, and many of the thoughts of the 'people' are now revealed to the historian."[4] The Church and African American history are inextricably linked, illuminating even that which goes beyond religious practice if we are willing to look past the pews.

Karl Ellis Johnson, in writing about "Black Church Activism in Postwar Philadelphia," argues that activism and the church could not be regarded separately at that time: "In studying black religious [Christian] institutions, it is a mistake to separate civil rights activities from the church's community-service role. Community service was often closely linked to social protest, because it displayed the ability of black institutions to provide some of the human and social services to their people that were often denied or unequally allocated by mainstream private, state, and local institutions."[5] Many narrators in the Krueger-Scott collection, including Madam Louise Scott, took it upon themselves to close that gap in services through voluntary works, within the church and without. Johnson's connection between church and community service also helps explain responses from so many of the narrators claiming no "political activity," while in the next breath describing active participation in their respective communities.

Listening to the Krueger-Scott oral histories, it is clear that church is integral to the life experiences of the majority of the narrators. Even those who did not attend church typically had stories relating to it. And those who were affiliated with a church revealed its role in so many facets of their lives. Very few interviewees responded to questions about church as if church did not matter.

Historian Timothy Neary writes, "It shouldn't just be religious history scholars but urban, labor, sports, cultural, and political historians who 'take religion seriously' as a category of analysis."[6] African American life cannot be understood without an accompanying and nuanced understanding of the African American church. In this chapter I hope to offer up some of that understanding through the lived experiences of those in and around the Black church.

"Community" (1930–1990). As one might imagine, at certain points throughout the Great Migration, the growing presence of African Americans was not always welcomed by other racial and ethnic communities. In his Krueger-Scott oral history interview, the Reverend Robert Woods of Newark's Morningstar Baptist Church tells the story of an alleged 1948 bombing of Bethsaida Baptist Church on Bloomfield Avenue in Newark. In answering his interviewer's question regarding "overall relations with Whites," Woods first notes that there were plenty of restaurants, neighborhoods, and shops in which Blacks were "not welcome" when he first arrived in Newark, somewhere around 1950. Then, addressing his interviewer Glen Marie Brickus directly, he says, "You remember they built [Bethsaida] there, they didn't want it there, they blew it up. They blew the church up."[7]

Clergy quite often becomes part of the political landscape, and their Sundays are not necessarily spent solely in the sanctuary. Reverend Woods recalled regular "informational meetings" held on Sundays, sometimes at a community hall located at 3 Belmont Avenue. (I include addresses whenever possible here. I have come to do this as habitually as the narrators themselves, who provide addresses for most every building in which they worked, lived, played, and prayed. Alessandro Portelli, in his oral history project *They Say in Harlan County*, explains that people "clinched discovery and possession ... with the act of naming."[8] Recounting addresses in the Krueger-Scott oral histories seems to be a part of this "naming.")

The "informational meetings" Reverend Woods references included such notable leaders as City Council President Ralph Grant, activist-artist Amiri Baraka (then LeRoi Jones), Mayor Ken Gibson, and Junius Williams, a lawyer and activist. Their goal, according to Woods, was to "hash out the problems that existed in Newark" and "formulate plans and ideas that would give some hope to African Americans."[9] Black church clergy regularly, and necessarily, took themselves onto the streets and into the communities, traveling outside the walls of the sanctuary in order to effect change.

According to most of the Krueger-Scott narrators, the church was also the place to turn for help. Time and again this response was heard in answer to question #67 of the questionnaire: "When you or others in your neighborhood got in 'trouble' or needed help to solve a problem, to whom did you turn?" Reverend Woods explained how in his younger days he had turned to the church when desperately looking for a job. Growing frustrated and impatient with the local unemployment office, Woods received word of an opening from a Reverend Jones, whose son had started working at Haydu Industries, a manufacturer of vacuum tubes in Plainfield, New Jersey. Woods contacted the company immediately and landed a job. He expounded in his interview on the importance of the Black church to the Black community:

> Most of our people find the church when they havin' a real social, or even political, or criminal problem.... They depend a lot upon the Black minister—I mean on the Afro-American minister—than they do on anyone else. 'Cause they think we have the solution for whatever problem exists in the community. At least they know that we will try to find out who they can contact.... The court system will write letters to the Black clergy about the young men and young women that's incarcerated in their system. How much we know about them, whether they're a member of our church, do we know their parents.... The Black church is our first line of defense.[10]

Lest we consider the reverend's perspective biased due to his vocation, there are many other non-clergy interviewees confirming this claim. Former Mayor Sharpe James said, in answer to the same question regarding where Black folks turned, that people would "start with the family, with them, and then if the family could not solve those issues, you would turn to the church. The church has always been a pillar of strength. Always there for guidance and leadership. So it was internally with the family, and if not the family, the church."[11] Sharpe James later laments what he contends is the modern trend toward disproportionate reliance on government—on welfare and Section 8 housing vouchers in particular. He argues that this practice has fractured the Black community.

In other interviews this sentiment is repeated, emphasizing the church's ability to take care of all things, and discouraging the idea of looking elsewhere for help. Funeral home director Franklin Banks put it this way: "Because the South was very family oriented. And also very racially oriented. Because they had to work and stick together because the whites were so much against them ... they had to depend on each other. And some of that came right up North with them. Like down at the church now, that was family oriented. If they could help you in any way, they would help. Or if you could help them, you'd go there and help them."[12] Councilwoman Mildred Crump agrees:

> Ninety percent of the time it was to the ministers in the area. There were some community leaders.... But for the most part it was to the church that we were able to turn for assistance.... Because they were the ones who were able to produce the results—to make, and to find and to create the action of adjudication of whatever the circumstances were ... you could pretty much know that your pastor would be willing to go to the judge and say something on your behalf, in your behalf, that might persuade the judge to give you another chance. But I think that was pretty much true of us traditionally. It was to the church that we went to for support in times of trouble and difficulties.[13]

This practice was most pronounced when municipal governments were made up of completely white administrations. However, once a few people of color finally began entering city halls across the country, African Americans were a bit more prone to call on local politicians and administrators to help in some formal matters. Numerous Krueger-Scott narrators easily listed the names of public servants, past and present, such as Newark's first Black City Council member, Irvine Turner, who won his seat in 1954.

Still, the listing of elected officials typically came after narrators had named the church as their first line of defense. Harvey Slaten, a deacon at Bethany Baptist Church, stated emphatically that if somebody in the community needed help, they went to their church. He echoed others, pointing out one big reason behind this: someone in the church was likely to know a judge—sometimes through employment as a domestic. Judges, Slaten noted, always showed compassion in court for their domestic employees.

In listening to the interviews, it appears that the words "trouble" and "problem" were a kind of code for legal issues. We hear, for example, that Willie Belle Hooper's father had to leave Alabama and change his name because of some "trouble he got into."[14] And Calvary Baptist Church member Zaundria Mapson May said, "Most of the times when there were problems, the people that I know called on the minister, who was able to counsel or to refer to various sources for a resolution of the problem."[15] As the criminalization of the Black body has long been entrenched in American history, it is not surprising that Black citizens' "problems" tended toward the legal.

Carolyn Wallace, a member of Redeeming Love Christian Center, lamented the lost opportunity for uplift, explaining that the church was once a way to elevate African Americans from their past. The "major accomplishments of the church," said Wallace, were that it "developed a people forgotten and that came out of what we now know as slavery. God rose up and [brought] people out of those ashes that really knew how to serve Him, okay, in the way Black people do. I mean, in joyful spirit. And I think we kinda gotten away from that."[16]

In her interview, Bethany Baptist's first lady (wife of the senior pastor), Dr. Beverly Scott, wanted to emphasize the economic support her husband's church provided to Newark's economy. For example, they employed Black-owned businesses whenever possible, Dr. Scott explains. "The church has certainly reached out to use the vendors—Newark vendors—for the needs of the church. Such as a cleaning service; it was African American, housed and located in Newark that this church uses."[17] At times when white society offers little to no help, the Black church steps in to provide support—practical and emotional—to their congregants, and often to the Black community at large. This remains the case still today.

A member of Bethany Baptist Church since the 1940s, Katheryn Bethea said in her interview that she always ended up at Bethany as a child, even while her family's membership was with Zion Hill Baptist Church, at 152 Osborne Terrace. One draw of Bethany was that it offered myriad youth services, whether children were members or not. It also had a strong community consciousness, taking care of its own, noted Bethea. This observation led Bethea to tell the story of a young white co-worker who, years later, asked whether if during the Depression Bethea had gone to soup kitchens with the proverbial pot in hand in order to receive free food. Bethea sounded indignant about that question, even so many decades later in her interview. "I don't know any Black people who was goin' down [to get soup]."[18] It was an insult to her, an affront to Black community collectivism as far as she was concerned.

Of course, we do know that many people during the Depression, including African Americans, needed help. But according to Bethea—and others in the oral history project—at one time churches did not even need to offer structured feeding programs (the common food pantries of today). Instead, church members simply took care of each other. There were private transactions made for those in need, avoiding public display. Bethea asserts, in accordance with Sharpe James, that the Black community always helped each other. "Churches played a large part—there were no organized community groups. . . . You did it within your church. . . . In the Depression days . . . if you had two potatoes and somebody had one you gonna give them part, you understand?"[19]

Even today, members of Black churches may privately approach their pastors requesting rent money or help paying the light bill. It is common for churches to supply pastors with a "benevolence fund" from which provisions are made at the pastor's discretion. In addition, more public organizations such as food pantries, free counseling, and shelters are regular staples of today's Black church. These more formal structures are necessary in part because church communities are not necessarily geographically localized anymore; members might be living some distance away, scattered from the site of the church. This makes the once private exchange method less effective.

In her interview, Katheryn Bethea recalled the strong influence that the women of the church had on her as a young girl, remembering them as role models and major contributors to the community. "I was only twenty-three when those people—they went and rented the Court Street 'Y' and sold tickets and gave me the money so I could pay for [swim] lessons [for the Girl Scout badge]. These were the women in my church. And so we had that kinda thing, you understand, where you had this kind of strength within your own community." Perhaps these determined women even inspired Bethea when, at sixty years old, she finally completed the college degree she had started back in the 1950s. Bethea went on to earn a master's, and ultimately became a professor of English literature.[20]

Newark enjoyed a robust social and religious Black community, according to Isaac Thomas, a member of St. James AME (African Methodist Episcopal) Church. That is most certainly where one turned to for help—to family, extended family, and to the church, said Thomas. He then added, by way of explanation, that race relations were quite strained in Newark—with the police most specifically: "They had total disregard—or tolerance—for Blacks doing certain things. I recall . . . when I first came here how one of the policemen interrupted a church service at Abyssinian Baptist Church and went into the church during the service and arrested the young man—not waiting until the service was over for him to come out but went in and took the person out. Well, that rippled through the community that this happened."[21] Those were the kinds of experiences, Thomas added with a heavy tone, that brought on the 1967 uprising.

Veronice Horne explained that in the post-rebellion era, after 1967, churches increased outreach to communities. "The churches, the priests—didn't matter the denomination, it was almost like it was fellow man helping fellow man. . . . There were times when I didn't have things and the church would open their doors. They would obtain things from businesses, and they would distribute it to the community." Horne was one of the few participants who spoke of her own reliance on institutional support, whether faith or government based. She saw things "coming up" in terms of community solidarity, and pointed out various ministries that her church, Bethany Baptist, was involved with at the time of her interview.[22]

Elma Bateman, a retired secretary at AT&T and member of Queen of Angels Church, somewhat countered her peers' tales when it came to seeking aid within the Black community. Bateman explained in her interview, during a discussion on race, that she held no animosity toward whites or Jews, in part because of the "good Jewish doctors" she knew. "When I left the government and went to look for a job—when I had three kids and couldn't keep the schedule up here, uh, I was interviewed by several [Jewish] doctors. . . . And the first Jewish doctor I worked for, he knew I had the background. . . . He said, 'I don't have to see anybody else; you got the job.'" Bateman worked for yet another Jewish doctor afterwards and noted that they both treated her well, even securing a lawyer for her son at one point. "Not only did I work for them, but they were always advising me. Some of the things I couldn't take advantage of because I didn't have any money. . . . [But] when my son got in trouble at one time, one of the doctors said to me, 'Wait, wait, let me call my lawyer.' You know, never had to put a penny out or anything, you know. They were always there for me."[23] Bateman was one person who found support outside the boundaries of the Black community early on.

Willa Coleman, member of Emmanuel Missionary Baptist Church, and a retired health care worker, said in her interview that the Black community was good at taking care of itself—as long as the people already knew each other. At one point she and her husband had taken ill at the same time, she explained. They needed help in caring for their children, and they looked to the city government for assistance. Coleman reports that the city was "ineffective," but that her neighbors were very helpful. She then makes a point of reiterating that Blacks would not help strangers—no matter their race.[24]

James Scott, pastor of Bethany Baptist Church, wrote in a 1995 article, "Segregation forced blacks to live in the ghetto, and the church served as a general-purpose institution, providing identity and status as well as social control and advocacy for greater opportunity."[25] As late as 2002, church was still central to the African American community. Church affiliation by African Americans remained high, with approximately 79 percent of those polled answering that they belonged to a church. However, just five years later polls showed only 53 percent of African Americans claiming membership in a church, and more than 12 percent claiming no religious affiliation. In 2014, the number rose to 29 percent unaffiliated, with 79 percent of African Americans still self-identifying as Christian and "religious" more often than whites or Latinos.[26]

Somewhere around the 1980s, American society hastened in its move toward a more individualistic center, people regularly cordoning themselves off from extended family and concepts of community. Yet still today there exists a large population of African Americans associated with a church, who recognize themselves through their church, and who contribute to—and benefit from—their church family.

Bethany Baptist (1870s–1990s). The words "pride" and "proud" are often utilized when the Krueger-Scott narrators speak of their churches. The point of pride for many was Bethany Baptist Church, a central figure among Newark's numerous houses of worship. Reverend James Scott explains contemporary Bethany to his Krueger-Scott interviewer, thirty years after first accepting his call as senior pastor: "This belief that Black people are superior or singular. We've already proved it. And so now we're able to welcome all people into our institution. Here in our church, it would have been very difficult [in the beginning] for us to have welcomed West Indians, Africans, people from Poland, people from this and that place—and we have now about twenty-three different nations represented in our congregation. But that would have been impossible until we had a sense of solidarity and an understanding amongst ourselves who we are and why we have a right to be proud."[27] Bethany is the church to which most participants of the Krueger-Scott Oral History Project belong. This is in part because the cultural center director, Catherine Lenix-Hooker, was a Bethany member. When it came time to solicit volunteers for the oral history project, Lenix-Hooker told me she made a plea to her fellow congregants, "Hey, I need help, you guys." She explained to me that people at Bethany had "time on their hands," as the congregation was made up of many retired professionals such as teachers and librarians. The church administration also strongly supported the oral history project, so much so that Reverend Scott became president of the project's board.

Figure 2.1. Bethany Baptist Church, circa 1900. Courtesy Rose Library, Emory University.

In our interview I pushed Lenix-Hooker regarding the possibility of a slightly skewed collection of oral histories as the result of this mining of Bethany Baptist members. But Lenix-Hooker assured me that the oral history project was publicized and "open to anyone," and that many people outside of Bethany came on board by "word of mouth."[28]

Approximately 28 percent of the Krueger-Scott interviewees who claimed church affiliation belonged to Bethany Baptist Church; St. James AME came in second, at around 16 percent. Suffice it to say that the presence of Bethany does inform the product that is the Krueger-Scott African-American Oral History

Project. That said, in Bethany we gain a useful lens with which to view varied issues, from status, to gender, to church worship. Acknowledging Bethany's strong presence in this project is a reminder that no set of oral histories can truly be a perfect sampling of a community; the term itself is misleading in its implication of homogeneity and accord. Thus, it is not a problem that more interviewees hail from Bethany, but simply something to keep in mind as we listen to these stories.

In his Krueger-Scott interview, Bethany member Richard Cooke reported that in 1922 his paternal grandmother wrote a book entitled *Faded Foliage and Fragrant Flowers from the Heart of Bethany*. This publication contains a history of the first fifty years of Bethany Baptist, from 1870 when a small group met in Deacon Jackson Watson's home at 187 Commerce Street, to their "adoption" by Peddie Memorial Church on Broad Street, to their official sanctioning as a church in 1871, on through the 1905 purchase of their first building, and up until the fiftieth anniversary celebration in 1921—which included a traditional mortgage-burning ceremony.[29] I have asked many Bethany members, historians, and local archivists about *Faded Foliage*, and all were unaware of its existence. Fortunately, thanks to Mr. Cooke's interview, this valuable primary source was brought to light.

Cooke's grandmother, Mrs. O'Kelly-Cooke, was a poet; thus, her syntax was a bit more elaborate than a traditional historian's might have been. O'Kelly-Cooke starts off the book by introducing the reader to her blind grandmother, Mrs. Nancy Thomas. "Softly I entered the room and found her sitting on the side of her bed. The massive frame of what had once been a strong and portly woman. 'How are you Grandmother,' and I reverently held within my own the hand which she extended."[30]

Still, *Faded Foliage* offers a valuable collection of photographs and stories illustrating the church's history—and Newark history more generally—from the rare perspective of urban African Americans at the turn of the twentieth century. Most of *Faded Foliage* consists of short biographies of various Bethany members. Descriptions include a man from a "prominent caste," a woman with a "spirit of christian piety," and a department store doorman who had "the respect of both races."[31]

O'Kelley-Cooke also interviewed a Mrs. Carter for her book, who explains that in New Jersey in 1870 there were no Black churches. African Americans were attending white churches. Carter adds that, naturally, African Americans were barred from participating and serving in these churches. That issue, she says, was the impetus for the creation of Bethany Baptist Church—and for so many other Black churches in the North during that time.[32]

Ongoing exclusion of Black Christians from white churches led to the continual growth of Black churches. Migrants grew many of these congregations,

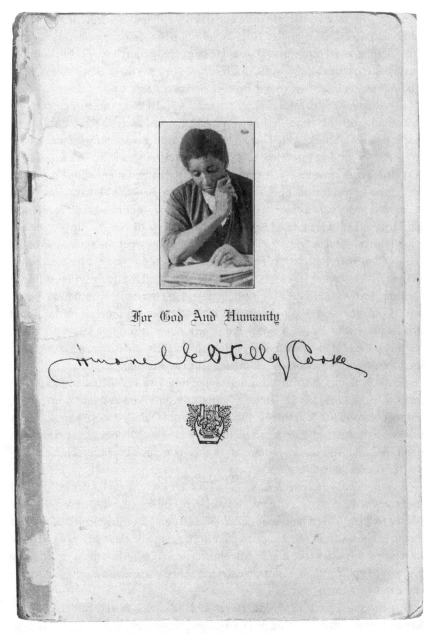

Figure 2.2. Dedication page from *Faded Foliage*. Courtesy Rose Library, Emory University.

bringing with them a slightly different style of religious worship. It was "more emotional and intense," notes Giles Wright in his book on New Jersey history. This "Southern" style of worship would inform many church services in developing Northern cities like Newark, disgruntling some northern Black churchgoers who wanted their services to remain more "respectable."

Faded Foliage illustrates that a particular mindset was established early on in Bethany's history, and Bethany Baptist today still carries a reputation as a respectable, slightly upscale house of worship. Ed Crawford, for example, said in his Krueger-Scott interview that growing up in Bethany he was exposed to very little gospel music: "Well, growing up in Bethany did not afford me a true picture on gospel music, I guess until I got grown. Because Bethany was a very staid, reserved type of a church. Our service was very—one thing that we retained between Reverend Hayes and Reverend Scott that the service is a fairly reserved, conservative, staid service. You're not apt to see folks 'get the spirit' too often, too frequently in Bethany. It's gotten better over the years."[33] I have attended Bethany's services on several occasions, the Reverend Bill Howard presiding at the time. Reverend Howard is an eloquent and intellectually stimulating orator, but the music—and the congregation itself—had much more of a traditional Protestant sensibility when compared to other Baptist services I have attended, including those at my own churches. Bethany has remained a place for those less inclined toward "emotional and intense" Sunday worship.

Franklin Banks, born in 1924 and a longtime deacon at Bethany, provided another insight into life at Bethany. "You weren't allowed to dance down there, but we had good times in there."[34] The stories from O'Kelly-Cooke's book, alongside the Krueger-Scott interviews, help explain the slightly bourgeois reputation that the church still carries today, a reputation perhaps based as much on its history as its present reality.

As famous as the church is, so have been its leaders. Ed Crawford recalled the renowned Reverend William P. Hayes in his interview, who served Bethany Baptist from 1932 until 1961. In 1954 Hayes had a public housing project at 71 Boyd Street, in the Central Ward, named after him. And to be clear, listening to these interviews, this was a true honor. After all, the "projects," when first erected, were symbols of uplift and hope, not yet carrying the negative associations that would come to haunt them later.

For the most part, Reverend Hayes and his wife are remembered in the Krueger-Scott interviews as pillars of the community, a power couple who brought all sorts of people together while still working for their "own." Retired law enforcement officer Henry Robinson pointed out to his interviewer that "Pastor Hayes was chairman of the Housing Authority . . . and a few white folks was with him . . . they all worked together at that time."[35]

Ed Crawford, who would have been eleven years old at the time of Reverend Hayes's retirement, did recall a sense of privilege enjoyed by the lighter-skinned

Figure 2.3. Hayes Homes, 1954. Photo courtesy Newark Public Library.

members of Bethany. Hayes himself, Crawford pointed out, had a fair complexion. When Reverend Scott accepted the call to follow Hayes as pastor of Bethany, Crawford said things "improved." Crawford described Reverend Scott as a role model, and a man of "true color."[36]

Edna Thomas, another member of Bethany, said emphatically in her interview that Hayes should have had a plaque erected for him in the city because of the major contributions he made to Newark. "Like I tell the members of Bethany Baptist Church every time I see them, 'Why did you let Reverend Hayes just pass away?' His contributions to Newark. . . . Just passed away . . . That project up on the hill, the Hayes Homes, that's Reverend Hayes."[37] Mrs. Thomas was concerned that people would forget Reverend Hayes if his namesake apartment buildings were demolished. And perhaps this was also part of her continued mission to keep Black history alive. Even as Mrs. Thomas was taping an interview slated to be stored in a public "museum" of African American culture, she worried that the Newark she knew would soon become nothing more than a pile of forgotten stories, "faded foliage" if you will. How might she have felt when Newark's African-American Cultural Center had yet to come to fruition at the time of her death in 2004?

Willa Rawlins, former administrative assistant with the Urban League, said that when she was young her family attended Bethany, but then some "trouble" came. She explained, "They threw the minister out, his name was Reverend Hurdle."[38] According to the Bethany website regarding Reverend Hurdle, "Through his solid, biblical preaching, Bethany became even stronger. Dr. Hurdle served with distinction from 1924 until 1930."[39] Mrs. Rawlins told her interviewer that Hurdle later opened a storefront church on Rutgers Street, which she and her family attended for a short while. I have been unable to locate any information on that church, and there were no other reports in the Krueger-Scott interviews of a pastor being dismissed from Bethany Baptist. This absence of information may be telling; if indeed a pastor was ousted, that sort of event would not be in keeping with the upstanding reputation recorded in the pages of Bethany's history. Perhaps Mrs. Rawlins's willingness to share this church drama characterizes her as a person less concerned with what was "respectable" than some of the other interviewees. After all, she and her family left Bethany, and she worked for an activist organization, the Urban League. Or, perhaps, the story of Hurdle's ouster is not, in fact, accurate.

Dr. Beverly Scott was also willing to paint a less-than-perfect picture of the Bethany of old. While interviewee Katheryn Bethea referenced its history of strong community, and Councilwoman Mildred Crump extolled its wide-ranging activities, Dr. Scott had a somewhat different experience. The first lady said that when she arrived at Bethany she found it to be much like an extended family, but that the welcoming embrace did not extend into the greater community. This echoes Willa Coleman's observation that African Americans were better at taking care of those they already knew.

In response to her interviewer asking about the initial reception that Dr. Scott received, Scott conceded that she was never fully accepted by Bethany's parishioners. In fact, Dr. Scott tells the story of one member who said to her, "you will never be the woman Mrs. Hayes [the previous first lady] was."[40] Putting this information together with Ed Crawford's memories regarding the alleged colorism at Bethany Baptist under Pastor Hayes, one might conclude that the Scotts' arrival at Bethany implemented a shift in culture. The couple apparently brought a different "look" and vision to the place. After all, the church website reads, regarding Reverend Scott's arrival, "The congregation accepted many new ideas, installing Mrs. Thelma B. Robinson in 1965 as its first female trustee."[41]

Bethany Baptist has had many lives. It has borne witness to myriad changes in Newark's African American community, as well as in its own congregation. Ed Crawford noted: "It's a church that has grown, felt its impact from folks moving out into the outlying areas. Obviously as people have become more economically stable and things have gotten better, folks have moved from the inner city of Newark out into some of the outer areas. So we've gone from being what might have been more of a neighborhood church to being more of a commuter church in our latter years now."[42] Many of Bethany's families departed Newark for the suburbs—or at least quieter urban quarters—during the last few decades. Yet the majority continue to return to Bethany each Sunday morning. Reverend Scott described what he believed was part of Bethany's staying power: "Bethany has always been a downtown church. . . . Curiously, Reverend Glenn Hatfield, the pastor of Peddie [Memorial] Church, when he came here to preach he said that Peddie Church, the large, white Baptist church, had organized about a dozen churches in its lifetime, and the only one that has managed to survive is Bethany. . . . It's not that, I think that we had, not only had an educated clergy, but we pushed education."[43] Bethany has played a prominent role in Newark and remains a touchstone for many Black Newarkers today. As it welcomed its latest pastor, Reverend Dr. Timothy Levi Adkins-Jones, in 2016, interested parties await the next phase of this important religious institution's life, looking to see how it will both affect and reflect the rapidly changing city of Newark.

While the Bethany bent of the Krueger-Scott oral history collection could be viewed as a limiting disadvantage, it provides opportunity for analysis of what middle-class life might look like in a majority African American city prior to the turn of the twenty-first century. This is a cultural perspective that deserves more attention, as it aids in the disruption of some common tropes perpetuated in history books and mainstream media regarding African American culture. The Krueger-Scott project reflects a more contemporary oral history practice by featuring middle- and working-class African Americans.

During the first generation of the oral history field, the academy spent little time on African Americans—or on poor whites and women for that matter. Oral historian Paul Thompson writes that early historians had "no interest in the point of view of the labourer, unless he was specifically troublesome; nor—being men—would they have wished to inquire into the changing life experiences of women."[44] The first half of the twentieth century can be described as a time in our country when powerful white men were still the primary storytellers. Modern oral history has helped diversify the narrative.

Even today, general teaching around the African American experience remains quite polarized, encompassing either "the greats" or those who have struggled "against all odds." Krueger-Scott's collection looks at many who lived between those two poles: middle-class Blacks, activists, those working for their communities through churches and social programs, and even those not particularly interested in changing the world but simply wanting to live a good life.

Queen of Angels (1926–2016). Bethany may have been the most visible church within the Krueger-Scott oral histories, but it was certainly not the only one that garnered pride among its members. And while there were many other home churches among the interviewees, space does not allow for the important urban history of each and every one.[45]

A handful of the Krueger-Scott participants mention Queen of Angels as their church, or at least as one that played an essential role in their Newark experience. Queen of Angels was the first Black Catholic church in Newark. The initial meeting of what would become Queen of Angels was held in 1926, organized by a group of African American women whose mission was simply to serve their community. The original edifice, on Academy Street, was ordered from the Sears Roebuck catalog for $1,400.

In 1958 the building suffered a fire, and the congregation was invited to share space with St. Peter's Church on Belmont Avenue, a predominantly German parish. By 1962, the white congregants had all but disappeared from St. Peter's and the church was rededicated as Queen of Angels that same year. The Reverend Martin Luther King Jr. visited the church in the 1960s, and meetings for Dr. King's Poor People's Campaign were held at the church thereafter. When King was murdered, the church organized a walk for racial harmony that drew 25,000 people.[46]

In her interview, Elma Bateman extolled the onetime leader of Queen of Angels, Father Thomas Carey, who created an artistic community in his church "to expand on church connections." Bateman explains, "He started Queen of Angels Players . . . and for ten years we gave shows . . . we put them on at Essex Catholic High School and then at St. Benedict's. . . . Things like that weren't being done in the church, you know, through the church. We brought people from all around Newark, not just Queen of Angels."[47]

Zachary Yamba, president emeritus of Essex County College in Newark, fondly remembered visiting Queen of Angels Church on Academy Street prior to the 1958 fire.[48] And Nathaniel Potts was an altar boy at the church, which he explained to his interviewer began as a mission for "coloreds."[49] Hortense Williams Powell was also a member of Queen of Angels, and had been since the age of seven:

> Back then, the Catholics were trying to get Negroes to join the church. Because most Negroes are Baptist, Methodist, scattered Presbyterians, scattered Episcopalians. . . . In fact, Queen of Angels was a missionary church. . . . They had a little car—or it was a car or bus or van or something that they would go around—and they would pick the kids up, you know, for Sunday school or, Protestants call it Sunday school, we call it catechism—for catechism and for mass on Sunday. You know. And they had that church there on Academy and Whitley [sic] Street. Was one story, had a basement. The men of the church, the men of the missionary, built that church. And, you know, we all went to that church.

Although Queen of Angels was the Black Catholic church in Newark, a few Black families also belonged to nearby St. Patrick's, a predominantly Irish Catholic church, according to Powell:

> Now, St. Patrick's had a church right there . . . on Washington and Central Avenue. But, you know, those—that was predominantly an Irish church. Mostly Irish went to St. Patrick's. But children who lived in that area, if you were Black, you didn't get your first holy communion and confirmation at St. Patrick's. You came up and you got your—you might have gone there for catechism, but when you got your confirmation and your first holy communion and any other sacrament, you got that at the Queen of Angels, which was the, I would just say, that was the Black church, the Black mission. You know. So the church was, the church was segregated. . . . I was very disheartened, too, when I came to the realization that all Catholics were not the same.[50]

Membership at Queen of Angels began to dwindle in the 1980s. Black church attendance nationwide was in decline, and because Catholics are a minority in the African American faith community already, this made a marked difference in terms of church sustainability.[51] The archdiocese finally closed the doors of Queen of Angels Church for good in 2012.

Queen of Angels remained an abandoned building until the summer of 2016, debris strewn within its walls and wire fencing surrounding the building. It was an eerie replica, in both image and narrative, of the Krueger-Scott Mansion. The church was finally demolished in July of 2016 after it had sat for two years with a demolition crane parked forebodingly in its driveway. The demolition, ordered by the Archdiocese of Newark, was initially slated for the summer of 2015. But as we have already witnessed, municipal wheels take long to turn. One of the delays in demolition was due to the discovery that the church was on the state and national Registers of Historic Places. Ultimately, the archdiocese prevailed, and the demolition was rescheduled despite the building's historic status.[52]

In a 2015 nj.com article, Matt Gosser, a member of the Newark Preservation and Landmarks Committee and professor at New Jersey Institute of Technology, claimed that he had attempted to purchase the building from the archdiocese in 2014 for $50,000. His plans were to turn it into a gallery or museum. His offer was declined; according to Gosser, the archdiocese was asking $500,000 for the property. Gosser believed that Queen of Angels could have been saved, but that "whenever a building owner wants a building to be demolished, they stop making repairs to it, so eventually, nature takes over and they say they have to knock it down."[53] Whether apartment house or house of worship, as with so many stories of the urban built environment, Newark's Black Catholic community lost its sanctuary to a diagnosis of "blight."

Still pursuing his mission, in 2016 in anticipation of the 350th anniversary of Newark, Gosser posted a call to artists asking for project proposals that celebrated Queen of Angels. Soliciting "artwork of any and all mediums that have some connection to the recently demolished Queen of Angels church in Newark, NJ," read the Facebook page created by Gosser. The exhibit, called "Queen of Angels: When a Church Dies," had its opening reception on October 23, 2016, in "an old auto dealership on Central Ave."[54]

Individuals (1919–1997). It is important to reiterate that church membership is not a given for every African American. Mrs. Marzell Swain in her interview, for example, was remembering her grandfather, a man who never knew his birthday, always wore a hat, took his grandchildren to church, and did not believe in God. Swain said in her interview that she asked him once why he would rouse the children each Sunday morning, deliver them to church, yet not attend himself. His answer referenced slavery, Swain explained, "He said, 'If there was a God why would He let me suffer the way that I did?'"[55]

Ed Crawford, a community counselor for halfway houses and prisons, said that while he had had family that belonged to Bethany Baptist Church since his grandfather joined in 1919, Crawford himself stopped attending church for a while. "As I finished high school, I thought I no longer needed that, so I walked away for a number of years."[56] (Crawford ended up going back to Bethany once he had children of his own, ultimately serving as an usher and trustee.)

The late teenage years are the age when several Krueger-Scott participants reported that they stepped back from church—if given the choice. Yet other interviewees decried the idea of giving children a choice when it came to attending church. Reverend Alvin Conyers said, "When I came north, I found there were a freedom of desire. If you wanted to [go to church] you could, if you didn't, uh, you didn't have to. . . . We lost our family church connection when we migrated to the North and adopted that method of freedom."[57] According to many interviewees, this departure from church, and the increased freedom given to children in general, were contributing factors in the downfall of the Black community.

Now for some, churchgoing was simply a luxury. Willie Bell Hooper, who belonged to Mt. Zion Baptist, reported that she did not regularly have the chance to attend church as a young mother, much as she would have liked to. She explained, "I had so many children that by the time I got them dressed I didn't have anything to wear myself."[58] Willa Coleman, a retired health care worker, told her interviewer that she had been a member of Emmanuel Missionary Baptist Church on Chancellor Avenue and Clinton Place since 1970. But "before that I was workin'; when I was workin' I didn't get to church much. When I did have a Sunday off, I would go to any church around," Coleman explained.

Of those who did carry on the churchgoing tradition, the Krueger-Scott narrators reveal numerous reasons why one church was joined over another. Quite often they were simply following family tradition; yet many also cited their choices as having much to do with the senior pastor. And upon occasion the sole reason for attending a particular church was geographical. Louise Epperson, who came to Newark as an African Methodist Episcopalian, explained, "The AME church was so far away, I would get lost trying to find it. I joined the Clinton Avenue Presbyterian Church."[59] Clinton Avenue was approximately one mile from Orange Street, where Epperson first lived.

By listening to the unique church stories of the Krueger-Scott collection, a better understanding of the complex role that religion plays in African American urban life can be constructed. And just the few previous stories confirm that African Americans, as with any other racial, ethnic, or cultural group, are not a monolith of thought and behavior. The role that the church played in their lives looked different depending upon the individual, even as there were strong commonalities surfacing throughout the interviews. While some were unwilling to participate in any kind of disparagement, others shared less flattering aspects of church life with their interviewers. The unique quality of this oral history collection is that peers were talking to peers; some might have even been members of the same church. The reticence and willingness may well have been affected by who was doing the interviewing.

Owen Wilkerson, legislative analyst for the Office of the City Clerk at the time of his interview, reported that, contrary to what some might claim, the Black faith community did not unfailingly embrace everybody. He explained there were rifts between classes and colors, and between the new arrivals and the old-timers. "The church has to change also to the norms of present day African American society and not African American society of the 1940s," Wilkerson cautioned. He blamed religious people for the creation of these barriers, while at the same time adding that the church also served as a sanctuary for those "new settlers" from the harassment of their own people.[60]

> Outside of the church, on the street and what not or within a community, I think I had mentioned, you know, we as kids we sort of ostracized the kid who came from the South and what not because of his or her talk or his clothing.... Those are one of the pluses that I have of the Black church. [It didn't do that.] That I really have a lot of respect for the Black church. I mean, there are other situations that are within the Black church as far as the gossiping and the scandals and everything that I detest.[61]

Amiri Baraka, native son of Newark, confirms this community fissure in his 1963 book *Blues People*. He writes, "There were now such concepts as a Northern and a Southern Negro, and they would soon be, to a certain extent, different people."[62]

Owen Wilkerson goes on to give an example in his interview with Glen Marie Brickus, of the troubling "mindset" of certain church people:

> I could just bring up an example. Zion Hill Baptist Church. There was this guy, Milton Wesley, fantastic organist. Gospel organist. He went to Arts High

School. Very creative, music-wise and what not. He was dating this young lady, Thelma. Thelma lived somewhere around here. She went to Westside. To make a long story short, he knocked her up. That's the expression we used to use in those days. And, you know, they had to stand before the deaconess board, the church board, and this board and that board. But they kicked them out of the church. You know, and I felt that this was the time when they needed God. They needed the church. You know what I mean? . . . That's when I really started, really started looking at the Black church, Mrs. Brickus.[63]

Louise Epperson, health care worker and community activist, shared a story in her interview about a rift she personally suffered at church. Epperson attended 13th Street Presbyterian, which eventually moved to Clinton Avenue and became Clinton Avenue Presbyterian Church. Epperson was head of "women's work," a sort of women's ministry. The minister, Reverend Collington [sic], and his wife, Epperson points out, were white. The demographics of the membership are unclear. Epperson explains in her interview that she suffered a heart attack at one point. And when a church member visited her in the hospital, at Epperson's bedside she produced a resignation letter from the women's ministry, which Epperson was asked to sign.

> When I had a heart attack, Vickie Booker, who was also a trustee or a deaconess at the church, she came to the hospital with a paper and asked me— She told me that the pastor's wife told her to ask me if I would sign from being—that I resigned from being the president of women's work because I was sick and they didn't want me to suffer with all of this heavy load on me. And they had someone else that they could appoint as president of the women's work. I said, "If you don't want me, that's fine. But I know I have served you well." And she asked me in the hospital. And I said, "But if you brought the paper to me and it came from the church then I will accept it and sign it." And that's what I did.

Epperson reluctantly relinquished her leadership position. She believed the pastor's wife had been waiting for an opportunity to get rid of her, due to her "outspoken nature." Epperson continues: "And years later Mrs. Collington met me taking a course at Rutgers [University], where she taught school also. Mrs. Collington told me then that she owed me an apology because what she thought I was about, she find out that I was not about that but I was speaking out and she respected my judgment now. And she regrets that she had turned some of the women from my church against me. But that didn't bother me, because I joined the church and not the minister."[64] It is not clear whether there were racial implications involved in this feud, but it seems likely as Epperson does mention the minister and first lady's race right off. It could also be that Mrs. Epperson uses her own trait of outspokenness as code for some cultural stereotypes of Black women, thus couching potentially racist accusations by the minister's wife for the sake of respectability. Ultimately, Epperson was disappointed in the comportment of people who claimed to be of a higher spiritual realm.

Hypocritical or less-than-gracious behaviors are, of course, not unique to the church; they are simply witnessed here through the church stories of the Krueger-Scott narrators. Holding church folk to a higher a standard is a habit many of us fall into. With the handful of tales that "tell" on the good church people of Newark, such as those of Owen Wilkerson, Bev Scott, and Louise Epperson, we can surmise that there may have been a few more that went left unsaid.

Politicians (1971–1997). In 1971, Wynona Lipman became the first African American woman elected to the New Jersey Senate; she was its longest-serving member at twenty-seven years. Countering common narratives regarding those who took part in the Great Migration, Senator Lipman also received a Fulbright scholarship to study at the Sorbonne, marrying her white husband in Paris.

As with many of the politically active participants in the Krueger-Scott collection, Senator Lipman noted that while she was indeed a member of a church, she did not attend regularly. After all, weekends were a busy time for politicians. An amusing conversation ensues between the senator and her interviewer, Glen Marie Brickus, one of the more animated Krueger-Scott interviewers:

> LIPMAN: Bethany Baptist Church. That's the church I belong to. I don't go very often. I'm not a real good churchgoer to tell you the truth. I know you were surprised to see me sit so long at the Zion Holy Church.
> BRICKUS: I really was. I expected you to leave almost as soon as you had made your presentation. And the reason I looked at you the way that I did because I go to Bethany and I never knew that you were a member there.
> LIPMAN: I go there.
> BRICKUS: Ahhh. It's nice to know. Okay. There'll be some changes made.
> LIPMAN: Yes ma'am. You're gonna call me up and take me to church.
> [Laughter.][65]

African Americans, especially in past generations, often feel compelled to ensure that those they love and care for are "churched." Lipman understood exactly what Mrs. Brickus was implying when she said some changes were going to be made. This push for church participation is partially motivated by the desire to preserve a Black community, but the urgency also stems from the Christian belief that if people are not "saved," upon death that they will bypass heaven for somewhere much less desirable. Erma McLurkin, 105 years old, said to her interviewer, Giles Wright, "Yeah, I'm a Baptist, gonna be a Baptist . . . Baptist is the way. What you is?" Wright responded that he was a Methodist. "You just got to be baptized. You don't be baptized, you don't make it in," warned McLurkin. Wright chuckled, then asked permission to take her photograph.[66]

Councilman and state Senator Ronald Rice said he refused to commit to a single place of worship. His home church was Allen AME on 19th Avenue, but he admitted he was not very active there. Rice believed that politicians were taken advantage of when they stayed at one church too long, with expectations placed upon them by ministers and congregants alike: "I understand the higher power, etc. I just haven't pinned down a church home. Um, I used to be a trustee at Allen AME when Reverend Druid was there. Unfortunately, when you're an elected official, and you pin a church home down, some of the ministers unfortunately expect you to do things—you know, it becomes more of a burden. You want to be active but you get taken advantage of and so I just keep movin'."

Rice, like Owen Wilkerson, was a man who seemed to have a complicated relationship with the church. He said at one point that the Black church "helped layin' the foundation to get us as elected officials, to push us in some of these positions where we can make decisions on people's lives." At the same time, Senator Rice was skeptical of some who called themselves Christians. When asked later in his interview about the "seamy side" of Newark, Rice described criminal communities that included numbers runners, craps organizers, and bootleggers. He added, "These same people at the church."[67]

Councilwoman Mildred Crump attended church only sporadically, according to her interview. But her absence was not so much for political reasons. In her interview she provided a unique explanation for her inconsistency, and another illustration of Bethany Baptist as "modernized" under the Reverend Scott: "In fact, our pastor [James Scott] is so wonderful and is so forward thinking—I won't use the word liberal because it constitutes another connotation. But as forward thinking . . . when I was really playing tournament bridge and I was traveling almost every other weekend, he would say to me, 'Okay, I missed you at church. What tournament were you at?' You know, that kind of thing. But Newark is famous nationwide for its tournament bridge players. And that's my favorite pastime."[68] Crump made sure to disavow any connection between Reverend Scott and the word "liberal." Perhaps even more so than today, the word had major connotations in the 1990s. After all, it was the 1988 presidential campaign that had Democratic candidate Michael Dukakis branded a "card-carrying liberal," a term some even associated with communism. As Mildred Crump suggested in her interview, "liberal" may have implied a kind of troublemaker—especially when attributed to a Black man. This was not a word she wanted to associate with the Reverend Scott.

Another elected official, Sharpe James, Newark's mayor from 1986 through 2006, said that he was invited to attend various churches frequently. Mayor James felt strongly about the significance of the church writ large, telling his interviewer that the African American community "has come this far from faith."[69] James went on to talk about his church wedding:

> Well, I met Miss Mary Madison, and shortly thereafter we were married in St. James AME Church. I believe in 1963 or '64. It seems like only yesterday so I can't remember the exact time. And I remember Reverend Blake was there. Because the wedding cost us fifteen dollars to use the church, and everyone was invited to bring their own brown bag. So we were married in the church upstairs. Everybody walked right down the back stairs of St. James AME Church, and then on Irvine Turner Boulevard and Court Street, and went downstairs for a reception of about a hundred friends who brought their own food.[70]

Although they were married at St. James AME, Mayor James's wife ultimately joined Elizabeth Avenue Presbyterian. Sharpe James was a Baptist and thus did not follow her, at least not at first. But in 1985, James did end up joining the Presbyterian church—after his son was shot, apparently in a mugging for his leather bomber jacket:

> When my son was shot in 1985, December the 5th, 1985—left for dead on the streets of Newark—that church, for the first time in twenty years, on Saturday had a revival. If it were not for them being open for the first time in twenty years on Saturday and having a revival meeting—. Then my son, left bleeding to death, crawled a hundred feet, hearing voices in that church, falling down the steps, and the church choir becoming angels of hope, taking off their white garments and wherever they saw blood mopping it up, wherever they saw a hole in his body sticking their white garment in it. One of them recognized that he was my son. Called up the house. Mary was in New York shopping with Sylvia Ross that day. My son would not be alive today. So our family belongs to that church. But that is a Presbyterian church and I'm a Baptist.

James went on to explain, echoing Senator Rice, that as a politician he was forced to make the rounds when it came to church. "So I find myself going to as many as possible out of respect for the work they do. Out of respect for their ministry. Because they don't want to see the mayor come just in election year. They hold that against you."[71]

Each African American politician in the Krueger-Scott collection had a somewhat different relationship to religious life; there was no collective performance of Christianity. In fact, Councilwoman Crump reported that she "flirted with Islam" at one point—although she quickly made clear in her interview that she was presently a "proud member" of Bethany Baptist. "I won't say I changed my name, but about the age of eighteen I started dating a young man who was Muslim. And what I did for a short period of time was stop using my last name, I remember, my 'slave name' as we used to call it. And I became Mildred X. But once Charles and I stopped dating, that was over."[72]

Politics and church have been married together for better and for worse throughout this country's history. The politicians' stories here are opportunities to consider more thoughtfully the ways in which we see our elected officials relate to religious institutions today. Perhaps it would prove useful to be more cognizant of both the private and public relationships behind the faith-based political performances we witness today.

This section has focused on two specific churches, and on Christianity as a whole. Yet across the country, as in Newark, participants in the Great Migration brought an assortment of religious practices to urban centers. And sometimes they took on altogether different religious practices once arriving in their new communities. In her 2017 book, *New World a-Coming: Black Religion and Racial Identity during the Great Migration*, Judith Weisenfeld tells a story about the Moorish Science Temple of America, an organization founded in Newark in 1913 by Drew Ali.[73]

The Nation of Islam, which came out of Ali's organization, was an important facet of Newark religious life. While only one Krueger-Scott narrator even mentions the Islamic faith, Newark included a large Muslim community by the mid-twentieth century. The radical 1960s was reflected in the community work of many Muslim women in Newark, as recorded in Cynthia S'thembile West's article, "Revisiting Female Activism in the 1960s: The Newark Branch Nation of Islam."[74] The expansion of Muslim entrepreneurship nationwide at this time also acted as a stabilizing economic force in many Black urban communities.

Weisenfeld's book additionally interrogates the role of Father Divine's Peace Mission Movement, referenced by several Krueger-Scott narrators—foremost in terms of the inexpensive meals it provided during the Depression era. A bit more will be said about the mission in a later section. Finally, Black Hebrews are also featured in Weisenfeld's book, African Americans who believe they are related to the ancient Israelites. One can find members of this group today doing street-corner preaching in downtown Newark.

It is not that these other religious groups and organizations were insignificant to the life of Newark, but simply that the members of the Krueger-Scott oral history project did not represent any of them. This is both an indication of the dominance of Christianity as a religious practice, as well as an illustration of the self-selective process in gathering participants for the project.

Not Just Church

Sundays are about more than church, we discover in these interviews—even for those who attend church on a weekly basis. Sundays can also be about what one wears to church, what one does after church, and sometimes what one does instead of church. Themes of clothing, food, and music thread themselves through the Krueger-Scott Sunday stories. Most memories shared here are positive ones, though not all. Ultimately, though, whether talking white gloves or baseball mitts, a lot of living was packed into this one day of the week.

Sunday Best (1924–1965). Councilwoman Crump, who came to Newark in 1965 from Detroit, was interviewed by Mrs. Brickus about churchgoing differences between Detroit and Newark:

> CRUMP: [I] found when I moved here a lot more flamboyancy, individualism. You know, we were kind of closed in the Midwest, you know, we wore gloves, three button to the wrist. You know that kind of thing. The old folks used to bring you up. There was just a certain way you dressed on Sunday. And I found that not to be true here.
> BRICKUS: Hats and gloves to church.
> CRUMP: That's right.
> BRICKUS: And you weren't dressed if you didn't wear hat and gloves.[75]

Fashion was and still is an integral component of African American history and culture. And in newly industrialized cities like Newark, at one point it clearly distinguished the Northerner from the Southerner.

The new settlers from the South were often schooled in the subject of dress. Once acclimated to their new urban homes, many migrants would return South for regular visits, often in the "homecoming" month of August. Wearing their best clothes—even renting apparel as well as cars—they intended to impress upon their Southern relatives and neighbors just how well things were going in the North. Isabel Wilkerson writes in *The Warmth of Other Suns*:

> At Easter and around the Fourth of July, the people from the North came. They looked like extras out of a movie at the Saturday matinee. They wore peplums and bergamot waves. . . . They flashed thick rolls of cash from their pockets—the biggest bills on the outside. . . . They said they were making all kinds of money. But they didn't have to say it because the cars and the clothes did the talking. They had been wiring more money to their families back home than they truly could spare and had been saving up all year for those gloves and matching purse. They made sure to show up at their mother-churches.[76]

The body is one thing over which African Americans have wrested some semblance of control during their time in America. Fashion has at times given expression to that which could not otherwise be expressed. In 1924, W.E.B. Du Bois gave a speech at his alma mater, Fisk University, admonishing the institution for its trend toward industrial education and conservatism as it moved away from the freedom and intellectualism Du Bois had experienced while a student there. Speaking about the proposed university dress code, Du Bois said, "All through the life of the colored people and their children the world makes repeated efforts to surround them with ugliness. Is it a wonder that they flame in their clothing? That they desire to fill their starved souls with overuse of silk and color?"[77]

Owen Wilkerson affirmed to his Krueger-Scott interviewer the importance of dressing up and standing out:

> On the weekends, that's when I—and I put this in quotes, quote, unquote—that's when the fashion show began. Sunday you had church. Everyone wanted to wear their Sunday best. And I mean, that was in the South. You know, the little girls would wear the white dresses and what not. I mean, I remember my mother used to put so much rouge and lipstick on, and, you know, perfume. And I used to say, "Gee whiz, Mom, you're just going to church." . . . [She'd say,] "Well, you know, if I don't dress up and everything I'm not serving the Lord right."

The night before Sunday had its own sartorial requirements, according to Wilkerson:

> You know, on Saturday nights, I mean, hey, you put on your best dress and your suits and your black and white shoes, and you go into the bar and you just leave all your tensions and frustrations that you had on the job, and you want to look sharp. . . . I used to shine shoes on Fridays and Saturdays, and I used to hit these bars and everything, and that's when you saw everybody in their—I guess their zoot suits and everything, red suits and yellow suits and everything. But I mean these guys were looking sharp, and the women were looking beautiful. But I'm sure come Monday morning everybody went back into their chauffeur's uniform or the laborer's uniform or their factory uniforms or whatever.[78]

It is unclear whether Mr. Wilkerson himself ever left all his "tensions and frustrations" at the club, or whether he simply witnessed that world from his shoeshine box. Either way, one can hear in his voice, and read in his words, a sense of pride in his people. And yet there is still resignation at the end as he acknowledges that the pageantry is only temporary. Inevitably, the revelers return to their jobs, the majority of which are in service to others, donning clothes no longer of their choosing.

George Branch also shined shoes for club-goers on weekends, as did several other men in the Krueger-Scott interviews. A shoeshine business was an easily accessible form of income, something a young boy could set up simply by purchasing a brush, some polish, and a cloth. In his autobiography, Malcolm X relates his own work as a "shoeshine boy" at the local clubs around Boston. Snapping the shoe rag for zoot-suited dancers and listening to Peggy Lee and Count Basie in the background, Malcolm X—much like Owen Wilkerson—soaked up the spectacle that was the dance club while making pocket money at the same time.[79]

Owen Wilkerson continued to talk about dress in his interview, wherein a dialogue emerged between him and his interviewer, Mrs. Brickus:

BRICKUS: But when I grew up in the South, we didn't go to church on Sunday without a hat on your head and gloves on your hands. You know. And then as time went on after I came here, you see more women in church without hats. And in recent years, I almost never see anybody with gloves....

WILKERSON: Except for an usher.

BRICKUS: An usher, yes. And I begin to see women wearing pants coming to church.

WILKERSON: Okay. No. When I was growing up here in the late '40s or '50s, no, a woman couldn't wear pants. As a matter of fact, the women who wore pants were looked upon as being manly.... Unless they were doing a particular occupation that required pants. Now, I remember Dr. Carroll [Dr. E. Mae McCarroll who lived on High Street] used to wear pants and what not, but again, she was in a whole different level and what not. And I remember she used to wear pants poking around in her yard, because she used to grow a lot of big flowers and everything and plant things and what not. And she'd be out there on her knees in dungarees and what not and everything. But.... No. I never, ever saw women wear pants in Zion Hill Baptist Church.

BRICKUS: Well, we were not allowed to wear pants. As a matter of fact, there was two things that my father was very strict on. His daughters didn't wear pants and they didn't whistle.[80]

Here Wilkerson and Brickus confirm shared protocol when it comes to church clothes, and to women's comportment more generally. While white women were quicker to embrace the new trend of pants wearing by the 1950s, African American women moved more slowly in that direction. Most generally, Black women were assigned to carry their race's respectability, assuring white society they were able to conform to the same gendered rules as white women. But Dr. Carroll was at "a whole different level," according to Wilkerson. Because of her elevated professional status, the doctor's responsibility was now different than that of a working- or middle-class Black woman. She could wear pants—on her property at least—and still be considered respectable.

Matthew Little worked on the factory floor at General Motors for thirty-two years, and belonged to Mt. Teman AME church in Elizabeth, New Jersey. Little was born in South Carolina and came to Newark in 1947 after finishing his tour in the navy. Interviewer Pauline Blount asked him, "In what way did people in the North dress differently from people in the South?" After a few moments, he chuckled and said, "Oh, in the South you wore what they call overalls, with suspenders, and here they even wore coveralls, which covered the whole body, you know. And in the South, especially in the country, they washed their shirts and overalls and starch 'em and wear 'em on Sunday. [Laughter between both.] Instead of dressing in suits and ties."[81]

Zaundria Mapson May, a teacher at the time, told the interviewer (her son) that church clothes were similar in the North and South. May recalled, "On Sundays we dressed up.... We were taught that Sundays were special and that you dressed differently going to church than you did during the week."

"What was dressing up for you?" asked her interviewer, Bill May.

"Putting on a dress with a wide skirt and a stiffened crinoline slip, where the skirt part of the dress would stick out and the crinoline would scratch my legs. [Smiling tone of voice.] Um, socks maybe, with ruffles or lace, uh, patent leather shoes, hair ribbons. And something a little extra special, a little pocketbook or even a pair of gloves. Maybe a hat."

"And your brother? What was the dress-up for him?" asked May.

"Uh, dress-up for boys would be a suit, maybe with short pants when they were very young, uh, long pants when they were older. Shirts, ties, and even hats for them."[82]

Mrs. May was raised in Newark. Her family came from Florida in 1947, when she was ten months old, after her father was called to pastor Mt. Calvary Baptist Church on Prince Street. As with many African American children, May returned South each summer to see family; her grandmother lived in Alabama. As a PK (pastor's kid), it is safe to assume that she was one of the more dressed-up children, even at her Northern church, and that her memories of Sunday dress probably reflected her social position.

Harvey Slaten, a retired postal worker, also grew up believing in the importance of dress. "In the Depression years, late '20s and '30s, we managed to have just about everything that came about as far as styles and customs. Easter was the time you got new clothing. My father would buy secondhand suits from the pawn shop so that we could have new stuff on Easter." Slaten learned early that clothes made the man. When asked later in his interview about important people in Newark, Slaten recalled the first Black county clerk, a Mr. Scotland. Slaten explained people called the man "Judge" because he always wore a suit and tie while working in the courthouse.[83] Respect and admiration was earned by those who dressed the part, even when they had not yet landed the role.

Mary Roberts's fashion memories took her back to childhood in North Carolina, and her mother taking in people's laundry. "My mother washed the little white girls' dresses, and I would just admire them, they were so pretty. I think that's why I have a lot of clothes now. Because I always said. 'One day I'm going to have those pretty dresses.'"[84]

Andrew Washington was a retired public school teacher at the time of his interview. When asked a question about his relationship with white neighbors as a child, he reported that he grew up in a community where his was one of the few Black families. "You know, they looked out for me if I got involved with some kind of trouble.... They would give us different things, you know. We always got clothing and stuff like that."[85]

While there were some interviewees who implied that they would never have considered accepting "handouts," especially from white people, others were willing to receive help outside their racial community. According to Owen Wilkerson, his mother at one time deliberated going "on the state" by moving into government-subsidized housing, but ultimately decided against it. Wilkerson then shared what his mother told him, that white people tried to make Black people think they were poor when they were doing just fine. "Because when you were on the state, you know, naturally you would have a white person to come by once in a while and check on you and everything. And then, you know, for some reason all the clothing looked alike. You know, the glasses looked alike. So, you know, you could say, 'oh yeah, he's on the state.'"[86] For some African Americans there were stigma concerns in their own community, coupled with responsibility to exhibit pride in front of the white community.

Style signaled agency, but its pursuit was not always an easy one. Clara Watkins, along with others interviewed, remembered how some of the downtown stores barred African Americans from using the fitting rooms. "Well, at that time they wouldn't let you try on clothes. You had to just look at 'em, pick out what you wanted. And you bought them."[87] African Americans were forced to take their chances on the garments they bought, hoping they would actually fit once tried on at home. This is just one more example of how the cards can be so easily stacked against a group of people; those with the fewest resources often were required to spend them on items that were not even guaranteed suitable.

Of course, not everyone followed the rules. Bernice Johnson, a retired educator, told this story:

> Stores downtown were mostly Jewish and they would sometimes didn't want you to try on hats or different things.... There was a hat mother liked. We knew mother wasn't going to buy that hat because then you bought things "on time": dollar and a half here, two dollars there. Lady said, "unless you buy that hat I can't take it out of the window." And I remember my mother say, "How do you know I'm not gonna buy it?" So the lady took it out the window, mother tried it on, gave it back to her, and walked on out the store.... She had a right to try it on. She was just like that, before her time.[88]

In religion and fashion, for so long, were rare opportunities for African American agency and expression. Today the Black church continues as a center of Black politics, culture, and history. And it continues to be a place for white gloves, for some.

On the Field (1938–1996). One Sunday pastime that did not involve pews, sermons, or fancy dress was America's "favorite." The Newark Eagles baseball team played in the Negro Leagues from 1938 to 1948, sharing Ruppert Stadium with the white minor league team, the Newark Bears. In 1946 the Eagles won the Negro League World Series. Team owner and operator Effa Manley was white

Figure 2.4. "Newark Clinches NL Title," *Pittsburgh Courier*. Photo by Richard Rosenberg. Courtesy Newark Public Library.

(or biracial, depending upon the source) and married to Abe Manley, an African American.. They lived at 71 Crawford Street in Newark. The Eagles were the first professional baseball team ever owned and operated by a woman. In James Overmyer's book on Effa Manley, Eagles player Max Manning is quoted as saying, "The Eagles were to [Black] Newark what the Dodgers were to Brooklyn."[89] The Krueger-Scott oral histories bear this out. James Churchman, funeral director, remembered:

> Oh, I used to swear by all the Newark Eagles. I used to go to the games. The thing that bothered me the most is they used to have opening day on Mother's Day. But my mother would always—we'd go to church, and she'd say, "I know you want to go to the ballgame. So you go ahead." ... And I can remember Mule Suttles and Ray Dandridge, all of the ballplayers. I remember when Larry Doby was playing with the Newark Eagles. 'Cause Larry and I finished high school the same year. Newark's own Larry Doby happened to be the second African American to break baseball's color barrier when he joined the American League in 1947.[90]

Right after internationally known Jackie Robinson became the first African American to play in Major League Baseball (MLB) in the modern era, Newark's own Larry Doby followed as the first African American to play in the MLB's American League.

Willie Belle Hooper recalled the Eagles games being a regular Sunday event. Perhaps surprising to some, it becomes clear in these interviews that the women were also quite involved in the culture of the team. Mrs. Hooper told her interviewer, "Well, the Newark Eagles was a baseball team, a Newark baseball team that everybody went—every Sunday they played in the stadium. Or any time they was in the stadium we went to the game. We didn't want to miss that. That was one of the highlights. And I think everybody used to go down there."[91]

Carolyn Wallace, a retired social services director, remembered the Eagles well, if not necessarily fondly. "My mother was a baseball fanatic, and maybe that's why I don't care for baseball now because she would go to every one of those games and take me. . . . I was so glad when I was old enough to not have to go."[92] Just as with church, apparently attendance at baseball games was mandatory for some.

Richard Cooke, a retired Newark public school teacher, used to go every Sunday to Ruppert Stadium. It was a "privileged life," he says, going with his "uncle and cousins," a reference to his "fictive kin"—family unrelated through ancestry. Cooke recalled, "I saw Satchel Paige when I was a little kid—and we'd have popcorn and a hot dog—we'd have a ball!" Cooke said that his grandmother was a baseball fan as well. "I got to see baseball games at the Yankees, and the Dodgers, when Jackie Robinson started playing. Oh boy, I'm tellin' you, I really enjoyed myself."[93]

The Eagles were important to Coyt Jones, a postal worker, too. "Well, my son and I have never missed a Sunday going down to see [the Eagles] play. Every Sunday we'd go down," he recalled.[94] Mr. Jones's son was LeRoi Jones, later known as Amiri Baraka. These kinds of moments in oral histories can illuminate the conventionality of some exceptional people, humanizing those who have otherwise become icons—or villains. Baraka was a man whose life was informed by the city in which he was raised. The late poet, playwright, and activist grew up watching Black men excel at their sport while being barred from participating on that sport's greatest stages. Early experiences shape people.

The Eagles were the Black team, the Bears were for the white fans. Whether on the field or off, the subject of segregation regularly enters the Krueger-Scott Sunday discussions. Sharpe James commented, "I've seen quote, unquote, not overt, but covert segregation in the North. And again, it was not based on neighborhoods. It was different in the South. In the South, you lived together, but you had to be a 'boy,' stay in your place. In the North, they didn't want to live together."[95] Or apparently go to baseball games together, either.

There were both advantages and disadvantages to the shift toward desegregation. Sharpe James noted that there were more Black millionaires when American society was segregated, and a better network of Black media outlets as well. "We had more restaurants, more of our own under a segregated society than we have now. Coleman Hotel. They had a restaurant. We had everything we needed under segregation. Our own hotel, our own stores, our own merchants began to grow. Integration brought competition where we lost many of our beginning industries."[96]

Baseball's Negro Leagues also fell victim to the decimation of desegregation, even as Effa Manley and other Negro League team owners pushed for that integration. Not foreseeing the ways in which that would ultimately shutter their league, owners believed that once white fans saw how talented the Black players were, they would flock to Negro League games as readily as they did to Dodgers and Yankees games.[97] But as a few Black players began playing for white teams, which offered more money and better resources, their peers were hard-pressed to remain behind in the relatively low-budget Negro Leagues. Alongside the new perquisites, however, Black major leaguers also had to endure the rampant racism incorporated into the fabric of American society. Integration, though not an end to racism, swept the professional baseball fields the way it did so many other industries. Owen Wilkerson explained in his interview:

> I sincerely believe that the worst thing happened to African American society was the lifting of segregation. I tell you the reason why. Because when you had segregation, you had your support system. Everybody worked. We had a common boogie man to fight. We had a common goal to reach in life and in society. The doctors lived with the laborers in the neighborhood and what not. Why? Because of segregation. So you had more of a family, you had more of a support system here. You knew the odds against you if you stepped out of that support system and tried to make it on your own out here in the, quote, unquote, white world.[98]

As sports so often do, baseball in the mid-twentieth century was reflecting what was occurring in American society more generally.

However things were shaking out, the sport of baseball continued to be a touchstone for many Americans, including African Americans. In an interesting moment during his discussion of leisure activities, Sharpe James declared, "I played on the Newark Eagles. Everybody thought I was going to be a professional baseball player."[99] The interviewer, Glen Marie Brickus, did not seem surprised at James's claim to have played for the famous baseball team. Yet, born in 1936, James would have been ten years old when the Eagles won the Negro World Series. Two years after that the league disbanded. James continued, expounding on how good the team was, so much better than the white Newark Bears. He then turned to reminiscing about attending games, watching the famous Negro League players he admired so much. The interviewer, in this case, was either disengaged or reluctant to comment upon her subject's apparently false claim. However, as oral historian Alessandro Portelli reminds us, this kind of moment is simply "another door" through which to enter history: "The first thing that makes oral history different, therefore, is that it tells us less about events than about their meaning. This does not imply that oral history has no factual validity. Interviews often reveal unknown events or unknown aspects of known events; they always cast new light on unexplored areas of the daily life of the nonhegemonic classes."[100] Clearly, the Eagles baseball team was meaningful to Sharpe James.

But Portelli also suggests that it might be that when someone spends a long time on a seemingly small event—or in Mayor James's case an untrue event—it may be because he is attempting to avoid or bypass another topic. "Dwelling on an episode may be a way of stressing its importance, but also a strategy to distract attention from more delicate points."[101]

It certainly is an interesting oral history moment, especially when considering Sharpe James's subsequent convictions for fraud while mayor of Newark. Perhaps James was more comfortable spinning tales of athleticism during his Krueger-Scott interview in hopes of avoiding "delicate" conversations about his political life, even as it was fairly evident that Mrs. Brickus had no intention of pushing James in any direction he did not want to go. In fact, James's athletic prowess was quite central to his public persona—an integral part of political campaigns, and a tool used to connect with constituents once in office. In the city archives, one finds piles of photographs of Mayor James variously swimming, playing tennis, or simply shaking hands with people while sporting a track suit. In 1996, the year of his Krueger-Scott interview, young Cory Booker had begun making his way into Newark politics. Consciously or not, perhaps James was even campaigning during his interview.

All told, the takeaway from these oral histories was that the Newark Eagles baseball team was ingrained into the life of many African Americans. The Eagles, and the Negro Leagues more widely, symbolized strength and ability in the Black community and were an example of success outside the white power structure. The Eagles brought families together, and even usurped churchgoing on occasion. By the time Effa Manley insisted in August of 1940 that attending an Eagles game to raise money for the Booker T. Washington Community Hospital was a "civic responsibility no one should shirk," the Eagles had become central to the lives of countless Black Newarkers.[102] Much of the scholarship on the Negro Leagues leaves Newark out of the discussion, as is so often the case for this city. Oral histories can fill in gaps that some people might not even know exist.

Leisure Activities (1927–1979). "What do you recall regarding the kinds of music that you heard in Black Newark, or do you remember listening to and/or seeing musicians perform jazz, gospel or the blues and at what places and what musicians?" So read question #76 of the Krueger-Scott questionnaire. Ministers and politicians might have been busy on Sundays, but that does not mean they forwent all forms of leisure. Bethany Baptist's Reverend Scott recalled Sundays as more than just time spent in the pulpit. "I not only went to church, but I did know something about nightclubs and so forth in our community. I like jazz."[103]

Senator Wynona Lipman answered the question, saying, "I used to think that the most of what we had in Newark were churches and bars!"[104] Both institutions certainly played a large part in the weekends of these Newarkers, although most narrators were more eager to discuss their churchgoing activities than their time spent in nightclubs. This was especially true of the women, although it may just be that they spent less time in musical establishments due to traditional gender roles and responsibilities of the times. Women's lives were, of course, typically centered within private domesticity, whereas men spent more of their time in public, whether working or socializing. Even so, there were always exceptions to these "rules."

Louise Epperson reported, for example, "When I came to Newark, I thought it was great to run to taverns and go to church. Those are the two main things that I did. [Laughter.] That's true. Church work and taverns. We just had a lot of fun doing that."[105] (Later on we will see that Epperson's familiarity with bars proved quite useful in her political organizing). Part of Louise Epperson's relatively nontraditional attitude may well have been informed by her aunt, with whom she lived when she first came to Newark, a woman who owned the first bar in the city after Prohibition.

There was a wide swath of feelings surrounding the subject of clubs and music. Some interviewees regarded these establishments as mysterious and exotic, while others looked upon them as locations of "the seamy side of Newark," as the questionnaire puts it elsewhere. Others yet embraced the club scene as just one more occasion to move about freely after spending so much of their lives barred from doing so.

"Again with that stereotype that after work our reward is to get drunk and to party and to act like a fool. Not to say, 'how much you going to pay me? What benefits I have, what health care I have.' Meet and drink, get plastered and forget the labors of the week and forget that you're being underpaid. And then, of course, you know, the real tragedy, forget to bring some money home," laments Sharpe James.[106]

Hortense Williams Powell remembered as a child peeking into the Bikini Club to look at the men sitting at the bar. And Mageline Little told her interviewer, "Newark had some good music—because I'm a Nancy Wilson, Sarah Vaughan kind of person." After mentioning some of the music she heard when she lived in the South, Little quickly interjected, "I didn't like the bars—but I liked the concerts they would have at Symphony Hall."[107]

Councilman Calvin West reported that when he was young, adults knew how to have fun at home. "They'd have a jolly good time.... Nothing out of line or what not.... It wasn't like goin' to bars and things of that nature. Didn't really know that that existed."[108] Owen Wilkerson, on the other hand, saw the taverns as a part of one's weekly routine, as long as it was balanced with some more wholesome activity. "Everyone was entitled to some relaxation," said Wilkerson, and then they "would take care of that on Sunday."[109]

Mary Roberts, a retired teacher, recalled watching entertainers at an unnamed downtown club in Newark. "Mostly we listened to our Black artists, you know, Sarah Vaughan, Louis Armstrong, all those people.... My brother used to take me down there. It was really a nice place to go. There was jazz.... I remember going on Sunday afternoons sometimes."[110] Going out in the afternoon with one's brother, perhaps right from church, may have been looked upon differently than venturing out after dark with an unrelated man, dressed in non-church attire. Davarian Baldwin makes mention in his book of the respectable "daytime image" that some African Americans sought to project upon Chicago's Stroll, and upon their leisure activities more generally.[111] Nighttime activities offered more potential for trouble, whether real or imagined.

Owen Wilkerson established that there were many options for one's weekend in terms of bars and taverns in Newark. He remembered gospel groups playing at various venues on Sundays, like Ronnie Williams with the Five Blind Boys of Alabama or the Mighty Clouds of Joy. Wilkerson provided a snapshot:

> I mean, everybody on a Friday night, you know, after you'd been working and slaving all day and what not and everything all week, you know, you would have a drink. You would go around the corner to the Meyer's [sic] Tavern on Belmont Avenue, which was right next to the Baer's supermarket. It was between the Baer's supermarket and Fisher's Bakery. And there was this one particular gentleman named Rudy. On Fridays, you know, Rudy would have a couple of drinks and come home and raise all kind of hell. And the cops knew him. I mean, every Friday they were there. You know, they'd just take him on the stoop and sit down and talk with Rudy and what not. Hey, Monday morning, Rudy's the nicest guy you ever want to meet.[112]

This is an interesting moment in terms of the relationship between Blacks and law enforcement, a moment that seems to illustrate a more "community policing" approach, like so many are calling for today.

Willie Bradwell recalled in her interview, "Laurel Gardens used to have—Ronnie Williams used to sponsor their gospel shows. And everybody came. That's the first place I saw Aretha Franklin.... Every Sunday practically we were in Laurel Gardens for a gospel show." Then Bradwell remembered another weekend leisure activity: Public Service would run buses on Sundays for excursions outside the city. They traveled to places like Roadside America, a miniature village tourist attraction, or the caves of Pennsylvania. Leaving a bustling city for the weekend continues to be a welcome distraction for so very many urban residents across the country.[113]

Figure 2.5. PSNJ GM No. 4081 at Franklin Avenue Loop, circa 1954–1955. Photo and permission by Brian Cudahy.

Of course, Sundays were leisurely in terms of eating, too; many enjoyed a meal or food specific to their Sunday traditions and observances. Calvin West, member of Friendship Baptist on Norfolk Street, said that Sundays were about "getting ready for Sunday meals and going to church, coming back home, having Sunday dinner, then going back to church. I used to say to myself, why do we have to go to church so much?!"[114]

"On Sunday we had corn bread that tasted like cake," remembers Reverend Scott.[115] Queen Elizabeth Wright James ("Queenie") reminisced on her father's good cooking. "My daddy used to love to cook 'cause he cooked in the army. He was a chef and that's what he got his diploma from. . . . He was a head chef in the service. And he was a good cook. And you talking about some corn bread. Whew! My dad could cook. He'd get up on Sunday morning or whatever and cook that corn bread."[116]

James Churchman's early memories of church had as much to do with what he got to eat afterwards. "And then we had an ice cream parlor there called Dellcrest, and it was a big thing on a Sunday after church—'cause we didn't go to movies on Sunday—that we would walk over to Dellcrest Ice Cream Parlor and sit down and eat ice cream there. It was quite a treat for us to go over there."[117]

Ice cream, in fact, turns out to be quite a memory trigger and place-marker for so many interviewees. For example, Joe Clark shared that he earned money as a young boy through the sale of Kool-Aid and ice cream. Using his mother's churn, he would make the ice cream himself and sell it for five cents a scoop. According to Katheryn Bethea, children who belonged to the Boy and Girl Scouts would get free hot dogs and ice cream at the Eagles games. And Owen Wilkerson remembered that his uncle would pick up a group of young people in his Hudson and take them to Weequahic Park for ice cream in the summertime. Louise Scott herself was savvy enough to ensure that her business empire included an ice cream parlor.

Calvin West was seventy-one years old at the time of his Krueger-Scott interview. At one point West is asked about birthday celebrations and responds that people did not need to go to bakeries "back then," but made their cakes at home. Considering his past comments about the excesses of bars and clubs, it appears that West highly valued a life lived at home. For the second time in his interview, he points out the merits of self-sufficiency that he witnessed as a child; adults created their own cakes, made their own fun. West's voice becomes animated in the interview when he exclaims, "We even made our own ice cream!" The interviewer says, "You're kidding," perhaps in response to the joy in West's voice more than to the impossibility of the statement. "Oh, certainly. We made our own ice cream in the churn . . . it was a wonderful thing," beamed West through the tape recorder.[118]

While one hears more of Saturdays as the day relegated to quotidian consumer activity, Sundays were also shopping days for some of the Krueger-Scott narrators. Queenie James shared that she and Madam Louise Scott used to treat themselves to a day of shopping in "the city" some Sundays. It is not clear whether this was after church or in lieu thereof.

> MRS. JAMES: Mrs. Scott, we used to go shopping on Sundays in New York. So I didn't really do a lot of big shopping here in Newark. I would go with her. We would go to New York, and she would drive. When she bought her first Cadillac. And we would drive to New York and go down, you know, where they, what did they call it? They used to go down where the big shopping area.
> BRICKUS: In the Village?
> MRS. JAMES: In the Village and all downtown and all that. We used to go there. I used to go with her. And we would pick up clothes and stuff like that.[119]

(It is not clear that Madam Scott and Queen James actually did their shopping in the bohemian stores of the West Village. Brickus's prompt negated the opportunity for Mrs. James to come up with the exact location on her own.)

Coyt Jones remembered that his Sunday afternoons were often spent window shopping, strolling Newark's downtown Broad Street. He also made note of the apparent ease of staying out until all hours back then, compared to present times.

"Come in any hour we wanted to. No one was afraid of anything. Now it's a different story. You can't do that."[120]

However, according to Rose Tucker, a onetime operating room assistant, one could not necessarily "come in any hour" even back then. Tucker explained, "You had to be home at a certain time, you didn't just walk in when you were ready. My time was 11:30. My brother could stay out longer." Mrs. Tucker did echo Coyt Jones's claim of safety, remembering how she would run from the "Y," down Court Street at 11:15 at night, returning home just in time to make curfew. The rules, and thus experiences, were clearly different for males and females of this era.

Tucker did certainly recall downtown fondly—highlighting the Griffith Piano Company on Broad Street, which opened in 1927. Sometimes, she remarked, they would have a live person playing the piano right there in the store window.

Downtown loomed large for numerous Krueger-Scott narrators; Mrs. Tucker and her interviewer, E. Alma Flagg, discussed this at length, summing up:

> TUCKER: You go downtown on Sunday. You could walk downtown, walk over High Street and go down Market Street and back up Broad Street. That was an afternoon out.
> FLAGG: I know what you mean.... You really went sightseeing downtown, didn't you?[121]

Downtown was an important locale; it was a site of awe-inspiring stores and coveted goods. Window shopping was quite often the only option for African Americans in Newark—and numerous other cities—during the first half of the century; those interviewed for the Krueger-Scott project by and large took segregation and discrimination as a given. Pauline Mathis proclaimed the beauty of downtown, but added, "I always felt that sometimes at some of the stores you could be waiting and there'd be several people waiting and sometime it took a little while for them to get to you sometimes. You know what I mean? Sometimes they'd take someone ahead of you and you knew you may have been there first."[122] The many qualifiers—*sometimes*, *little*, *may*—in Mathis's explanation speak to her possible concerns with sounding too negative even as she describes what were clearly racist practices.

As children, many of the narrators accompanied their parents on pilgrimages downtown just to look at merchandise outside many of their families' reach—whether financially or logistically. And there is some tension in the interviews between shopping downtown and spending one's money on Springfield Avenue or Prince Street. Ethel Richards remembers that her mother bought her shoes at Allison's Shoe Store on Springfield. "There was no need to go ... downtown," said Richards.[123]

All in all, there was a sense among the narrators that, even if they no longer would have gone downtown by the time of the interviews, they certainly wished

Figure 2.6. Griffith Building, 605 Broad Street, 1952. Courtesy Newark Public Library.

it was still there as they remembered it. Marion Williams recalled, "Having Bamberger's and Hahne's downtown allowed people to know what was in style."[124] At the time of the interviews, those department stores were long gone. Malls and chain stores had commandeered consumer culture, in Newark and across the country. The downtown that these women and men once knew was less a site for strolling by the 1990s and more a site of corporate industry. What shops still existed were mostly catering to the nine-to-five employees of Prudential or the Gateway Center, not necessarily the city's permanent residents.

Across the country, downtowns continue to be places of contestation. In Beryl Satter's book, she writes about how Chicago's Metropolitan Housing and Planning Council (MHPC) had its eye on transforming the city's downtown into a more inviting locale: "In the early 1940s, the MHPC began studying a problem that concerned many of the prominent businessmen on its board—the fact that Chicago's downtown Loop shopping district was surrounded... by dilapidated housing. These slums created a physical barrier between Loop businesses and their middle-class customers. Slum dwellers not only did not patronize these upscale department stores but scared off those who did." And so, as is often the case in these stories, the impeding majority Black neighborhoods were "blighted;" residents were evicted from their homes through eminent domain; and urban renewal came in with "more profitable structures." Longtime city dwellers across the country later watched as their downtowns morphed once again from family-friendly shopping areas into shiny high-rise landscapes thanks to generous municipal tax abatements—even as their own neighborhoods continued to lack basic resources such as garbage pickup. The story of urban America has so often centered upon its relationship to the city center. So it was, and remains, with Newark.

Radio (1936–1997). The Krueger-Scott community spent a lot of their leisure time at home, and the radio was the foremost supplier of news, information, and entertainment. As Robert Woods explained in his interview, his family could not afford a television, so he listened to a lot of radio, especially stations WWRL and WNJR. He remembered Sunday radio shows playing music from the local Black churches.

Other interviewees recalled Father Divine's voice coming through the radio on Sundays. Born George Baker, in 1936 Father Divine broadcast six live radio shows over station WBHI in Newark.[125] Divine was a national figure, considered by some God incarnate. He started his multiracial International Peace Mission Movement sometime around 1915, and during World War II Newark became Divine's center of operations. Although he died in 1965, Divine's followers still participate in some of the mission's prescribed rituals today, carrying on his traditions and ideology throughout the country.[126]

Several oral history participants mention Divine's lavish meals that he regularly offered to the public at the nominal cost of fifteen cents. (Sometimes they were altogether free.) In Newark, most of these dinners were held at the Riviera Hotel on High Street and Clinton Avenue, purchased by Divine's organization in 1949 for $500,000 in cash. Some members of the extended "family" also resided there. According to the Newark Public Library: "In April 1935, the *Newark Evening News* described a banquet attended by Father Divine where there were

Figure 2.7. Father Divine and his wife leave Newark Tax Board, 1949. Courtesy Newark Public Library.

baskets of fruit and candy everywhere. More than 500 men, women, and children were seated at the table and at least that many stood around the perimeter. From the audience a woman shouted, 'Oh, Father, our Savior, I love you.' Father Divine sat in a satin-backed chair at the head of the banquet table. Every course passed through his hands."[127]

Eugene Thompson, an attorney, described the importance of radio in his lifetime as instrumental in getting a lot of information.

> I remember during the war there was a radio announcer called Gabriel Heater. And he used to come on every night to bring you up on the events that were concerned during the war. And he had an old saying. He used to say, "Ladies and gentlemen, I've got bad news for you tonight." . . . And, of course, there was a famous correspondent, Edward Murrow. I didn't know who he was then as a kid. We used to listen to him when the bombs would drop—they dropped in London. It wasn't funny, but when you was a kid this was just something you couldn't visualize in your world . . . because you didn't have television so you had to use your imagination on exactly what was really going on. But we knew that there was a war going on.[128]

Louise Scott had her hand in radio as well. Station WBHI broadcast from her Scott Hotel. And Scott later aired a radio show from the auditorium at the Scott Cultural and Civic Center. Kitty Taylor remembered, in her interview, Scott's radio show playing gospel music and featuring assorted guests, including Amiri Baraka. "He performed for her in many ways," said Taylor in describing the admiration so many varied Newarkers had for Louise Scott.

Radical radio personality Bernice Bass and highly respected journalist Connie Woodruff "were two of the most important women who took part in Louise Scott's life," added Taylor.[129] Bass and Woodruff were indeed a central part of Scott's community—and Newark's—during a volatile historical era. It is unfortunate how little has been recorded about these two women. The journalistic and activist work of Bernice Bass is worthy of at least its own publication, while Woodruff, a leading activist in her own right as well as an outspoken newspaper columnist, also deserves much more public attention than she has received. Her longtime friend, Barbara Kukla, has made great efforts in keeping Woodruff's story foregrounded.

Bernice Bass's weekly *News and Views* show on WNJR, which aired from the 1950s through the 1980s, was mentioned in most every single Krueger-Scott interview. Kitty Taylor said about Bass's show, "On Sunday nights, Newark's seniors would rush home from church to listen."[130] And Louise Epperson remembered, "We always had, at that time, *News and Views* on the radio with Bernice Bass. Bernice Bass was one of the first persons that ever give me free access to the airwaves to talk about the dilemma of Newark [and the fight against the medical school]. And she continued to help us up until she left."[131] Elma Bateman recalled listening to Bernice Bass as well; it was the only time she "got involved in politics"—she wanted to see what was "going on." Bass supplied that information.[132]

Figure 2.8. Connie Woodruff (left) presents an award to Bernice Bass at the Essex County Civic League's Crispus Attucks Luncheon at the Downtown Hilton, n.d. Courtesy Newark Public Library.

This radio show, *News and Views*, was a part of the cultural fabric of this African American community, and the wider New York metropolitan area as well. An outspoken, intelligent, politically astute woman, Bass—who worked days as a clerk at the downtown passport office—regularly stirred the political pot. Unfortunately, Bass was not interviewed along with her peers in this oral history collection. She had reportedly become quite reclusive in her later years, and passed away in 2000.

Mrs. Bass's obituary in the *Star-Ledger*, written by veteran journalist Barbara Kukla—also a friend of Bass—included testimonials from various friends and co-workers, several of whom were participants in the Krueger-Scott oral history project. "Because of Bernice Bass, I'm a better person," Mayor Sharpe James was quoted as saying. "Newark is a better city, and America is a better place." Kitty Taylor, often a guest on Bass's show, said to Kukla, "You had to be quick and witty when you were on Bernice's show. You were better off saying nothing than saying the wrong thing." Councilman George Branch agreed: "If you said the wrong thing, she'd get you."[133]

Oral histories so often highlight just how important one person's contribution can be, even as so little is known about it. This is especially the case when it comes to women and people of color. In his Krueger-Scott interview, George Branch remembered visiting the "Scott Mansion" regularly and hearing Bass's early shows in person. "We used to go in there for the radio shows at Miss Bernice.... We always invited to come and sit and listen to ... to raise questions on political issues, you name it, what have you—she was tough.... And everybody listened on Sunday night to hear Bernice Bass.... Nine o'clock at night."[134] Mageline Little, project director for the oral history collection, recalled that most of the community's news came from Bernice Bass's radio show, that it was listened to every Sunday night, and that after Bass stopped hosting the show there was no "pipeline" anymore. "That's the one show nobody has thought of to replicate.... That's something that's missing in the Newark community," noted Little.[135]

Frank Hutchins responded to a question regarding where he got his information, explaining that he learned about his community from attending council meetings and listening to Bernice Bass's *News and Views* on WNJR and WABO. Bass's show was controversial, and Hutchins recalls the community even having to "stick up for her" at one point.[136] This was probably in reference to the radio show's temporary cancellation after Bass refused to follow the mandates of the station manager regarding her "spontaneous" on-air conversations. It was requested that she begin prerecording her interviews, but Bass refused for reasons both ethical and logistical. The case went to the city's Human Rights Council, and eventually the restrictions were lifted and the show returned.[137] *News and Views* had become as close to a Sunday ritual as church for many, and its avid listeners were not about to let those in power interfere in their weekly routine.

Bernice Bass's radio show created and nurtured political actors in the Black community. But it also may have put off some who continued to toe the line of "respectability." Listening to Tommy Dorsey on the radio was one thing, but not everyone in the Krueger-Scott community—or the larger urban audience that Bass reached—could have been pleased with a woman of color speaking up for civil rights and speaking out against city administrators. Yet within the Krueger-Scott interviews there is no criticism of Bass, and only a few in the oral history collection neglect to even mention her name when asked about the impact of radio in their lives.

There is scant archival information available to document Bass's obvious impact on the African American community of Newark and beyond. Images of her are elusive, even as she was famous enough to have a street named after her in the city. As with so many of those interviewed in this oral history collection,

Bass was an "everyday person" who greatly affected history. Forgotten by many, left unknown to others, Bass's story is yet one more example of the importance of oral narratives in the restoration of Black history, and Black women's history more particularly.

The radio was certainly a pipeline for the African American community, according to these interviews—for entertainment as well as news. Joe Clark and many others remembered the feelings of excitement when Joe Louis's boxing matches were aired on the radio, for example. Clark brings this up in response to a question concerning traditional "ethnic" celebrations. "That was a celebration when he would knock people out . . . up and down the street."[138] James "Chops" Jones also remembered Joe Louis as a hero, one who grew in stature thanks to radio. "Joe Louis was like our idol. . . . Anytime Joe Louis fought, everybody stayed up. . . . The first time Joe Louis lost to Max Schmeling, well, everybody was outside cryin' like somebody hit 'em. Grown people."[139]

Much like clothing, radio offered a location in which to practice and experience Black agency. Radio was where African Americans could hear about themselves, as well as simply hear themselves. At first, African American popular media basically limited itself to the foregrounding of performers and athletes, but by the 1950s Black intellectuals and activists found space on those airwaves. Radio sustained most of the Krueger-Scott narrators and allowed for shared experiences within this Black community. Black radio programming contributed to the affirmation that there was indeed a place in American society for African American culture and thought, and that society could benefit from its existence. Radio cannot be underestimated as a tool for the progression of Black thought; much has been written on this subject. Unfortunately, as is so often the case, this research tends to privilege stories of the men involved, overlooking so many of the influential women of radio, including Mrs. Bernice Bass.

Conclusion

If one based conclusions solely on the Krueger-Scott interviews, then it would be safe to say that the majority of urban African Americans attended and relied upon church throughout most of the twentieth century. Yet this fact is borne out through national polls and research as well. Although the Newark group in question leaned especially toward one particular church membership, the fact is that most every person interviewed was connected to a church—through family, music, or tradition, if not direct membership.

Those narrators who were church members invariably had diverse relationships with their churches. Coyt Jones loved Bethany Baptist and seemed to have volunteered for most every post available. "If they paid me I would give it back to them," he said.[140] George Branch, who belonged to St. James AME, cautioned, "I never looked for just to do anything but just go to church. I didn't want to take an active part because I know when you take an active part—all I know is that they work the devil out you."[141]

At the very least, Newark's churches played an integral role as landmarks throughout these interviews; so often a building was "down the street" or "across" or "one block over" from a house of worship. This foregrounding was probably due in part to the sheer abundance of churches in Newark, as well as to their importance in Black life. As Jacob Lawrence captioned his fifty-fourth panel of the *Migration Series*, "For migrants, the church was the center of life."

Using the lens of Sundays to look at activities such as church—but also leisure activities like baseball, radio, and food—provides a snapshot of the twentieth-century life of an African American urban citizen. This picture also shows us that not everyone's Sundays looked the same. We hear stories about Sunday socializing, while others demur; we hear facetious reactions to organized religion, and sorrow over its "demise." And sometimes the unsaid provides its own stories, too.

Dr. Martin Luther King Jr. lamented the segregation of Sundays, but these interviews allow us to consider a possibly different analysis of this "most segregated" day. During the core of the twentieth century, and throughout most of American history in fact, Sunday was a day that brought African Americans some of the most freedom available. Whether a respite from field work, or a day off from delivering the mail, Sunday has been for a very long time a rare day of rest for the working class. It is "the day the Lord has made," and in many and varied ways these Newarkers chose to "rejoice and be glad in it."

CHAPTER 3

Workdays

Paid Work

Newark helped build this country, and African Americans helped build Newark—first as enslaved laborers, then soldiers, entrepreneurs, and educators. As with so many agricultural areas in the Northeast, early Newark profited from slave labor, directly and indirectly. By 1800, there were 12,422 enslaved people in New Jersey, 5.8 percent of the state's population.[1] As time progressed, African Americans' work continued to be extraordinarily difficult. Even post-Reconstruction, most African Americans would work their entire lives. In 1890, more than half of all Black Americans of all ages were working: 57.7 percent, compared to 46.6 percent of whites.[2] On the whole, African Americans' jobs were more arduous and less lucrative than those of other racial and ethnic groups, especially in the increasingly crowded and competitive urban boundaries of the Great Migration.

Throughout the Great Migration era, there was a limited list of job opportunities available to Black workers in America's cities. This dearth is confirmed in the Krueger-Scott oral history collection through the responses to question #56, which reads, "What were the common occupations for black men/women in Newark when you came? Did blacks enter new occupations during your residence in Newark? If so, what occupations? When?"

Repeatedly, the narrators listed the common jobs as domestic workers, porters, and delivery(men) for the first half of the twentieth century, with positions for skilled factory workers, teachers, secretaries, and civil servants beginning to open up in the latter half. The most common employment for Black men in the early 1900s was within the "unskilled" labor force, which meant they were typically underpaid and without job security. Choices were even more limited for African American women; most all were domestic workers at one point or another, no matter their educational background or experience.

The concept of work, by the way, will not be limited here to that which one does to draw an income. African American Newarkers spent much of their time working for the betterment of their communities, their families, and the city itself. For some, it was by way of educational engagement, attending PTA and school board meetings; others were concerned with the upkeep of their neighborhoods, calling City Hall each time requisite services were withheld; and still others directly fought injustices perpetrated upon them by systemic racist practices. Whether working on the job or working for the people, Black Newarkers spent a large part of their days laboring.

W.E.B. Du Bois wrote in his 1899 sociological study, *The Philadelphia Negro*, "The humblest white employee knows that the better he does his work the more chance there is for him to rise in business. The black employee knows that the better he does his work the longer he may do it; he can not hope for promotion."[3] A century later that statement still held some truth. While some change had been effected, and race relations were slowly improving, the Krueger-Scott oral histories provide us an understanding that throughout the century, even as job opportunities improved for African Americans, it was not quite a sea change.

The Krueger-Scott narrators' experiences in the workplace certainly reflect a positive trend. We hear many stories of parents in low-level jobs and how, subsequently, their children were able to secure more professional and higher-paying work. While many of the de jure racist employment policies of the early part of the century were erased by the 1950s and '60s, this does not mean that Blacks had anywhere near equal opportunity compared to whites when it came to employment. Throughout these interviews there are numerous stories of continual racist labor practices in Newark, right on through the 1970s and '80s.

Our inegalitarian labor history is well documented along this nation's urban landscape. In the 1904 "Twenty-Sixth Annual Report of the Bureau of Statistics of Labor and Industries of New Jersey," the committee considered the ongoing "negro problem": "It may be said that with equal educational facilities enjoyed for so many years the negroes should make a better showing in the superior lines of employment, and that their failure to do so is due to racial incapacity for anything higher than the commonest forms of labor; that if they possessed the necessary mental qualifications, ambition to advance and a capacity for something better than the menial work, they would, through their own exertions, have succeeded in establishing themselves at least to some extent, in the superior grades of labor."[4] Deep-rooted racism in the workplace has pushed many African Americans into activism. Historically, their efforts to secure, and then hold onto, fair employment has entailed challenging many well-entrenched cultural and legal structures. Black city dwellers especially continue to challenge additional deeply rooted systems within urban development, education, and retail policy. These advocacy efforts are often akin to second jobs. Sometimes they are collective efforts, and other times folks are forced to fight these battles alone.

Mandi Isaacs Jackson writes in her book *Model City Blues* about New Haven, Connecticut's activist community during the 1960s in a predominantly Black neighborhood called The Hill. Much like how Tom Hayden and his majority-white Students for a Democratic Society (SDS) came into Newark's Clinton Hill neighborhood to "organize" the residents, New Haven's mostly white Yale students entered this majority-Black community in an attempt to rally support of anti-establishment activity. Jackson writes: "The story of neighborhood organizing in The Hill also offers an alternative microhistory of the New Left. Although an infusion of young white activists who moved to the neighborhood in 1964 facilitated the establishment of a neighborhood union and a number of other community programs, the concurrent emergence of an organized group of black parents—demanding improvements at their children's school—laid the foundation for more comprehensive and radical community organizing in the years to come."[5]

Oral histories, alongside work by scholars such as Jackson, provide a more nuanced understanding of community activism than is sometimes taught and reported. Stories of outsider organizations with familiar names tend to be foregrounded in the historiography, while the ongoing work of ordinary neighborhood residents—before, during, and after an issue is brought to light—can receive less attention. This is especially true when the local advocates are of color, or women, or members of other marginalized groups. This narrative absence hinders potential future civil rights activists from observing varied models of grassroots organizing. When one considers the number of local activists in any given city today, whether banding together over detention centers or police shootings, imagine if even more people were aware of, and inspired by, the history of their very own community heroes. The Krueger-Scott oral histories offer up just such stories.

Newark was not always a city of color, of course. But the Great Migration changed that as so many African Americans came North looking for better work and a healthier life. By the summer of 1940 there were 45,760 African Americans living in Newark, of whom 11 percent had paid employment. By 1950, 17 percent of Black Newarkers were employed.[6] We will learn from the Krueger-Scott interviews that which has already been addressed by so many scholars and artists, that those participating in the exodus to Northern urban spaces did not always find themselves in a land of milk, honey, and steady employment.

A 1941 Works Progress Administration (WPA) report notes that, prior to 1917, approximately 75 percent of African Americans in the country were "gainfully employed, mostly in domestic and 'personal service' jobs." But (as would happen again post–World War II) after World War I, when white soldiers returned home to work, suddenly the recently hired Black laborers (and women) were deemed no longer competent or capable enough to remain in those positions.[7]

Price and Wright understood the centrality of work to the lives of Great Migration participants. The questionnaire used for these interviews has a robust section devoted to questions surrounding "work." From "What kind of work did you do in the South? . . . What was your wage?" to "What were your work conditions? . . . How were you treated by your supervisor?" Thirteen questions regarding work and all that entails appear on the questionnaire. The answers bring up issues not always addressed in traditional labor history studies.

For example, one might surmise that the emerging union presence in factories and other industries post-Depression would have helped dismantle racist labor practices and provide more and improved job opportunities for African Americans. And certainly, there was a cultural shift happening; in 1935 the Congress of Industrial Organizations (CIO) split from the well-established American Federation of Labor (AFL), the latter known to many as a racist—and sexist—organization. The CIO worked to organize all employees on any given worksite, gaining an inclusive reputation.

But still, as Joshua Freeman writes, this kind of progress "stirred fears among whites and men that their advantageous positions in the labor market would be undermined."[8] A familiar national pattern was reemerging: backlash lurking just around the corner as soon as African Americans made headway.

Domestic Work. Louise Epperson told her story of domestic work to Krueger-Scott interviewer Glen Marie Brickus:

> EPPERSON: My first job in Newark [in 1932], my friend asked me if I would hold a job for her while she tried to get a better job. Because she didn't want to lose that job. It was a part-time job. I had never been in a white person's house to work, and I was very nervous and excited over it. And she said I could do it, and I did it. I did all the cleaning. I did the cooking. And I received five dollars a week.
>
> BRICKUS: So that was a domestic job.
>
> EPPERSON: Domestic job. Then I got a second domestic job working for Dr. Swain on Roosevelt Avenue. And I thought I was really coming into something then because I started off with twenty-five dollars a week. I was his receptionist, and when the people would all leave the office, he would come into the house. Then I would take my uniform that I was a receptionist in and change into another uniform and cook dinner.[9]

Epperson told Mrs. Brickus in her interview that she hated the first family that she worked for, but noted that the Swains were very nice. However, she explained, she had no intention of being a domestic her whole life. After another "hold" job in nearby Montclair, as a chauffeur and cook, Epperson landed a job at the Western Electric factory. Because of this relatively lucrative position, Mrs. Epperson was able to purchase her own home a few years later, a fact of which she was very proud. She subsequently left the factory and took what she thought would be her final job, the one she held as she famously battled the expansion of the medical school. She was employed by the ultimately notorious Willowbrook State School on Staten Island, working with developmentally challenged youth.

Many of the Krueger-Scott narrators' mothers performed domestic work, if they worked outside the home at all. The domestic tasks varied, depending upon the family for whom they worked. Joe Clark made a distinction between a domestic worker who merely cleaned and one who was given the responsibility of an employer's children. "My mother took care of the children up to a point, but on occasion did domestic work," he explained.[10]

Eugene Thompson's mother was a domestic in Virginia; Katheryn Bethea's mother was a domestic in Newark; and Carolyn Wallace's mother worked as a domestic in Bernardsville while living in Newark, some thirty miles away. Mildred Crump's mother stayed at home with her children in Detroit until Crump's father lost his job; then Mrs. Crump also took a job as a domestic.

In a discussion with Senator Wynona Lipman, interviewer Glen Marie Brickus noted that when she herself arrived in Newark, in the 1950s, most African American women were still domestics. Lipman agreed, adding that it had been the same in the South. "When I first came to Newark, it was the early '50s. And most women, most Black women, were doing domestic work. And most Black men were laborers."[11] This is an important moment in employment history if we are to understand some of the racial issues we face today. Only some seventy years ago, the majority of African Americans were still relegated to jobs of servitude, jobs that carried little to no status in American society. The consensus was that was where they belonged. And while it may not be a consensus anymore, there are still too many employers with this thinking today.

One might surmise that what with the long civil rights movement, new labor laws, and the shift in social attitudes toward race, employment equity gaps between whites and Blacks would be minor by now. But of course, even those who may have believed such a possibility a few years back have had the benefit of a global pandemic to witness just how distinctly different the experiences of whites and African Americans can be in this country.

A 2020 report by the Center for American Progress called for, among other things, "the establishment of a national trust fund resourced through a small levy on large corporations." This is one approach to attaining racial equity in the labor market, the report argues, as the consistent level of unemployment highlighted in their research is clearly the result of decades of discriminatory systems.[12]

Reverend Woods told his Krueger-Scott interviewer, "My wife was a domestic. And most of her friends were domestics. Even though she was a beautician. They felt that they could make out better by doing . . . 'day's work' . . . 'cause they didn't have to pay any income taxes, social security at that time, which was wrong. They thought it was right because they didn't have to pay anything out of it."[13] Of course, this practice of under-the-table pay continued on throughout the twentieth century, benefiting employers at least as much as their employees. It is only somewhat recently that laws have been enacted against this practice.[14]

Marzell Swain told her interviewer that even though she graduated from high school in 1940, the only work she was able to secure was that of a domestic. "That was the only job I could get. Until I was workin' for a lady and she said, 'How far did you go in school?' So I told her and she said, 'What are you doin' doin' domestic work?' She said, 'You got an education, you should not be doin' domestic work and you should not be takin' care of babies.' So then she tried to help me get into a store and she still couldn't help me. Some friends she knew. They wouldn't touch you."[15] Mrs. Swain ended up working as a domestic until she married. Later she was employed by a Mr. Strauss, who owned a small clothing store on Prince Street. Swain explained that her responsibilities at the store were to "help put up merchandise, take care of customers, sweep what had to be swept, you know, I did domestic—you know, took care of the customers—you know, salesperson." Swain's interjection of the word "domestic" into her job description might have implied that she was so used to that form of employment that she naturally utilized the descriptor. Or perhaps her tasks felt so much like those of a domestic that she naturally made the association.

Domestic work was the most available option for the majority of African American women during at least the first half of the twentieth century. It was not ideal by any means, but it was also not a job that carried with it the dishonor that some might project upon it today. Too often history is viewed through the lens of the present. Shifting to the sensibilities of a past historical moment can help us understand that moment in a more nuanced fashion.

A few years back I conducted an oral history project at my historically Black Baptist church in Madison, New Jersey. In an interview with our former first lady, she included her story of live-in domestic work in New Jersey. Mrs. Johnston reported to me that the Jewish family for whom she worked used to drive her to our church every Sunday, and then wait for her until service was over to bring her back to their home. It is worth noting that they were Jewish, as that meant that they did not have any traditional religious obligations of their own on Sundays.[16] The point I want to make here is that Mrs. Johnston, at approximately eighty years of age at the time of her interview, told her story with great pride. She felt fortunate to have been driven to church each Sunday, but also reflected a sense of agency in her demand to attend church weekly. Make no mistake, Mrs. Johnston added, she would have been attending weekly services one way or another. That was nonnegotiable.

The opportunity to attend church was not all that common among live-in domestic workers of this time, according to Elizabeth Clark-Lewis in her book *Living In, Living Out: African-American Domestics and the Great Migration*. In fact, Clark-Lewis explains that the inability to go to Sunday services contributed greatly to the social movement that had domestics liberating themselves from live-in to "day's work." This is just one example of a person's job spurring on activism, and why discourse around quotidian jobs and social justice should not be siloed or dismissed. There are so very many examples, even today, of those in the service industry organizing for better treatment.

As addressed in the last chapter, what was worn—and when—was of great importance to many in the African American community. In the case of domestic work, it was also political. In interviewing ninety-seven past domestic workers for her book, Clark-Lewis learned just how essential—financially and emotionally—was the shift from live-in, twenty-four-hour servitude to the relative luxury of a distinct work schedule and pay scale. One benefit to "living out" was that domestic workers no longer lived in their uniforms. Instead, carrying one's uniform in a bag on the way to and from work became a sign of liberation. "To these women, their shopping bags full of work clothes meant no less than their hard-won personal freedom," writes Clark-Lewis. One of her narrators, Sadie Jones, explains that those bags in which the women carried their clothing came to be called "freedom bags." Jones added, "Mostly I guess I wanted to show I didn't wear a uniform. I wasn't a servant."[17]

Donald A. Ritchie, in his handbook *Doing Oral History*, suggests that students will find "Oral history challenges their preconceived notions and makes them rethink how they research and analyze."[18] After wresting myself away from my own preconceived notions of domestic work, I was able to understand the pride that emanated from the women in my church—and the women in the Krueger-Scott interviews. The pride was not necessarily in the job of domestic work itself but in the women's fortitude and self-determination to make those jobs their own.

The women of the Krueger-Scott collection came North from places like Georgia, South Carolina, and Virginia—often by themselves, or at very young ages with family. They found work, which meant food and shelter for themselves, and often for extended family as well. While this form of servitude is certainly a reflection of the caste structure of the time, there soon came a period when most of the women in these positions decided that changes were needed in their work situations. Black women who were domestics worked very hard, and subsequently succeeded in challenging the very definitions of their vocation.[19]

Non-Domestic Work. Not every woman was employed as a domestic. For example, Queenie James worked at the Scott Beauty School beginning in 1941, when she arrived in Newark. "She was a gem," said Mrs. James about Madam Scott. According to many interviews, Louise Scott was a generous employer, among her other attributes. "She never had any children, and so the girls that worked for her, you felt like she was a mother," said James. Mrs. James worked five days a week at the beauty school at Scott Mansion, "doin' heads." James trained under Scott for three years and then, "Well, after I left her, I opened my own shop on West Street.... And I had that, and I kept that for maybe fifteen, twenty years."[20]

Katheryn Bethea, who ultimately retired as an assistant professor of English literature at Rutgers University–Newark, worked multiple jobs in her lifetime. She followed a fairly typical employment trajectory for a Black urbanite of the time, according to the Krueger-Scott interviews, and in keeping with much of the literature on the Great Migration.[21] "When I got out of high school in 1940, there were really no jobs for young Black women except takin' care of babies," said Bethea. After a stint working for her father in a Cleveland grocery store, she returned to Newark and worked in a "war plant." There she helped make "inflatable mechanisms" for use on life rafts. "When the war was over, of course, that job ceased," Bethea explained.[22] As was the case for the majority of African Americans and women hired during World War II, once the white male soldiers returned from war and to their jobs, those last hired—predominantly African Americans and women—were typically fired.

After the war, the next phase of Bethea's employment was as a seamstress. As her reputation grew, she opened her own tailoring shop on 13th Avenue, with a financial contribution made by one of her clients. This situation allowed her to care for her young children while at the same time bringing in a salary. When business was slow at her shop, she would take on additional work, sometimes in a local dress factory or at the post office. Mrs. Bethea recalls one Christmas season, in 1942, when she sought to supplement her income by working at Bamberger's department store. She was hired as a "floor girl," carrying up clothing from the basement to the various departments. Because of her diligence as an employee, she was asked to stay on after the holiday season. Bethea agreed to do so, but only if she could work as a clerk and not haul around stock anymore. "They weren't hiring any Black women—girls ... to be clerks. We could go down there and lug all that stuff," but the position of salesperson was not available to women who looked like Bethea. Her manager told her that while she was personally ready for an African American "on the floor," Bamberger's was not quite there yet. Bethea declined the store's offer to stay on.

There were some, although very few, Krueger-Scott interviewees who stated that they accepted government aid during especially difficult times. Some referred to it as being "on the state." Broad welfare statistics during this period are difficult to find for Newark; many of the census figures only report overall numbers of those living below the poverty line. From the Krueger-Scott community, one fact we can glean is that a low socioeconomic level did not necessarily equate to acceptance of government assistance. As noted in the previous chapter, the Black community at large was expected to help each other, avoiding the need to turn to outside sources for aid. But for some there was just no choice.

WORKDAYS 93

Figure 3.1. L. Bamberger & Co., Newark, NJ, 1940. Courtesy Shorpy Historical Photo Archive.

According to an October 1933 Unemployment Relief Census, 15,376 "Negro Persons" were recorded as "on relief" in Newark. This is compared to 42,027 whites. Interestingly, the summary of the full report states, "The percentage of the urban Negro population receiving relief was three times that of the urban white population." Yet a simple scan of the listings of cities shows that every one had more whites on relief than Blacks.[23] History's narratives sometimes tell tales that differ from fact.

We have already heard stories of whites helping their Black employees when it came to legal matters. Material aid was also offered at times. Owen Wilkerson recalled such an event involving his mother, who cleaned houses in Summit, a town about twenty minutes away from Newark: "She would take the Summit bus, the 70 Summit, you know, and go to Summit, and she would, you know, clean white people's homes and what not. And there was this one particular family that used to give her—their son Jimmy, I think, was, oh, about six or seven years older. And this lady would give me—give my mother Jimmy's clothes to give me and what not. You could really tell they were very expensive clothes."[24] There are several stories told of these types of donations, and often the clothing would come with a sewn-in label bearing the white child's name on it. More than one African American child grew up in this country thinking that the name on the label was a designer's.

Hortense Williams Powell tells her interviewer, Annemarie Dickey-Kemp, that her family received welfare because Powell's father had died in 1938:

> So then the family continued to receive the state help from the State Board of Children's Guardianship until about 1945. [Then] my youngest brother was old enough that my mother could go out and work, and she got a job at National Union Radio Tube Corporation. That was in Newark. And she worked there for ten years.... They had labor problems, and the union walkout, and all of that type of thing. It was after the war, the Second World War.... The factory closed down and it never reopened, and my mother stopped working. But by this time, this was about 1955, all of us were grown up then.

Powell was explaining to her interviewer that when her brothers were too young to work, the family had to go "on relief" until their mother secured the factory job. The interviewer, apparently unfamiliar with this system, asked, "Exactly how did that work?"

Powell answered, "If you didn't have any job and—or like the father was dead, uh, then—and you had children and you couldn't work.... Even if you could find work you couldn't work because the children were too little, right? Then they had the Board of Children's Guardianship, and they would send you a check."[25]

Powell's mother subsequently lived on a widow's pension as well as unemployment, due to her husband's military service. She did not have much choice, Mrs. Powell reminds the interviewer; there were just not that many jobs available for a fifty-five-year-old Black woman in the 1950s.

An inference can be made here that, based upon the median economic status of the Krueger-Scott group, some of the peer interviewers might not have had personal experience with government subsidies. The interviewer in this case, Dickey-Kemp, lived in Upper Clinton Hill and was a member of the middle-class St. James AME Church. In this case it helped that the interviewer

Figure 3.2. National Union Radio Corporation ad, *Radio Craft*, April 1945. Courtesy radiomuseum.org.

was unfamiliar with the system, so that the oral history contains that informative explanation from Powell.

On this subject of welfare and the Krueger-Scott narrators, worth considering is the possibility that some felt shame or embarrassment in sharing tales of poverty. It must be remembered that there is someone else from their immediate community in the room, and the narrator has been told that these interviews will eventually be publicly accessible at the Krueger-Scott African-American Cultural Center. An account of taking government "handouts" might also have challenged the collective narrative of a close-knit Black community that many were enthusiastic to portray. At this point, the actuality of Black community support could well have been ingrained in the collective memory.

In any event, while some of the Krueger-Scott interviewees certainly grew up poor, only a handful in the cohort fell outside of traditionally middle-class professions once they reached adulthood. This fact, combined with a likely good dose of resistance to "leaning on the government" in general, might well be one explanation for the dearth of Krueger-Scott participants reporting any experience with government assistance.

Reverend Alvin Conyers's first job in Newark was as a porter at Columbia Laundry in 1946. He then became a professional barber, and later a teacher and ordained minister. The employees at Columbia Laundry were 90 percent Black, Conyers reported when asked whether there were "certain tasks reserved for certain groups" at his job (Question #50). "Whites were mostly truck drivers, checkout men," explained Conyers, who worked at the laundry three summers in a row while home from college. He called it a "nice job."

"I swept the floor, uh, dusted the machines and, uh, took the clothin' that were washed from one area to another.... I enjoyed it. That was my first employment. I remember vividly I was making $30 a week.... It made me feel like I was becomin' a young man."[26] In Conyers's voice we hear no form of resentment, even as he relays information regarding apparent racial disparity in job assignments. Perhaps this is simply a reflection of accepting "how it was" at the time, much as with the women who were performing domestic work. It certainly is not apathy or naïveté on Mr. Conyers' part; his future engagement in numerous social justice groups, as well as the degrees he secured in education and theology, indicate a very present person indeed. But as he noted, Conyers was glad to have a job at the time, to bring some money home to the aunt with whom he lived, and to be treated fine if not necessarily fairly. At least that was what was acceptable to him in 1946.

Within these interviews there is a noticeable trend toward people becoming more proactive and "political" about their work as time—and opportunities—pass them by. This is not surprising. Certainly by the early twentieth century, African Americans had established themselves as a labor force to be reckoned with through consistent collective and individual activism on the job. It is only recently that some Americans are realizing that, since the beginning of slavery, African Americans have consistently protested discriminatory labor practices in myriad ways, from work stoppages to property destruction, to walkouts, to political participation. Du Bois speaks to this in *Black Reconstruction*: "But this slow, stubborn mutiny of the Negro slave was not merely a matter of 200,000 black soldiers and perhaps 300,000 other black laborers, servants, spies and helpers. Back of this half million stood 3½ million more. Without their labor the South would starve. With arms in their hands, Negroes would form a fighting force which could replace every single Northern white soldier fighting listlessly against his will with a black man fighting for freedom."[27] This legacy of self-determination, and an understanding of where power lay, is also apparent in the Krueger-Scott interviews.

Willie Bradwell started working as a domestic when she first came to Newark in 1939, at the age of eighteen. She did not like domestic work, neither the tasks nor some of the people for whom she worked. "I hated it. I don't like housework, not even my own," she told her interviewer. One day her employer insisted that Bradwell get all her work finished before eating lunch. "So when I had my lunch it was time to come home," said Bradwell. "I didn't go back."

Bradwell next found factory work, which she liked much better. She started out at a paper cup factory in North Newark at fifty-five cents an hour, minimum wage at the time. After a few months she secured a better factory job, with H. A. Wilson at 97 Chestnut Street, sometime around 1946. "They didn't even hire Black people till after the war. So when we went in there after the war, it wasn't too much of a problem." It is worth noting that, according to Bradwell, this factory was not hiring African Americans during World War II. This implies there may well have been other businesses willing to suffer through an inevitable labor shortage in order to keep the racial status quo. The racial makeup at H. A. Wilson, when she worked there, was about 25 percent Black and 75 percent white, Bradwell reported.

Soon after she started at H. A. Wilson, a union came in, explained Bradwell. The employees received insurance benefits and a raise to seventy-five cents an hour. At this point the interviewer, Cleta Bradwell, asks about benefits. "Did you not get paid vacation before the union came in?"

Bradwell replied, "No."

"Oh, that's interesting," said the interviewer, "because my whole work experience, you know, that's always been, you know, part of it." With that comment—from the interviewer who appears to be Mrs. Bradwell's daughter—we can see that after just one generation, compensation for vacation days was considered a reasonable expectation of employment. This can be attributed in part to the efforts of Willie Bradwell and her peers, who transformed the workplace into a more equitable space.

Mrs. Bradwell became involved in the union, eventually taking on the position of shop steward. Later, the Engelhard Company took over H. A. Wilson and, according to Bradwell, the working conditions remained essentially the same. In 1953, Bradwell said, she was able to buy a car and no longer had to rely on the #140 Somerset bus to get her to work. (It seems to have taken her approximately seven years to save up for that car.) Bradwell also related that, as the union's shop steward, she did have to challenge management on several occasions. Bradwell's stories of union organizing are told in a most straightforward manner.

"Did you guys ever have a strike?" asks the interviewer.

"Yes," replied Bradwell.

"What was that like?"

"That was rough 'cause we were out there about six weeks. And I don't even, now, I don't even remember why we struck. And don't know if we got what we struck for."

The interviewer encourages: "So you, well, I guess being the shop steward, you were out on the line."

Bradwell says, "Yes. But I just don't remember the details." Her daughter the interviewer then comments that it must have been dangerous. Bradwell replies, "No. It wasn't dangerous. 'Cause there wasn't anybody attempting to cross the line, just the foreman. And they didn't attempt to bring in any strikebreakers, anything like that. Our biggest problem was attempting to stop the trucks that was comin' in with materials and things." Apparently, Mrs. Bradwell did not deem any of this especially intimidating.

The Engelhard Company eventually relocated to Union, about six miles south of Newark. Bradwell continued to work for the company for thirty years, yet she was not offered a retirement package or any other benefits upon leaving.

> BRADWELL: They shut down that division where I worked. They closed out that division where I worked. And they put us out of a job.
>
> CLETA BRADWELL: So how did you feel?
>
> BRADWELL: I felt very badly because they didn't even give us our benefits or anything. . . . They told—I don't know who was responsible—maybe the union sold us out. Because we had a closing clause in our contract. But they called in the union to negotiate a closing contract, and they did us out of our severance pay.

Soon after leaving Engelhard, Bradwell became ill and went on disability. She was "having a problem with the muscles in her arms" and applied for Social Security. It was approved three years later. She worked "here and there" along the way, and it certainly sounds as if she may have been due some kind of workers' compensation payments. But we cannot know whether Bradwell took advantage of such insurance.

The talk of work continued in the interview:

> CLETA BRADWELL: Were you ever unemployed from the time that you went to work when you came to Newark, other than when the company, you know, closed down on you all, were you ever unemployed?
>
> BRADWELL: Not really. Because I went from one factory to the other, and then I stayed there for—this happened. I mean, until they shut down. And for one small, I mean, one eight-month period in there, I went on welfare while I was waiting for my Social Security to come through.

As with so many of the interviewees, Bradwell's voice sounded proud of the duration and consistency of her work life. The term "work ethic" is referenced on a regular basis in these oral histories. Working was a sign not only of financial achievement, but of respectability for many of these Newarkers. We get little sense that Bradwell was looking back and envisioning how things might have been better—save for the Engelhard Company's summary closing of her division. She worked hard, but she worked—and that seems to be what mattered to so many of the Krueger-Scott narrators. Bradwell's interpretation of the following question sheds even more light.

> CLETA BRADWELL: And what were the common occupations for Black men and women in Newark when you came here?
>
> BRADWELL: Oh, there was plenty of work in Newark at the time. 'Cause this was a manufacturing hub. There was plenty of work in Newark. They had the chemical plants, and they had all kinds of manufacturing. So there was plenty of work.[28]

What was important to Bradwell was that there were many jobs available. What kinds of jobs they were seemed less relevant. For a long while, simply having a job as a Black American was an achievement. Remember that in 1950 only 17 percent of Newark's African Americans were officially employed.

Getting Work (1940s–1950s). Elma Bateman, a retired secretary with AT&T, said in her interview, "Once we got out of school and began to work, then we got into the problem of . . . race relationships." Bateman was answering questions about race relations and school, explaining that she recalled few problems as she made her way through Robert Treat High School in the early 1940s. Yet she also mentions that she asked her school counselor for permission to register for a "commercial" course that taught typing and stenography, instead of one of the "basic" courses to which Black students were typically steered. "The counselor wanted to know why, when Black people aren't hired as secretaries," said Bateman. Following the basic curriculum, Bateman explains, "All you could do when you came out was work in a factory." Bateman signed up for the commercial course without permission.

"I took a secretarial class and I'm so glad I did.... I came out and was able to get a job at the VA [Veteran's Administration]."[29] Bateman would be one of a number of women in the Kruger-Scott interviews who would later say she was "not political" when asked. Yet this move as a high school student, registering for a course against an authority figure's advice, might be considered political by some.

Exclusion and discrimination, starting from a young age, was a common experience for the narrators of the Krueger-Scott collection—and for African Americans in general through at least the first half of the twentieth century. As historian John Cunningham points out, these issues started early on in Newark. By 1900, city government was moving quickly to create an education system for the city's growing immigrant population, yet at the same time they continued to ignore the educational needs of the city's "colored" residents.[30] Even as we hear in the Krueger-Scott interviews just how "good" the Newark schools were, in the next breath often come anecdotes regarding the predominantly white teaching population and the extremely low expectations placed upon Black students.

And still today, African American students find themselves routed into vocational courses that prepare them for limited career paths. The term "tracking" has been a euphemism employed to describe this continued practice, wherein students of color are regularly denied access to upper-level courses in myriad ways. I witnessed this in my own children's high school in suburban New Jersey in the early years of this twenty-first century.[31]

Elma Bateman told her interviewer, Pauline Blount, that she was very pleased to get that government job at the VA as a Black woman, and that the atmosphere was fairly civil among the mixed-race group of co-workers. But when she moved into a new job with the Air Force, sometime around 1950, Bateman came up against pronounced racial tensions that jarred her.

> BLOUNT: Do you recall any personal discrimination?
> BATEMAN: [Long pause.] For me? Well, I had one incident, well it wasn't really... discrimination... when I was working for the Air Force.... I was to be promoted, you know, to work for this captain.... There was this one white woman... boy, she put up such a fight.... I ended up gettin' the job anyway.... She just felt that, you know, how dare I get the promotion and she was white.... That was the only incident I can remember.... Made me realize what you can come up against.[32]

For the second time we hear Bateman resist the characterization of racism per se, even as she shares stories of a negative personal experience based upon her race. These oral histories might indicate that there are varied definitions of "discrimination" among the interviewees. There could be several reasons for this, including investment in the aforementioned respectability politics.

African Americans attempting to assimilate into the world in which they are placed have often been expected to comport themselves to "sustain the comfort of others," according to Sarah Ahmed. Writing in *The Affect Theory Reader*, Ahmed argues that, for example, the "angry Black woman" persona can be considered a "killjoy," so much so that "some bodies are presumed to be the origin of bad feeling insofar as they disturb the promise of happiness."[33] Ahmed describes "affect aliens" as those who essentially refuse this paradigm of playing by socially constructed rules. In the case of Bateman's interview, calling out discrimination may have been considered inappropriate by both women participating in the interview process. Perhaps neither wanted to sound like that "killjoy."

The fact is that Elma Bateman was kept from taking a particular class in a public school due solely to the fact that she was Black. Later she went through a stressful situation after rising above a white person in the hierarchy of her job. This is, of course, discrimination and racism. But Bateman hedges in her interview, framing her experiences as simply a few occasions when she believed she may have been treated less than adequately due to her race. At another point in her interview, Mrs. Bateman also expresses concern that she is coming off as "negative." She was a woman who was clearly very conscious of the tenor of her responses.

Pauline Faison Mathis was born in 1932 in Clinton, North Carolina. She arrived with her husband in Newark in 1951. He had read about Newark's burgeoning job market in the newspapers. This common experience is reflected in the artwork and literature inspired by the Great Migration era, for example, as noted in the prologue regarding Jacob Lawrence's panel #34. Simply by accessing the newspaper in which he read about Newark's job prospects, Mr. Mathis was probably taking some sort of risk. This is just one example of why so many refer to the Great Migration as a protest movement.

Mrs. Mathis said in her interview, "Well, it wasn't exactly what we thought when we got there. We thought the opportunities were greater.... You could read in the paper there were opportunities ... and the next thing you knew, because of your color, because of your voice or whatever, you wouldn't get the ... job." Mathis goes on to tell a story illustrating just how racism did not stop at the Mason-Dixon Line. In 1952, Mrs. Mathis started her first job in Newark, as an office clerk working for the Newark Newsdealers Supply Company on Halsey Street. She had gone to an employment agency and secured a position that she was told would pay $38 a week. She headed straight to the office to begin her new career.

"When I walk in, I am surrounded by nothing but whites. 'Uh oh,' that is the first thing you say to yourself. I don't know if I'm gonna get this job or not." According to Mathis, as soon as she handed over her employment papers to the general manager, the office manager and the owner quickly huddled together with the GM as Mathis waited nervously in her chair. The three men finally turned to address the woman, informing her that the employment agency had made a mistake and that the pay would be $35 a week, not $38. (That would equal approximately a $30 difference in weekly pay today.)

Mathis continues, "Now I know what's goin' on here. . . . I'm Black, they changed the salary on me. 'Cause I heard about that kinda thing going on." But Mathis decided at that moment that she was there to integrate that office—the only other African American there, she observed, was a man sweeping the floor. So she called the men's bluff, assuming they were trying to dissuade her from working there by offering the lower pay, and accepted the salary. "So I guess they had to hire me," she said, with a lilt of satisfaction in her voice.[34]

In 1952, the Reverend Robert Woods was hired as a manager at Allied Electric in Irvington. This was not his initial life plan. Woods arrived in the city with the purpose of attending Newark Academy of the Arts, studying to be a commercial illustrator. He was promised a job at the *Newark News* once he graduated. But this did not come to fruition. "Upon graduation, I guess they discovered that I was not Caucasian. I didn't get employment in the *Newark News*. They couldn't hire me because the rest of the artists would leave the studio. So that created a bad taste in my mouth," said Woods. He never did become a professional artist.

Woods said he felt fortunate in finally landing the position that he did at Allied Electric. He told his interviewer that it was a coup as a Black man to be hired for anything other than simple labor at the time, and he assumed his college degree probably helped. Even so, people like Coyt Jones and others noted in their interviews that Blacks with college degrees were still having a difficult time finding jobs at mid-century. African Americans graduating from college in the 1950s were far from an everyday occurrence, as many of the country's universities were only just beginning to accept African American applicants at all. Between 1950 and 1960, less than 5 percent of Blacks over twenty-five had completed four years of college.[35] This statistic is another reminder that the Krueger-Scott participants were not necessarily reflective of the African American demographic as a whole, as over 30 percent of the Krueger-Scott participants had college degrees or higher. On the other hand, if one figures in the college completion statistics of urban African Americans specifically, then the percentage of the Krueger-Scott interviewees with higher education degrees is more in keeping with the norm.

College-educated Jessie Johnson said in her interview that Blacks with college degrees became trainers at their jobs. She worked for the Office of Dependent Benefits (ODB) and remembers training white employees with high school educations who would then end up supervising her.

JOHNSON: I was a processor at the ODB and a trainer for new people coming in. Because they used the people with the degrees to help—after they trained us—to help train others while we remained in the same job. And after we trained other people from the Pennsylvania area, they would get to be the supervisors of whatever.

BRICKUS: Oh, I see. Are you saying then that the people you trained were basically white folk?

JOHNSON: The people we trained were basically white folk.

BRICKUS: And they moved up while you stayed where you were?

JOHNSON: And they moved up while we stayed where we were.

At this same time, when Pauline Mathis applied for a job at Bamberger's department store, she was told that she "wouldn't like it" because she was so educated. "That was the word going then, 'You have too much education, you wouldn't be too happy here,'" explained Mathis.[36]

Reverend Woods's new job at Allied Electric was not without its racial complications either:

WOODS: I was the manager of forty women.... [Laughter.] You know how that was!

BRICKUS: No, I don't really know how that was.

WOODS: Well, they wasn't used to an Afro-American manager ... boss....

BRICKUS: Most of these are white women?

WOODS: Yes. They wasn't used to that—wasn't used to taking orders from nobody like me. And sometimes it became difficult, and we'd have to wind up in the president's office with a grievance.[37]

Woods's first remark could have been misconstrued as sexist, but it soon becomes evident that he is simply describing workplace racism. While these white women were not allowed access to jobs with authority, they felt enough agency to challenge their Black superior. And they carried enough power to file grievances against their manager that got addressed by the president of the company. Jacob Lawrence's panel #50 about racial conflict in the workplace might foreground an angry white man wielding a club, but sometimes racist frustrations were transmitted more subtly.

Many companies simply refused to hire Blacks in order to avoid the racial conflicts considered inevitable in an integrated workplace. In a 1956 State of New Jersey report on employment practices in retail stores, shop owners and managers were interviewed surrounding employers' attitudes toward minorities. The respondents claimed that either no "Negroes" ever applied for the jobs in which they were conspicuously absent, or that they were sometimes turned away from employment because of potential discomfort for white customers being waited upon by a person of color.[38] Katheryn Bethea was told the latter outright at Bamberger's in 1942, and Mr. Woods was a victim of the same attitude a decade later.

By around 1955, after leaving Allied Electric, Robert Woods became the first Black machine glass blower at Chris Electronics, "blowing the nets" for the television tubes. When Chris Electronics folded, he was unemployed for two weeks but then moved to a similar operation at Haydu Brothers. He left soon thereafter to work for Progressive Life Insurance as a collector, but disliked the job. Aside from the amount of work and time he had to invest simply to earn a "couple dollars"—eight hundred visits a week, according to Woods—he did not like the idea of "collecting from our people." He later moved on to North Carolina Mutual Life Insurance Company, presumably tasked with a different set of responsibilities.

Pearl Beatty was born in 1935 and came to Newark from Pittsburgh with her family as a baby. Her father had been injured in the Pennsylvania coal mines, so they left the area in order for him to find different work. Beatty's aunt lived in Newark, and so the family moved to the city. Everybody had to pitch in, Beatty recalled: "Well, my first job was in a factory two blocks from here. From the beginning we lived on Baldwin and Washington Streets. And one day I was walking down the street and I saw this sign, 'employment needed.' And I went in and applied. I was sixteen. And they hired me. And I was thrilled because my job was just two blocks from home. We're talking about, let's see now, we're talking about '52." Pearl Beatty was biracial—. This arises in her interview when she is asked by Geri Smith about her racial status. Smith was apparently well acquainted with Mrs. Beatty.

> SMITH: I don't know whether we talked about—I know you're multiracial, and I don't know whether we talked about whether your mom or your dad was—
> BEATTY: My mother was Italian and my father was Black.
> SMITH: How did that affect you when you were coming up in the neighborhood, and how did people perceive you?
> BEATTY: Oh, we used to get beat up.
> SMITH: You did?
> BEATTY: Oh yes, we did. Going home from school.
> SMITH: Was that by Black children or by white children?
> BEATTY: Black.
> SMITH: They were Black?
> BEATTY: They were Black.
> SMITH: What was your feelings about that?
> BEATTY: Oh, it's very hurtful. I mean, why couldn't we belong? They sort of us held us standoffish. [Long pause.] There was a lot of teasing. Not—not too much fighting. Here and there a fight. But a-a-a lot of teasing. [Another pause.] Awful lot of teasing. And name calling.
> SMITH: Did this affect you, you think, when it came to . . . your first job?

BEATTY: ... In fact, when I walked in [to the factory job], the white girls thought I was, uh, white. And this one white woman said to me, "I want you to know that the Black girls that work here are very clean." [Chuckling between Smith and Beatty.] And at my lunchtime I went over to the Black girls and introduced myself. And when I came back to my bench to work—[pause] the white lady said to me, "Now, just because I said that the Blacks were clean here, that didn't mean that you have to go over there and eat with them." And I politely let her know that I was Black. . . . Now the Black women, they knew I was Black.[39]

Pearl Beatty worked at this factory for eight years. The name of the company is not mentioned, but geographical clues suggest that it may have been the Imperial Manufacturing Company at 297 Washington Street, which produced parts for typewriters.[40]

Joe Clark noted that the highest-level jobs for Blacks, when he was in the job market, were "preaching and teaching." And Hortense Williams Powell explained that "Newark was a place of entry" when it came to work. During this period, when many of the Krueger-Scott participants were looking for work, Blacks were still barred from most "public" jobs, such as bus driver or retail clerk. Once integration started taking effect, African Americans were hired with more regularity to work in shops and stores, but even then those positions rarely included visibility—or the handling of money.

Ed Crawford was born in 1950, late enough so that he was able to secure a job at Bamberger's department store after high school. He performed multiple jobs, all behind the scenes. At one point Crawford's manager acknowledged him as an excellent worker. In turn, Crawford tells his interviewer, he requested a raise:

CRAWFORD: So I remember having to sit with him and somewhat plead my case to get a nickel raise, a nickel an hour raise. However, when I transferred out of the section and went on to another section to work, and the next fur storage season started, they hired two guys to do the job I did by myself. . . . Made me wonder why I had to work so hard to get that nickel out of them when they had to pay two salaries for the salary they paid me.
BRICKUS: Were these white fellows that they hired to replace you, or were they Black guys?
CRAWFORD: White guys. Another irony of the situation.[41]

It is evident that the African Americans of the Krueger-Scott project simply had fewer job opportunities than whites during their prime employment years. Decades later, in some of the promotional materials for the proposed Krueger-Scott African-American Cultural Center, the creation of more jobs for the Black community is presented as one of the restoration project's selling points. Whether during construction, or subsequently as service and retail employees, it was promised that the center would provide much-needed work for the surrounding community. Late into the twentieth century, job opportunities for people of color continued to be a major issue.

Part of the vicious cycle of underemployment was propelled by the fact that Blacks did not own numerous businesses, nor typically work in positions that could facilitate the hiring of their peers. African Americans simply had less economic power than whites, and still do. Wynona Lipman told her interviewer that the same thinking that was behind the idea that neighborhoods declined once Blacks moved in also carried over into the workplace. White employers wanted to keep the status quo in their factories, offices, and stores—and they had the power to do so.

Nursing Work (1948–1969). One occupation less well represented in the Krueger-Scott oral histories than in African American history in general is that of nursing. Only a few of the women interviewed for the Krueger-Scott project worked as nurses or nurses' aides: Lenora Means, Lurline Byass, Carolyn Wallace, Shirley Sylvan, Bernice Rountree, and Hortense Powell. Vivian Berry trained as a nurse but for various reasons never worked in that capacity. Mageline Little told me that the oral history project staff had hoped that by hiring retired nurse Annemarie Dickey-Kemp as an interviewer they would attract more nurse participants. The project directors were aware of the relevance of this occupation to African American culture and made an effort to secure stories related to the field.

Nursing is an occupation that African American women fought very hard to enter into. And in the Black church, nursing was—and still is—a highly respected profession. Part of this pride in nursing comes from the fact that the job was just so hard to access for so many. The more traditional churches today still include Nurses Guilds to honor working and retired nurses. Typically, one Sunday service a year is set aside to celebrate Black nursing, wherein the women (for the most part) congregate together in the pews, smartly dressed in their white, starched uniforms.

In a 1950 nationwide study, only 3 percent of those who identified themselves as nurses were African American women. That is just a little over 13,000 Black female nurses. Professors Patricia D'Antonio and Jean C. Whelan, both registered nurses themselves, published a narrative study in 2009 entitled "Counting Nurses." This project provides statistical and biographical sketches of the history of the profession through the lenses of race and gender. They write: "The dominance of white women nurses, however, did not come at the expense of African American women. Throughout the early decades of the twentieth century, the proportional representation of African American women who identified as professional nurses remained fairly stable at an approximate average percentage rate of 3% of all women nurses for the first five decades of the 20th century."[42]

Seated: Rev. Mapson. Standing, Left to Right — Marie Jones, Johnnie Card, Rutha Guyton, Katie Dailey, Lorena Ryan.
(Not Shown) — Thelma Lynn.

BEST WISHES ON YOUR THIRTIETH PASTORAL ANNIVERSARY

THE NURSES GUILD

LORENA RYAN, Leader

— 96 —

Figure 3.3. The Nurses Guild, Mount Calvary Baptist Church, 30th Anniversary program, 1977. Courtesy Newark Public Library.

Mabel K. Staupers might have challenged the claim regarding the dominance of white nurses. Staupers was the executive secretary of the National Association of Colored Graduate Nurses (NACGN). At the beginning of World War II, Mrs. Staupers battled the ban on, and subsequent segregation of, Black nurses in the military. Once Black nurses were finally allowed into the military, it was only to care for prisoners of war, not American soldiers. Meanwhile, the navy continued its refusal to induct Black women into their Nurse Corps altogether for many years to come. And the Red Cross, supplier of nurses to the military, did not look to the NACGN as a viable labor resource; only members of the all-white American Nurses Association (ANA) were recruited. (Another longtime racist practice of the Red Cross included the separation of blood donations by race.)

At one point during the war a draft was called due to a nursing shortage, although there remained a large pool of Black nurses available and eager to serve. Echoing the segregationist rhetoric that confronted the Krueger-Scott participants so often, the military's argument to those fighting the racial exclusion was that white people would be uncomfortable serving with, or being cared for, by African Americans. Apparently, whether waiting on customers or tending to patients, there was a strongly held belief that Blacks were not as capable as whites.

Fourteen years after the battle began, in 1948 the ANA was finally desegregated, and in 1950 Mrs. Staupers deemed her organization of Black nurses no longer necessary.[43] It should be noted that twenty years later the National Black Nurses Association was founded to advance health care for African Americans and elevate the positions of Black nurses in education and leadership. Evidently, things had not evolved quite as much as Staupers had imagined.

How many of the Krueger-Scott women who worked in the medical field knew the history of activist Mabel Staupers, a history that was being made even as some of them were in training? It might well have been an inspiring story, an uplifting narrative for someone growing weary of the obstacles placed in her way. As Charles Payne and Adam Green write in their introduction to *Time Longer Than Rope*, "An alternative understanding of the past can help people envision alternative futures and the steps that lead there."[44] The relevance of Black women's historical narratives is more than just what happened in the past.

Hortense Williams Powell was interviewed by fellow nurse Annemarie Dickey-Kemp. Powell attended nursing school at City Hospital in 1949, as part of the third graduating class to ever allow African Americans. She had hoped to become a doctor. The initial plan was to get through nursing school, make enough money to go to medical school, and eventually become an MD. "But it didn't work out that way," Powell said.

Powell's graduating class had eight women in it, three white and five Black. They lived in segregated residences. Although Powell was one of the few women to speak consistently about race during her Krueger-Scott interview, she claimed she was treated fairly during her time in nursing school:

> There were only two incidents that gave me cause.... During the senior year, the alumni association usually took two students to the convention, the American Nurses Association Convention in Atlantic City. And during my

senior year, two students were selected, I being one of them. The other one being a white student. And two of the white representatives from the alumni association went down with us. I recall we stayed in the Claridge Hotel. It's the first time I had ever been to Atlantic City and the first time I had ever been in a hotel that big. And it reminded me of a castle. And the girl I was with, I don't think she had been any place like that either. So we were both rather awed with the whole experience. But when we got to the hotel, we didn't—neither one of us understood why we had separate rooms.... There was an adjoining door, but we had separate rooms. And the two ladies, they stayed together in a room.... But the feeling that dawned on me was that I was in that room, and she was in that room because she was white and I was Black. And it hadn't really come to the point in New Jersey wherein you had integration in these hotels. In fact, it was still hotels that you really couldn't go in at all.

According to the ANA's Expanded Historical Review, the last convention the association held in Atlantic City was in 1926. There is no record of a convention in 1939, the year Powell graduated. The 1938 convention was held in Missouri and the 1940 event took place in Philadelphia. Perhaps it was another group's convention that Powell attended.

The review lists 1962 as the year "all state nurses' associations accepted all qualified registered nurses into membership, regardless of race, color, or creed." And as early as 1908, "52 Negro nurses met in New York City and founded the National Association of Colored Graduate Nurses. Martha Franklin of Connecticut, a graduate of the Women's Hospital in Philadelphia, was chosen first president of this group which proposed to work for higher professional nursing standards, the elimination of discrimination, and the development of leadership among Negro nurses. It merged with the ANA in 1951."[45] Powell continued her story:

And the other thing was when a scholarship was given to the student who had the highest academic and general all-around achievement upon graduation. Had never gone to a Black student before.... But I was the one that was in contention for this scholarship. It was a five-hundred-dollar scholarship. Doesn't seem much now, but it was a lot at that time. You had to go before the board ... they put me through a rigorous question [sic], almost as if they didn't believe some of the things I said.... And I remember it was sort of amusing. You know, there was one person that just kept questioning me and asking me about my activities, and I just said, "Do you think that's enough or shall I go on?" [Interviewer laughs.]

And somebody kind of chuckled a little bit. I guess maybe, I don't know whether because of the way I said it or because that they were thinking that it was a bit too much, too. Well, in either case, the end story is, I think that what they were trying to do—certain factions were trying to do—is to not give this scholarship at this time to a Black student. So they interviewed the others, they had two other candidates, two white girls . . . but they really didn't want to go on to a get a degree. One said, she told them clearly, she really planned to get married. And the other one, for some reason or other, she didn't really want to go to school right at that time. . . . They were faced with a dilemma because they either have to give it to me—

DICKEY-KEMP: 'Cause you wanted to go on to school.
POWELL: Yeah. Oh, I wanted to go on to school. And either give it to me, not give it, or give it half to one of them and half to me. And I think after some deliberation, I guess, or some compromise or whatever goes on behind the doors . . . they decided that they were going to split the scholarship and give two-fifty to one and two-fifty to the other. So, which was all right, you know, it's all right with me.
DICKEY-KEMP: So you got two-fifty and someone else—
POWELL: I got two hundred and fifty dollars instead of the five hundred.[46]

In "Counting Nurses," D'Antonio and Whelan tell the story of Florence Jacob Edmunds, an African American nurse who "turned to sewing to supplement her husband's salary during the 1930s." Edmunds had trained at Lincoln Hospital in New York City after the white nursing school in Pittsfield, Massachusetts, refused her admission. "[The school] had never entertained the possibility of an African American student," write the authors. Edmunds won a scholarship to further her study at Teachers College and worked at the Henry Street Settlement House after receiving her degree. She and her husband then returned to Massachusetts because they thought it a better place to raise their children. There Mrs. Edmunds took in sewing because, as she was quoted as saying, the town "wasn't ready" for a Black nurse.[47]

One cannot consider African Americans and jobs in the twentieth century without considering racism. Each job that a Black person wanted, applied for, worked in, and was fired from included experiences linked to race, typically negative. Most employers and business owners of this time, according to these interviews and myriad other studies, were not especially concerned with racial issues, nor the possibility of being perceived as racist. This was just "how things were done." Yet, in large ways and small, from demands for raises to refusals of jobs, the Krueger-Scott narrators disrupted the deeply entrenched system of employment discrimination. And things did begin to change. Reverend James Scott made the following observation in his interview:

Well, during the late 1960s, early 1970s, a lot of occupations broke open. There were jobs in banks—in the public sector there was a general opening up, civil service became much more concerned about having a good repre-

Figure 3.4. Class of 1950, Newark City Hospital School of Nursing. Courtesy Newark Public Library.

sentation of Blacks. The professional schools, the law schools, the school of pharmacy, the social work school, the library school, and so forth, began earnestly looking for Blacks. And as a result, Blacks moved into many areas, whether it was architecture or engineering, driving a bus, veterinary medicine. For the first time you began to see Blacks and you weren't surprised when you saw this.[48]

Willie Bradwell noted the same trend: "Well, you got to remember that affirmative action came along during those years. So it made it much easier for Blacks to move into certain jobs that they weren't in before. . . . Back with the civil rights movement."[49]

In 1961, President John F. Kennedy employed the term "affirmative action" upon establishing his Committee on Equal Opportunity, under Executive Order 10925. The order reads in part, "The contractor will take affirmative action to ensure that applicants are employed, and that employees are treated during employment, without regard to their race, creed, color, or national origin,"[50] This decree continues to be tested to this day.

Reverend Woods believed that the real shift in job opportunity for African Americans, in Newark at least, came with the 1967 rebellion. By 1968/1969 there was a new kind of thinking he said, "a brand-new generation was born as a result of those riots."[51] Black Muslims were rapidly opening businesses, more Black nurses were graduating, and African American teachers were finally being promoted. Echoing Reverend Scott, Woods described a stark visual change in the employment landscape. The more that African Americans were seen working, the more (little by little) employers and consumers accepted their presence in the workforce.

Sociopolitical Work

In the introduction to *Time Longer Than Rope*, Payne and Green lament what many call the master narrative surrounding the civil rights movement. They write that while stories filled with charismatic leaders and dramatic redemption are compelling, they do not "take seriously the 'ordinary' people whose years of persistent struggle often made the big events possible."[52] This "politics of the everyday," as Robin D. G. Kelley might call the counter to the master narrative, has become more prevalent in Black activist historiography only recently. The expansion of terms like *activism* and *politics* is one necessary step toward the inclusion of "ordinary" people's work in this discourse. The Great Migration, scholars are now arguing, is more than a simple mass departure, but the most powerful and long-lasting labor action against systemic white supremacy in America. Many recent studies, according to Kevin Gaines, for example, have "rooted black activism in the urban migrations of black working people and their encounters with labor and the left."[53]

The Krueger-Scott participants did not necessarily see themselves as activists, in part because of their understanding of the term—an understanding solidly based upon the master narrative. Yet it becomes apparent while listening to the interviews that this community was made up of many an activist. As Payne and Green write, "everyday life for Black folk was invariably politicized," and "everyday life constitutes the core substance of Black politics."[54]

As Langston Hughes wrote, life was "no crystal stair" for the majority of African Americans of the Great Migration era. It required many battles before "reachin' landin's, And turnin' corners."[55]

Robin D. G. Kelley writes in *Race Rebels*: "Writing 'history from below' that emphasizes the infrapolitics of the black working class requires that we substantially redefine politics. Too often politics is defined by how people participate rather than why: by traditional definition the question of what is political hinges on whether or not groups are involved in elections, political parties, or grass-roots social movements. Yet the how seems far less important than the why, since many of the so-called real political institutions have not always proved effective for, or even accessible to, oppressed people."[56]

The Krueger-Scott narratives answer the "hows" in order to provide illustrations of this historical era. But the emphasis in their words is on the "whys." And in this chapter, the answer as to why has a lot to do with a need to battle racism and injustice in the workplace.

In addition, these oral histories provide some understanding as to why it might be that participants often differentiated between political and community activities—and why the questionnaire itself was designed to acknowledge this differential. Question #60 asks in part, "How much have you participated in political activities?" while #61 asks, "How much have you participated in community activities?" This separation probably indicates an understanding on the part of the project leaders of the possible connotations attached to the word "political." What is evident is that had there been no question based on "community" activities, the interviews would have missed out on a great deal of "political" stories.

Contemporary activist and seminary student Frances Lee recently wrote about just this as they struggled with the often-concretized expectations of a socially conscious person. They write: "I want to spend less time antagonizing and more time crafting alternative futures . . . that may look like shifting my activism towards small scale projects and recognizing personal relationships as locations of mutual transformation. It might mean carefully choosing whether I want to be part of public disruptions or protests, and giving myself full permission to refrain at times. It may mean drawing attention to the ways in which other people outside of movements have been living out activism, even if no one has ever called it that."[57]

The workplace, it is pointed out in Paul Ortiz's study of early Black voter registration, has long been an important location of everyday Black activism. "Contrary to the assumptions of much of the literature on modern protest," Ortiz wrote in 2003, "it is not charismatic individuals who create movements: it is the relationships between individuals that convince ordinary people to take risks and engage in politics."[58] In the Krueger-Scott interviews, we hear about a lot of ordinary people taking risks.

Women Working (1965-1994). Much in the way that the majority of activists live in the shadows of the few who are celebrated, women's stories of activism continue to be overshadowed by men's. While there has certainly been newfound attention paid to women's activism, their erasure from the historiography is a difficult habit to break for even the most conscientious of scholars. Because women of the Krueger-Scott generation often moved to activism through domestic issues—and then performed this activism frequently in private spaces—some have been misidentified as apolitical.

Dr. E. Alma Flagg told her interviewer all about the changes occurring in the Newark Public Schools (NPS) during the 1970s. She had been appointed assistant superintendent in charge of curriculum services in 1967, a major coup for an African American woman at the time, she explains. But by the mid-1970s reductions in state requirements for administrators signaled the beginning of the end as far as Dr. Flagg was concerned. Those hired were no longer the specialists she believed necessary to take the district into the next social and political era. Her position was eventually eliminated altogether, and she received a demotion. Explaining in her interview that she did not want to change jobs, nor was she ready to retire, she instead registered for advanced math courses at the National Science Institute, taking advantage of the New Jersey Board of Education's paid tuition plan. In 1980, Flagg published a math textbook that became part of the NPS curriculum.[59] Flagg had found a backstage way of contributing to a cause she deeply believed in. Similar to Pauline Mathis's situation at the Newark Newsdealers Supply Company, simply remaining where one is not wanted can be a form of rebellion in and of itself.

Carolyn Wallace stood out as a rare woman who answered her interviewer in the affirmative when asked whether she was politically active. "Since 1969," she declared.[60] The more typical reply from the women of Krueger-Scott was a denial of any sort of political activism. Yet later, in response to the question about "community activities," these same women would share stories that positioned them as heavily involved in a world that many would count as political.

Even Carolyn Wallace's claim that her political activity began in 1969 seems a bit modest, as it turns out that she began organizing unions even before that time. In the mid-1960s Mrs. Wallace organized at a sewing factory:

> I did some union organizing for the Ladies Garment Workers. I lost a job behind that, too. . . . The company that I was working for on Freylinghusen Avenue—I had got promoted down there and they asked me to go to this other place and . . . help organize the other shops in the area. And, uh, went up to Dickerson Street, and they were makin' shower curtains. I will never forget the shower curtains—they would slide through the machines—made me so mad. And a lot of the girls were getting hurt up there and I had started that union.

Wallace subsequently received an offer to go to Switzerland for a training program in labor organization. She explained to her interviewer that she had refused. "My vision was not that wide at that time. I shoulda went. But . . . I didn't want to go no place but Newark."

Wallace worked many jobs, including as a nurse's aide, legislative assistant, and social service director. And as with so many in the Krueger-Scott community, she leveraged her work into activism. Wallace agreed with other interviewees in that she saw her relatively good job prospects as related to the fact that she was one of the early Black college graduates. She also believed that the increased access to higher education contributed to increased activism as it raised the consciousness of Black workers—Black women in particular.

And Wallace continued to work for the greater good. With her husband, she founded the International Youth Organization (IYO), established in response to the 1967 uprisings. Approximately 35,000 children had benefited from its services at the time of her interview, according to Wallace. A 2010 news article covering the fortieth anniversary of this social services organization reported that it first started meeting in the basement of the Brick Towers housing projects in 1970.[61] Prompted by her interviewer, Wallace explained that the organization first came out of her job as part-time management agent for the newly built government-subsidized Hill Manor housing project (the housing project next door to the Krueger-Scott Mansion, whose impending demolition was a contributing factor to the project's delay). In keeping with the federal government's Great Society model, and its short-lived mission to facilitate equitable local allocation of federal funds, Mrs. Wallace and the Hill Manor management temporarily carried influence in the selection of tenants at the development.

Focused especially on the well-being of local youth, Wallace wanted to ascertain whether families were "ready" to live in the brand-new housing complex. She told her interviewer that once the federal government discovered that she was doing the "picking and choosing" of who would live in the complex, their funding was threatened. "Whatever we try to do for Black people the federal government messes up," said Wallace. Ultimately, this experience led her to see the need for "Giving kids a route off the streets," as described on IYO's website. Notably, all that we learn of IYO comes as a result of the question regarding "community activities. ".[62]

Councilwoman Mildred Crump had not always planned for a career in politics; she had gone to college in her hometown of Detroit to train as a Braille instructor. Arriving in Newark in 1965, her first job was as a traveling Braille teacher.

> When I first started, Sussex County was part of my territory. You talk about being afraid in race relations. When I would drive through those towns early in the morning before the major highways, the white kids would throw eggs and rocks. They knew I was coming through there. . . . And they pretty much knew my schedule, and they'd step out and, you know, go *whoo*, you know, in front of my car. It was quite terrifying sometimes. And I almost never wanted to stop because I never knew what to expect from any of those persons.

Crump worked for a Dr. Kelley, then head of the Special Education Department based in Jersey City. The job entailed constantly crisscrossing the state by car as there were very few trained Braille teachers at the time. But this was not the job that Crump had been offered initially; she had accepted the position of director of the program for the blind and visually impaired. She tells her interviewer:

Here again, this was one of those incidents, a promise that was made sight unseen. And, I mean, at that time I was the first African American Braille teacher in the city of Detroit, and [Dr. Kelley in New Jersey] was not expecting a Black person. I know that. But when I walked into his office to say, "Hi, here I am," he tried to fake [unintelligible]. So what he did is he said to me, "If you will work for Jersey City in another capacity and while we find funding for this position—" All of a sudden they lost their funding for the directorship. And he said, ". . . we'll fix it up for you, don't worry."

Crump stayed at the Jersey City program until the end of 1965, fulfilling her three-month commitment to Dr. Kelley. Then she moved up to a job working for the State of New Jersey, and her salary moved up with her. "Actually it was more than just Braille teacher. . . . I was actually an education consultant. . . . What I did is I set and monitored programs for students who were officially impaired throughout the state of New Jersey." Mildred Crump went from making $3,000 a month to $7,000 a month, and she loved her new job, although being the only Black Braille teacher did entail constantly having to prove herself, she explained. What Crump witnessed and experienced in her job as a teacher ultimately propelled her into the political arena.[63] Mildred C. Crump was sworn in as Newark's first African American councilwoman on July 1, 1994. She later became the first female Municipal Council president, an office she held until August of 2021.

Mildred Crump's remarks when talking about her idol Shirley Chisholm shed some light on the meaning of "politics" for some in her generation. Crump said about Chisholm, "I continue to marvel at what she's accomplished as an African American woman. . . . Now this is a woman who is political, but she's accomplished a lot." *But*, emphasized Crump. Clearly the word "political" is weighted with multiple meanings for these Newarkers, including that of all-talk-and-no-action, as Vivian Berry would make clear in her interview.

At the time of her Krueger-Scott interview, Vivian Berry was retired as director of senior citizens for the City of Newark. She was also an ordained minister. Berry believed that "political" organizations were full of people merely talking about what they would do. Berry said she just did things, that she was "a doer, not a talker." Perhaps this is another explanation as to why so many of the interviewees demurred in response to the question surrounding "political activity." The connotation of the word appears to carry a sense of inaction for some. Even as city governments began to feature a smattering of African American politicians by mid-century—and Newark welcomed its first Black mayor soon thereafter—ordinary Black lives did not necessarily improve commensurate to that increase in Black political presence. Thus, there were some African Americans who remained unimpressed with all things political.

In the beginning of Vivian Berry's interview, we hear a bell go off in the background. She explains, "I'm not gonna answer . . . I have a little candy store." Later she discusses the candy store when asked if she contributes to the economic life of Newark. While acknowledging that she does not take in any "earth-shaking" amount of money at the store, Berry said, "I consider this my mission field.... I use the time to talk to children, to encourage them to stay in school.... I try to encourage them by giving them a little gift." Vivian Berry used her shop as an outpost for young people, for teaching and encouraging children who might have thought they were just coming by for a soda and some chips. Like Carolyn Wallace, Berry's community work focused on the youth.

Berry's interviewer, Glen Marie Brickus, pushed Mrs. Berry about the candy store income, "Do you consider the volume of business you do significant?"

Berry repeated, "No ... not 'earth-shattering.' I consider it more of a mission field. Nothing I could live off of." Berry had made her point: sometimes work is not about income but output. Later in the interview, she responded that she had never been especially political, but she always voted—and volunteered at the polls. She also served as a board member of the antipoverty United Community Corporation and acted as a Democratic district leader for two years—an unpaid position.[64]

Mrs. Berry was, in addition, a member of her block club, alongside political activist Louise Epperson. They were part of the larger Association of Community Organizations for Reform Now (ACORN), a well-known national advocacy group for low- and moderate-income families. "No [political] activities, but we were responsible for a stop sign being installed there on Second Street," said Berry. And "as a result of us forming this block club we were able to convince ... Councilman Carrino [of the North Ward] to get involved."[65] If these sorts of undertakings were Berry's idea of not being political, then we can only imagine what other activities Berry—and others—may have left out had they not been asked about other, nonpolitical, experiences.

Another "community-minded" woman, Mary Roberts, complained in her interview that men needed to step up, noting their lack of participation in her block association as an example. (She also announced at one point in her interview that she would be running a clean-up initiative for her block that coming weekend, sounding a bit as if she was attempting to recruit her interviewer.) Roberts worked at her church, Sacred Heart Baptist in Brooklyn, New York, as an ordained minister and licensed counselor. She was also an elected district leader. Having retired from teaching in 1992, Roberts did not especially want the position of district leader, she explained, but people in her community petitioned for her to run. Roberts explains her hesitation: "You know you have a different opinion of political people." Her interviewer responded, "Right.... Don't trust them a lot."[66]

For Mildred Crump, her politics consisted of community work early on, and only later became her paying job. Crump has devoted much of her life in Newark to politics, and explained to her interviewer that her interest began while growing up in Detroit. Crump's mother had told her daughter early on that she "wouldn't be able to help herself" and would eventually go into politics, just like so many others in the Crump family—all men, emphasized Crump. Once in Newark, a place that she "didn't know beans about," Mildred Crump indeed became involved. In 1966 a neighbor asked her to help support the election of Calvin West, who would end up becoming the first Black elected official in the Addonizio administration. "Well, I fried my first chicken wings for Calvin West, believe it or not, in 1966. I guess you could say 'and the rest is history.'"

Once the political question had been answered to her interviewer's satisfaction, Crump was then asked about her "community activities."[67] Was she very active in her community? "Well, I think, I'd say a great deal," replied Crump. She relayed one story of "community activity" as a member of the Weequahic Partnership, when Crump battled the city's plans to demolish Weequahic Park's stadium: "The first day that they sent the bulldozers out to tear down the stadium, I laid down in front of the bulldozers so they couldn't come. And Wilbur McNeil [president of the Weequahic Park Association] said, 'Mildred, please get up off the ground,' so they didn't run over me. That's how passionate I was about what was done to Weequahic Park. And I know that had it remained a Jewish community, they never would have—The county would not have done that."[68]

I was unable to find more information on this urban showdown. Essex County did eventually raze the beloved Weequahic Park stadium, a place where, among other things, Newark's young athletes trained. A St. Benedict's Prep alumnus told me he remembered running the stadium stairs in preparation for his fencing competitions. There were also horse races held there, under the aegis of the New Jersey Road and Horse Association, until 1943, when the track was converted into housing for World War II soldiers. The neighborhood, as Crump references, gradually went from majority white (and Jewish) to majority Black, before and around the 1967 uprising.

In her book *Bulldozer: Demolition and Clearance of the Postwar Landscape*, Francesca Russello Ammon looks at the ways that the bulldozer—and other demolition equipment—symbolize the destruction of so many urban neighborhoods, as well as the lives lived within them. The bulldozer became a tool of postwar America's "clearance as progress" thinking, a symbol against which urban activists consistently fought. One only need recall the image of that crane sitting in front of Queen of Angels Church for so long, just waiting for the go-ahead to dismantle the historic Black house of worship.

"Minority communities were the primary victims," Ammon explained in an interview. In fact, 60 percent of those who were displaced by what many across the nation came to call "Negro removal" (i.e., urban renewal) were minority groups.[69] The bulldozer was a symbol, but also, in the case of the Weequahic Park stadium, an actual machine—one in front of which lay a very respectable middle-aged African American woman named Mildred Crump.

Men at Work (1974–2006). Frank Hutchins, who worked for the Housing and Urban Development Tenants Coalition, wanted to talk about others' work before his own. Hutchins had clearly contributed to his city, so much so that Mayor Gibson declared a Frank Hutchins Day, which featured an annual festival in Weequahic Park. In his interview, Hutchins chose to highlight Amiri Baraka's work, for example. He said that after Ken Gibson's election as the city's first Black mayor, Newark became a site of political awareness. Hutchins credited Baraka for helping to bring Blacks together as a community after what Hutchins saw as an extended period of individualism and focus on upward mobility.[70] Hutchins, notably, was atypical of the Krueger-Scott men, who tended to spend more time speaking of their own efforts rather than others'. In keeping with other related studies, generally the men's stories here included themes of bravery, independence, and fortitude, while the women spoke more in terms of community uplift.

The initial lack of collectivity in Newark's Black residents, as perceived by Frank Hutchins and others, was not necessarily due to lack of desire. As so many writers and thinkers have observed, the reinforcement of the everyday citizen as an individual in a "colonized" situation keeps those in power where they are, while holding the proletariat at a distance where they focus solely on self. Jean Paul Sartre writes in his preface to Frantz Fanon's *Wretched of the Earth*, "The different tribes fight between themselves since they cannot face the real enemy—and you can count on colonial policy to keep up their rivalries."[71] We have already heard examples of these "tribes" in the Kruger-Scott narratives, for example, in the form of Black Northerners and their more recent Southern migrant counterparts. Those rivalries in Newark were encouraged through, among other things, political campaigns and propaganda.

In Alessandro Portelli's oral history collection from a Kentucky coal mining community, *They Say in Harlan County*, there appear multiple parallels to stories of the Great Migration. One similarity is in the sabotaging of potential collectivity. In the case of Harlan County, the coal mine operators might be cast as the "colonizers," ensuring that no strong bonds were forged among the coal miners—keeping Black and white workers separate even as they all labored together under similarly brutal working conditions. Race has always been a handy divisionary tool in this country. In the days of American slavery, landowners ensured that poor whites—often exploited in their own right—still had some sense that they were better, and better off, than the enslaved Blacks. After all, they were "free" to come and go, and to receive pay (however nominal) for their work.

As Johnny Jones, a Kentucky coal miner, tells Portelli, "You take this race hatred and stuff, all that sprung from the money man. They get betwixt you and me and make us distrust each other, and make people kill each other for a lousy dollar."[72] The necessity of bridging these divisions was evident to many in the Krueger-Scott interviews, and an integral part of their sociopolitical work.

Frank Hutchins described Amiri Baraka's community-making efforts:

> He had the ability to bring people together. In the early '70s, right after Ken Gibson's election, on a given Sunday morning, there would be over two, three hundred leaders meeting at his headquarters. All the fields that dealt with the quality of life in the Black community. Health, education, church leadership. People used to come and meet prior to going to church on Sunday morning.... It's a shame that it didn't last longer and that more couldn't have been achieved by that. I think had that concept continued to go... the strides that would have been made in this city would have been terrific.[73]

This is not, however, the story everyone tells of Amiri Baraka. To some he was just another faction-maker, doing exactly what "the money man" wanted, fanning flames of disunity in the Black community. In the Krueger-Scott interviews, we hear some accuse Baraka of tearing at the fabric of a cohesive Black community with his Afro-centric focus on education and politics. In her interview, for example, Willie Belle Hooper remembers when she was teaching at the Robert Treat School. Amiri Baraka (then LeRoi Jones) and Eugene Campbell (a teacher at the time, who ultimately became superintendent of the Newark schools) wanted to make the school a more Afro-conscious space. Campbell started wearing dashikis and speaking Swahili to the students, according to Hooper. Together with Baraka, the two men battled for an updated cafeteria menu that reflected a more African flavor. Hooper and others did not agree with this plan: "And I went back to Robert Treat. And I stayed there until there was all of this confusion with LeRoi Jones.... They came in there running the school. And raised so much Cain. I don't know how they got them out. But the principal and the vice principal were white. They got them out of there. How he did it I don't know. But he did it.... I'm as Black as anybody, but there are certain distances I'll go."[74]

In the case of the Krueger-Scott interviews, because both interviewer and narrator share the same general civic space, the former plays an especially central role in this oral history process. Perhaps the lack of response on the part of interviewer Pauline Blount, for example, when listening to Frank Hutchins wax positive about Amiri Baraka was an indication of the feelings she held about the famous artist and activist. Not once did she comment upon the praise Hutchins was lavishing upon Baraka. Yet in Willie Belle Hooper's interview, the same interviewer encouraged her subject to expand upon the details regarding that push for Afro-centricity at the school. A lack of engagement on the part of an oral history interviewer might not be so notable in a different situation, but in the case of the Krueger-Scott interviews, consistent, spontaneous interactions were the norm. When comments are met with no response, it often feels significant.

Ronald Rice's life's work was in politics. He was a Newark City Council member from 1982 through 1998, assuming the office of New Jersey state senator in 1986. Rice was also deputy mayor from 2002 to 2006, he ran for mayor against incumbent Sharpe James in 1998, and he ran against Cory Booker for mayor in 2006. But, as with so many of the politically active interviewees, he started his life somewhere else entirely. In response to a question about his first job, Rice answered that he shined shoes. From there he performed a string of menial jobs, explaining that by the time he took a position after high school at Skyron Corporation in Belleville, he was committed to furthering his education. "It was a sweatshop," he remarked.

When subsequently asked about his political activities, Rice said that he preferred performing his political work within the community, but that, "if the Democratic Party calls me to an event or a meeting, I'm there. I'm in leadership." At the time of the interview he was both state senator and City Council member, a double duty one was able to perform at that time. (A state law would later be enacted prohibiting public servants from holding dual government positions.)

Rice was also asked, in a separate question, whether he had any experiences with "racial discrimination in Newark." He replied, "Oh yeah," wherein he referenced his 1978 campaign against Mickey Bottone for the West Ward council seat, a race he ultimately lost. "They did not want a Black to represent the West Ward," Rice says. At the time the West Ward was majority white, largely inhabited by European immigrant families and people from New York City looking for affordable housing. It appears Rice was somewhat understated as to exactly what he went through during that election.

In 2015 the *Observer* ran an article entitled "Six All-Time Newark Ward Contests and Why They Mattered." Number two on the list was entitled "Ronald L. Rice versus Michael 'Mickey' Bottone and a New Day in the West Ward," which described a "rematch from an especially brutal 1978." A newcomer to the primarily Italian and Irish West Ward, Ron Rice moved to its Vailsburg neighborhood in 1974, working in law enforcement at the time. According to the *Observer* article, Rice claimed ballot fraud in the 1978 election—although he does not mention this in his Krueger-Scott interview. Reportedly, the official ballot count had him losing by 760 votes. One can only imagine the backlash he received as a Black man challenging the status quo, accusing the government of voter fraud. (All these years later, African American Stacey Abrams was initially castigated for saying the same thing about the gubernatorial election results in Georgia.) Rice noted in his interview that part of the reason people did not want African Americans in power was, "you can't do backroom deals with certain Black folk."[75] Four years later Rice ran again for that council seat and won. Bottone became mayor of Lavalette, a shore town in southern New Jersey.[76]

George Branch was another political worker, and one of the council members who was an original backer of the Krueger-Scott Mansion project. Branch had been a professional boxer at one time, a career that eventually led him to train other young boxers. He subsequently found himself invested in Newark's youth, especially in terms of public housing advocacy. As with Carolyn Wallace, Branch noted the ways that youth were excluded and affected when it came to discussions of fair and adequate housing.

Branch tells a story of his first reluctant and problematic foray into politics:

> Yeah. But let me get back to the first part, why I got involved in politics. I had developed a household name. Then I didn't like, really like politics that much. And was a guy because I had the name recognition, his name Ray Burgess. He came to me, and he was slick, slick as an onion. He came to me, he said, "Councilman," he said, "why don't you run?" He said, "You got name recognition, everybody knows you. Why don't you run?" I said, "Ray, I'm not interested in that stuff." He said, "You should run." He says, "I'll be your campaign manager. I help you raise the money," what have you. And I like an old fool—goddamn—trusted that boy. Come to find out he was using me to raise money... He was packing in money. I ran third in the race and lost. That was in 1974.[77]

In 1975 Mayor Ken Gibson appointed George Branch to the Board of Education. In 1982, Branch won a seat on the City Council. Meanwhile, Ray C. Burgess has a park named after him in the nearby town of Irvington.

In the Krueger-Scott collection we find so many stories of everyday women and men redefining what politics and activism look like. It also becomes clear that indeed, "everyday life for Black folk was invariably politicized," as Payne and Green write. So many of these Newarkers were forced into the fray of politics simply in order to get through their day. Yet other African Americans sought out politics as a proactive tool for change. In the analysis of these narratives, it only makes sense to look at *why* these actors did what they did and not just *how*.

Ministry (1912–1969). Black ministers have alternatively suffered criticism and received praise when it comes to their work in local politics, an issue touched upon in the previous chapter. Theirs may be the voices most often heard in Black civil rights historiography, yet one can find many people who are quick to criticize Black clergy's lack of activism in the face of so much injustice. Ron Rice points out in his interview, "Ministers are people, too, and they have their faults. You know, we can all be critical."[78]

African Americans have had a complicated relationship with their pastors since the first church was ever planted. At one time the only authority in a Black community, ministers were generally revered by their African American peers. This relationship persisted even as African Americans rose to higher levels of status and economic stability through a variety of other professions. However, as times progressed, the old-guard attitude of pastor devotion began to rankle more than a few African Americans, who came to regard Black clergy—and the Black church more generally—with suspicion and skepticism. Today, Black clergy's tendency toward more conservative social and political stances has kept them too quiet for some, too distant from activist movements. And those faith leaders who do make themselves known through public pronouncements on policy and law are sometimes accused of grandstanding for their own gratification. The role of Black clergy is not an easy one to define or take on.

As early as 1912, W.E.B. Du Bois railed against Black preachers in an editorial in the NAACP's *Crisis* magazine. While he acknowledged the hard-working and "self-forgetful" ones, Du Bois wrote, "The paths and the higher places are choked with pretentious and ill-trained men and in far too many cases with men dishonest and otherwise immoral. Such men make the way for upright candidates of business and power extremely difficult."[79] Du Bois looked upon these sorts of men (Black women would not serve in the church as ministers, for the most part, for decades to come) as hindrances to Black progress.

In 1952, in a speech to the National Negro Labor Council, Paul Robeson differentiated his minister father from others. "Never to forget the days of my youth . . . inspired and guided forward by the simple yet grand dignity of my father who was a real minister to the needs of his poor congregation in small New Jersey churches, and an example of human goodness. . . . If it were not for the stirrings and militant struggles among these millions [of Negro Americans], a number of our so-called spokesmen with fancy jobs and appointments would never be where they are."[80]

And in a 1967 *Time* magazine article about the Newark uprising, a citizen is quoted responding to the accusations by Mayor Addonizio that the uprising occurred due to a lack of Black leadership. The article reads: "Another Negro, one of some 900 who assembled in Newark for a conference on black power, told the *New York Times*: 'There was only one man who could have walked on Springfield Avenue and said, "Brothers, cool it." That was Malcolm X. We have no such leaders now. Whitey doesn't understand this. Some little Negro pork chop preacher who is hustling pot and girls in a storefront church goes to city hall and gets all sorts of promises. That's not grass-roots leadership, but Whitey thinks he's dealing with responsible Negroes.'"[81] Lest we conclude that the influence of respectability politics is unique to the experience of African American women, there were many men seemingly caught up in the same. Black clergy, as with the larger African American population, were susceptible to the constantly shifting social stances and cultural expectations surrounding Black American behavior and activities. L. H. Whelchel Jr. points to the experience of the Reverend Fred Shuttlesworth in Birmingham, Alabama, as an example of this shifting ground. Contrasting his approach with Dr. Martin Luther King Jr.'s more educated, "conciliatory" style of preaching and organizing, Whelchel describes Shuttlesworth's reputation as "crude, uncouth and dictatorial," according to the Black elites of the time. Shuttlesworth attracted the "masses," who were in turn admonished for following someone so clearly ignorant of the need to "uphold the status quo." Whelchel adds that these upper-echelon detractors also tended to stay "a safe distance away from the trenches of the civil rights battles," while Shuttlesworth placed himself right in the thick of things.[82]

There are, of course, numerous occasions when Black clergy have made valuable contributions to American society, stepping in voluntarily, courageously, and without fanfare, to battle racial and civil injustice. Robert L. Allen in his 1969 book *Black Awakening* argues, "The black minister remains today an important, if not the most important, social force in most black communities." Yet Allen also goes on to acknowledge that those in the profession can at times deserve the "Uncle Tom" moniker, due to what looks like "collaboration" with the power elite.[83]

The bottom line is that there are a wide assortment of ideas on how the role of Black clergy should be performed. Professional religious leaders of the African American community live under scrutiny when it comes to their work and the ways they utilize their bully pulpits. Some take advantage of their position to build themselves up, others utilize their visibility to effect change for others—and some do a little of both. In her Krueger-Scott interview, Elma Bateman said there was a time when there used to be more "jackleg preachers," but that the profession had increased its education level, and this in turn strengthened their leadership abilities.[84] Needless to say, this was a subject that engendered much conversation in these oral history interviews.

One example of Newark clergy active in the "struggle" is the Reverend Henry Cade. According to Louise Epperson's interview, Reverend Cade opened Central Presbyterian's church doors to the Committee against Negro and Puerto Rican Removal meetings. This was the organization spearheaded by Epperson to fight the medical school expansion in her University Heights neighborhood. "We went into the church and had many, many meetings. He was always for us," explained Epperson.

In fact, Reverend Cade's work was later acknowledged by Rep. Donald Payne through a tribute in the House of Representatives in 1996: "Over the years Newark's Central Presbyterian Church has recognized the need for the church to become more than a site for worship. The Central Presbyterian Church has opened its doors to programs and services that truly help the community and its residents. The church sponsors programs like SHARE, a food program; preschool-head start programs, senior citizen programs; young adult ministries, homeless ministries, as well as others. It takes a certain kind of leadership to make things happen. For the Central Presbyterian Church that leadership has come from Rev. Henry Cade for 30 years."[85] Reverend James Scott was also praised by many Bethany Baptist Church members as a minister who not only changed the church he was called to lead, but also the city within which it stood. Under his leadership, Bethany initiated numerous community outreach programs and was a strong supporter of the NAACP and Urban League. Reverend Scott explains to his interviewer, Glen Marie Brickus (a Bethany member), why there existed a perception that African American religious leaders might be less than responsible sometimes:

> Maybe I should tell a little story that kind of highlights how Newark was and show you what it is today. We moved here to the city of Newark, uh, maybe May, June, something like that, 1963. Sometime early in the summer, before August, I got a call from City Hall asking me would I take such and such a job. The job paid almost twice as much as what I was making. And I said, "What do I have to do?" And they said, "Nothing." And I said, "God, I want a job [unintelligible]." And someone came and visited me and asked me, and their rationale was "everybody else—every other clergyperson in the city—has a job, why shouldn't you?" My feeling was from the outset—and this was during the Addonizio administration—my feeling was that I did not want to be anybody's house n——. That if I was to have any integrity as a leader in this community, I had to be free. And while I needed the money—and I was not being paid very well—I at the same time valued my independence more highly than a handout. So that was my first introduction to the social and political culture here in the city. I've never—and I just decided that I would never be a politician. I didn't see how I could balance the demands of being a leader in the church and being a leader in the political realm.
>
> BRICKUS: So you have not had any direct participation in political activities in Newark?
> SCOTT: That's right.[86]

Dr. Scott was committed to the separation of church and state. As with so many of the narrators in this collection, he did not consider himself "political," and claimed no interest in being a politician. Once again we see that the arena of politics can come with a severely tainted reputation.

Reverend Robert Woods had strong opinions about what made a good pastor and did not consider the traits commonplace in contemporary ministry. This was evidenced in his answer to Mrs. Brickus's question regarding what made pastors "great." Woods explained that in the past, "Even if they reach a level that most ministers don't reach as far as pulling together congregations and this sort of thing—they were men that was down to earth, that you could sit with. You could talk with. They were willing to help and aid other ministers and give them directions." Woods added that those ministers "would give you a lesson in life, just like you're having in this interview."

Reverend Woods certainly fell under the heading of politically engaged clergy. When answering questions about social and cultural activities, he named his work with block organizations as well as his position as chaplain for a New Jersey human rights association. When asked about his political activity specifically, he and his interviewer Mrs. Brickus laughed. "Bob," said Brickus, "I know about your extensive involvement in politics and associations with politics but just give me—"

Woods interrupted: "I was twenty-one years, I was a district leader in the West Ward." (The women, notably, quite often listed that same job as apolitical.) Woods was also city chaplain when Mike Bottone—Ronald Rice's nemesis—was in office. Woods went on to name many organizations for which he was chaplain, and politicians with whom he "function[ed]. "I designate myself as a Democratic [sic] but I really, I really only go for the people I think can help my people the most."[87]

Reverend Alvin Conyers, who experienced racial discrimination early in his job as a laundry porter, ended up becoming active in the fight for racial equality. One issue he tackled as a member of the Social Action Committee of the Ministerial Conference was that of discrimination in hiring Black firefighters. There will be more about that effort in the next chapter.

Newark is typically characterized as a political town. Whether it is made such by the people who live there, or whether those who come are drawn to the complex politics that power the city, it is hard to say. All in all, according to the oral histories, a good number of Newark's Black ministers were regularly involved in community and political activities. Those who were not, we hear much less about. And that might be just how they want it.

Conclusion

A lifetime of being denied service in restaurants, of seeing no one who looks like you driving the buses you take to work, of being assigned separate swim days at the public pools ... all because you are not white. In the case of the Krueger-Scott participants, these experiences often ended up inspiring action. There was no lack of motivation when it came to leveling the workplace playing field. According to the U.S. Census Bureau, in 1947 the average income for an American white family was $3,157. That same year, a Black family averaged $1,614. Matters improved through the decades, as many Krueger-Scott interviewees noted, but not markedly; by 1970 Black families were earning almost 62 percent of what a white family was making. Yet in 1997, the year most of these interviews took place, an average Black household brought in 56.9 percent of what an average white household brought in that same year.[88] The economy was going in the wrong direction when it came to racial earning equality.

In the grand scheme, quality of life did improve for the Krueger-Scott group. Many of those who came north were children of sharecroppers, working with their parents in fields of cotton, peanuts, and tobacco to help support the family. Few saw African Americans in professional careers or positions of authority when they were young. Of course, the South was not alone in this; many of the interviewees born in Newark also witnessed their parents being turned away from jobs or working long days in menial positions. The majority of the participants grew up poor, even if it was not apparent to them at the time. Yet, upon reaching adulthood, most would gain greater freedoms and opportunities than their parents ever had. Expectations around labor equality and opportunity motivated many of the Krueger-Scott narrators to invest their time advocating for their people, whether they called that work political or not. Maybe their own children were no longer shining shoes or being denied advanced courses in school, yet there was still a long way forward to equitable opportunities among all races and classes in Newark.

In decades past there were generally two schools of thought when it came to labor and the African American, two basic ideologies voiced by those of the race—as well as those outside of it. This is sometimes personified as the Du Bois/Washington binary. Most generally, Booker T. Washington exhorted his people to learn a trade, to do whatever they could to participate in the social system as it stood at the time. Newark's Joe Clark could perhaps be considered a member of that ideological camp:

> But my major types of work came from carrying groceries, delivering newspapers, shoveling snow. These were all the types of things that gave me a work ethic, a sense of punctuality, a sense of profit too, sense of being in charge of your destiny, a sense of not sitting around holding a pity party for yourself, being an oversensitive crybaby, expecting others to do for you what God has given you the strength to do for yourself. So that's been going on since I was four, five, six years old. It has not stopped and it never will. Because I feel that we must be in charge of our own destiny.[89]

Du Bois, believed that many (though not all) African Americans had talents that would go unrealized as long as white supremacy was the prevailing social model. Du Bois believed in dismantling inequality through the mind, learning and then speaking up about what had been learned. Senator Wynona Lipman, a highly educated politician working tirelessly to change the system, may have been more Du Boisian in her approach to Black progress. Her interview is full of observations on society's racial inequities:

> I don't think that the justice system is the best that we have. And I guess it does the best we can. But I don't think that's fair to African Americans either. I used to say when I was in the Hall of Records, if I could just blindfold the

judge so he wouldn't see that the lawyer is Black and that the prisoner is Black, then maybe some of these juveniles would get better treatment. Because just go in a prison, just go in a young person's prison, all you see is Black faces. Occasionally, a Latino face. Lots of Latino faces now. It used to make me almost cry to go to the prison just to see the Black faces all around.[90]

Listening to these interviews, it is apparent that the African Americans of the Krueger-Scott oral histories were often forced to make Herculean efforts to earn a paycheck. But that does not make them victims, nor imply that their experiences were all the same. Some had financial goals primarily based upon survival, and then later perhaps on increasing their quality of life. Others were bent on changing the way things worked in their city, battling a system structured to ensure Black failure. When asked to sum up life in Newark at the end of each interview, most narrators answered that they were pleased to have lived and worked there, that they cared very much for their city. But many also pointed out at the end of their interviews that there was still more work to be done.

CHAPTER 4

Hot Days

The Setup

Perpetuated Narratives and Actual Stories (1961–2011). For many people, the city of Newark is synonymous with the "riots" of 1967.[1] Burning stores, broken glass, and armed forces are the optics in much of the public imagination, even all these years later. There are several reasons for this. First, it is a convenient way to dismiss Newark's problems as unique, thus avoiding acknowledgment of urban crisis as a national issue. The term *riot* implies dysfunction, and so the African American "rioting" that happened in Newark during that long, hot summer (and at so many other sites across the country) can be regarded as isolated and irrational.

Second, Newark itself has not done an especially good job of framing its own story of civil unrest; decades passed before the city began to come to terms with this small sliver of its long history. It was not until 2008, for example, that Dr. Clement Price and colleagues succeeded in their efforts to place a commemorative plaque on the police precinct building where taxi driver John Smith was taken into custody on that fated July day. The plaque reads, "On this site on July 12, 1967, there began a civil disturbance that took the lives of twenty-six people and forever changed our city. May this plaque serve as a symbol of our shared humanity and our commitment to seek justice and equality. Dedicated July 12, 2007, by the People of Newark."

Newark is over three hundred fifty years old, colonized by Puritans in much the same way as many other more celebrated American cities. And Newark quickly became a center of American industry, hosting an international exposition in 1872 where President Ulysses S. Grant was in attendance. In the first half of the twentieth century, as evidenced by the Krueger-Scott oral histories,

Figure 4.1. Plaque commemorating 1967 Newark uprising, Fourth District Police Precinct. Photo by Jake Ephros.

Newark was also a hub of entertainment and commerce. The "Four Corners" at Broad and Market Streets were known as the busiest intersection in the country. Additionally, Newark played a vital role in the World War II production of war materials. But then, as with many industrialized cities nationwide, troubling trends affected the economy and the morale alike. And in 1967, three hundred years after its founding, a five-day urban uprising occurred, and suddenly the city's history became that one moment.

And just in case there were opportunities to thwart the foregrounding of that uprising as the pinnacle of Newark's story, various forms of production continue to fan the flames of that memory. John T. Cunningham, in his 1988 edition of the coffee table book *Newark*, writes about the rebellion in a chapter entitled "The Whole Town Is Gone." The title is in reference to then-mayor Addonizio's response to Col. David B. Kelley's query as to the state of the city at the time of the rebellion. Cunningham concludes his chapter with, "Newark had reached bottom. If it ever could rebuild, its new foundation would forever rest on the ashes of July 1967."[2] This kind of dramatic narrative has been spun through many cycles over the years.

HOT DAYS

In 1997, Newark's own Philip Roth published the novel *American Pastoral*, whose main character, "Swede" Levov, is a successful Jewish Newark businessman. One scene in the novel has Levov reflecting: "the riots, Springfield Avenue in flames, South Orange Avenue in flames. . . . In Newark's burning Mardi Gras streets. . . . The surreal vision of household appliances out under the stars and agleam in the glow of flames incinerating the Central Ward . . . the old ways of suffering are burning blessedly away in the flames, never again to be resurrected, instead to be superseded, within only hours, by suffering that will be so gruesome, so monstrous, so unrelenting and abundant, that its abatement will take the next five hundred years."[3] Sometimes fiction can actually be stranger than truth. And in 2011, Tom McCabe published *Miracle on High Street: The Rise, Fall, and Resurrection of St. Benedict's Prep in Newark, N.J.* In this piece of nonfiction, McCabe refers to the rebellion that occurred forty-five years prior to publication as "The watershed event in Newark's recent history." It was "six days of looting and rioting, death and destruction," when "fire seemed to be a lasting image." The chapter entitled "'Camelot Is Dead': The Newark Riots and the Closing of St. Benedict's Prep, 1967–1972" describes the rebellion as viewed by a monk standing atop the school's roof, where he "looked down and watched the riots through his horn-rimmed glasses. African American teenagers looted nearby stores along Springfield Avenue."[4]

Whatever the intent of these authors in their various portraits of the 1967 uprising, what is rendered is a constant flow of theatrical depictions of Newark's mean streets filled with Black marauders, flames, and death. This is a hard image for a city to shake.

Those five days in July of 1967, as with so many of the urban uprisings of that era, are part of a much more complicated moment than is often reported. This is evidenced, in part, by the multiple perspectives shared in the Krueger-Scott oral histories. Ida Clark, for example, described Newark's peak as "behind the riots," when people started to realize there was "a better way," and Black people became more involved in their community.[5] Carolyn Wallace responded that she could not call the riots the lowest point because there was some "coming together" that occurred. Vivian Berry answered that the low point for Newark was actually prior to the rebellion; after all, Berry remarked, before the uprising, "they just thought because nobody complained about anything that people were just generally happy with the ways things was goin'." But afterwards, said Berry, "People's eyes had become open."[6] This is, in fact, a common response to rebellion found within this oral history collection, and within urban scholarship more generally. Rebellion brings change. We need look no further than the summer of 2020 and the protests by and for Black Lives Matter.

But, of course, not all African Americans see rebellion the same. Mary Roberts stated in her oral history that Newark was at its peak when she arrived in 1961, and that the riots brought it to its lowest point.[7] Marion Williams agreed, claiming that the lowest point of the city came in the 1960s with the riots, when people tore up their own homes and stores and "went wild."[8] And while Pauline Mathis argued that the uprising brought a positive change in terms of the hiring of Black teachers, John Martin believed that the riots truly divided the city. Meanwhile, Lewis Turner brought up the 1971 teachers' strike—not the rebellion—as a "watershed moment" in the city. He claimed it was the beginning of a loss of respect for each other and for authority.

Historical narratives are packaged to be remembered in assorted ways, and for a variety of reasons. The palatable narrative—one that tends to place blame elsewhere than on those in power—is often the result of a process much like the children's game of Telephone. One person begins the story, and then perhaps a journalist relays said story with a particular slant (however unwittingly), and then the story is modified just a bit more—through the media and other public communications. The end result is often a narrative that does not necessarily match up with the original events. Later down the line still, someone writes a history book based in part upon this detached narrative, and so it goes.

Cities wrestle with all sorts of unique challenges: innumerable people per square foot, multiple tiers of social and economic classes, old attitudes bumping up against new. And in our country, there is always the matter of race. Racism, whether meted out through individual slights or systematic operations, has eclipsed a lot of what is good about Newark. Tribulations experienced by most Black residents in Newark came from living in a crowded urban space as a Black person. Through these oral histories it becomes evident that the African American residents of Newark suffered the overwhelming burden of their city's twentieth-century problems. And one longstanding problem within urban centers has been destruction by fire.

In Newark's extensive history, as in numerous American cities, fires play a dominant role. Fire is also a powerful symbol in the lives of many of the Krueger-Scott narrators, one often deployed in the process of their remembering. Once again we witness the intentionality behind the questionnaire designed for this oral history project; Giles Wright and Clement Price seem to anticipate the importance of the element of fire in eliciting stories. Question #81 reads in part, "What would you consider to be the five most important events/developments that have occurred in Newark during your residence here (e.g., strike, election, riot, fire, natural disaster, black in-migration)?" It is useful to note that the question uses the word "riot," as opposed to "the riots." Yet many of the interviewers automatically say "the riots" when posing this question to their subjects. This places emphasis, of course, on the 1967 uprising and perhaps encourages a particular discussion that might not have ensued in quite the same manner had the more generic term been used.

In any event, from the Krueger-Scott interviews we learn that fire seared childhood memories, devastated Black churches, and ignited subpar tenements.

Figure 4.2. *Time* magazine cover, July 21, 1967. Courtesy Newark Public Library.

And Newark's fires were battled by a primarily white fire department all the way until the 1980s, the face of the fire department itself becoming a measuring stick for progress. And, of course, fire was present during the 1967 rebellion, sometimes by way of Molotov cocktails and other times through the media's visual and written metaphors announcing the demise of Newark, New Jersey. The July 1967 "Embattled Cities" issue of *Time* magazine, for example, included an article entitled "Races: Spreading Fire." The piece began, "Even as the fury of

Newark abated last week, other Negro ghettos flared like gunpowder dropped in a fire." The scene had been set.

The subject of the uprising—and of destruction and violence more widely—has been left for last here, intentionally. I sought to first foreground the everyday tales of the Krueger-Scott narrators, recentering the story of Newark as a place where people lived regular, if not uncomplicated, lives. In first acquainting readers with some of the residents of Newark, I hoped to offer respite from the well-worn tropes of a city constantly under siege.

The following section will concentrate on two subjects: urban fire and the heated uprising which started on a hot summer day in July 1967. When it comes to the subject of tough times in Newark, these two topics—both intertwined and separate—play a sizable role in the Krueger-Scott narratives.

Firefighting (1950–1994). The addition of Black members to the fire department was significant to many of those interviewed, a sign of advancement in equal rights. The Krueger-Scott narrators were asked in question #66, "What do you remember about such public servants as the police, firefighters, social workers, etc.?" Or, as Glen Marie Brickus put it to Mr. Churchman in his interview, "What about Black folk in the police department and in the fire department?"

Funeral home director James Churchman told Mrs. Brickus the story of Richard Freeman, who grew up across the street from what was known as the busiest firehouse in Newark, at 93 Belmont Avenue. Freeman longed to be a firefighter when he was a child, explained Churchman. After finishing high school, Freeman took the fire department exam and passed. He was assigned, at his request, to that station on Belmont Avenue he had been eyeing since he was a child. But Mr. Freeman, because he was Black and it was the 1950s, was not allowed to sleep at that firehouse with the other firefighters. Years later, when he made captain, Freeman changed those rules. Said Mr. Churchman in his interview, laughing, "I thought that was a very good story."[9]

The increasing African American presence in various occupations was referenced frequently as a marker of progress. Retired social services administrator Vivian Berry noted that, along with more Black school administrators, the visibility of Black firefighters was encouraging to the Black community. Retired factory worker Matthew Little was—among many others when asked to name important people in the city—quick to name the first Black Newark firefighter, a Mr. Thomas.

Incorporating Black police and firefighters into the respective departments was a cause worth fighting for, judging by the actions of numerous narrators. Reverend Alvin Conyers said he worked with the Social Action Committee to increase the number of Black firefighters, and Senator Wynona Lipman told her interviewer that she wrote numerous recommendation letters for men applying to the fire department. (Lipman added that she was, however, disappointed at the continued lack of women's presence in the police and fire departments.)

Reverend Robert Woods told his interviewer that he participated in the preparation of Black firemen for the written exam as soon as the affirmative action mandate went into effect, sometime around 1983. Woods noted that before the early 1980s there were perhaps two African American firefighters in the whole Newark fire department. Lurline Byass confirmed the paucity of Black firemen when discussing her first home at 95 Clinton Place, where she lived from 1962 to 1963. It was in the Homestead Park area, a mostly Jewish neighborhood. She recalled that the nearby fire station (probably the one at 395 Avon Avenue) was staffed entirely by white men. A similar image is evoked by many of the interviewees; wherever they looked there was still little reflection of themselves, a regular reminder that Jim Crow had followed them north.

Especially during the lives of the Krueger-Scott narrators, civil services often conflated Black urban material poverty with a poverty of importance. Ethel Richards, born in Newark in 1918, explained in her interview that during her lifetime firefighters showed little concern for Black people, rarely entering into their neighborhoods. Another native Newarker, Bernice Johnson noted that all the firemen and policemen were white when she was growing up; but she also said that everybody knew them, suggesting some semblance of relations across the racial divide. Dr. Beverly Scott, who arrived in Newark in 1963, observed that initially the (white) police were insensitive to African Americans' needs. She said that as time went on, she witnessed progress in this area. "It was gratifying to see the changes . . . within the police force. It was gratifying to see the changes in the fire department in terms of their hiring practices."[10]

It was not until the late twentieth century that a systematic movement was in effect to make these well-paying and prestigious jobs available to African Americans. In 1988, *Ebony* magazine published a feature on Black fire chiefs. Echoing the Krueger-Scott narrators, the article stated that while fire departments were once called "White men's country clubs," now there were actually some African-American men in charge:

> From Newark to Kansas City to Sacramento, Black fire chiefs are running departments of 400, 600, 1,000 people. . . . They are men who entered the field 20 or 30 years ago with a handful of other Black firefighters, all of whom were relegated to segregated firehouses. The most intense heat they ever felt was not from the blazes they fought, but from their White counterparts who demanded that they prove themselves daily. . . . They worked their way up to driver, lieutenant, captain, battalion chief, assistant chief, and finally to what one chief referred to as "that pot of gold at the end of the rainbow."[11]

Claude Coleman, who was remembered by many of the interviewees as Newark's first Black fire chief, is featured in this *Ebony* article. He had worked as legal adviser for the Newark police department for fifteen years prior to becoming a firefighter. Coleman was forty-seven years old at the time of the article's publication. Many in the Krueger-Scott community also mentioned the fact that Mr. Coleman ultimately became a judge, his ascension held up as a great point of pride.

Unfortunately, in keeping with an all-too-common pitfall of Black American life, in 1994 then-judge Coleman was accused of using a stolen credit card at the Short Hills Mall in New Jersey. He was handcuffed and subsequently suspended from the bench. It was soon confirmed that the accusation was in error and public apologies were made by the department store whose security had apprehended him. In a *New York Times* article written by David Margolick, author of several books on historically racialized events, Coleman was quoted as saying, "So long as any black person is thought of as a n——, until all persons of color are looked upon with respect, none of us are going to be. And it doesn't matter whether you're a lawyer or a judge or a prosecutor."[12]

"Important Events" (1949–1968). When asked in his interview about "important events" in Newark, retired city clerk assistant Owen Wilkerson recalled a large fire on Avon Avenue, as did many of the other narrators:

> I remember on Avon Place [*sic*], this was back in '49 or '50, there was one hell of a fire. And I think that was in Gene Campbell's building . . . big, bright orange building. But anyway, that place burned to the ground. And I remember the Red Cross trucks and what not and everything out there. You had the NAACP went on a clothing collection drive and what not. I'm surmising a lot of the families, victimized families, were taken in, you know, by families within the community. . . . There was also a sense of embarrassment. I mean, here you were burned out and everything, and you're walking down the street with someone else's clothes on or shoes and everything. Because, you know, I've never been burned out. God forbid, I hope I'm never burned out. But I imagine that's a humiliating experience.[13]

Issues of respectability creep into the conversation as we listen to Wilkerson objectify those who suffered disaster through no fault of their own. He saw them as involved in an embarrassing situation and made sure to distance himself from it.

Youth counselor Ed Crawford named three major events in Newark that he thought were important: the rebellion in 1967, the runoff for Mayor between Kenneth Gibson and incumbent Hugh Addonizio, and a big fire on Avon Avenue: "Okay. I remember a very bad fire happened over on Avon Avenue just below the Avon Avenue School there. It took out the church and, matter of fact, that whole area in there—they since started rebuilding with townhouses. But it wiped out, oh, a block and a half, two blocks. About two blocks worth of housing over there . . . and it took out the church, took the church too. I forget the name of that church."[14] Notably, the interviewers felt tasked to retrieve certain stories, but the dates did not always seem as important. This can be frustrating when listening for chronology, a potential compromise as a result of the interviewer not being a professional historian. On the other hand, it is certain that some stories in this collection would never have been told had the interviewers not been peers.

Remembering (1920–1972). Fires are a useful tool in the marking of historic timelines. The famous Chicago fire, one hundred years before the fires of Newark's rebellion, has much in common in its telling with many contemporary urban fire reports. Carl Smith writes about "The Fire and Cultural Memory" in his book *Urban Disorder and the Shape of Belief.* "No matter what anyone thought the [Chicago] fire meant, for good or ill, everybody agreed that it marked a moment of major transition in Chicago history." Smith goes on to say that much as the South did with the Civil War, Chicagoans structured discourse of their city into a before-and-after paradigm. "The local population seized upon the disaster as an historical marker that would help them frame and understand urban experience and this period of rapid change."[15] This seemed to be the case with Newark's 1967 uprising as well. There was a "before the riots," and then there was an after.

Fires are often featured in the oral folklore of a community, memories of disaster handed down through generations. Alessandro Portelli explains, "oral narrators have within their culture certain aids to memory. Many stories are told over and over, or discussed with members of the community; formalized narrative, even meter, may help preserve a textual version of an event."[16] In the case of fires, this mode of memory preservation seems important as there is little in the way of recorded history when it comes to the many fires discussed by the Krueger-Scott interviewees.

In theorizing collective memory, Jacquelyn Dowd Hall writes that "Personal memories tend to disappear unless they are rekindled through repetition, and we repeat what is considered significant by the groups with which we identify."[17] The fact that a question regarding fire is included in the Krueger-Scott questionnaire, and is being asked by an interviewer for a project that is to be located in an African American cultural center as part of a historical archive, seems to imply the significance of fire. This implication, in turn, seems to rekindle memories of—and associations with—fire.

Take, for example, early in the interview, when Pauline Blount asks Coyt Jones if he remembers the taxi fare for the ride from Newark's Pennsylvania Station to his aunt's apartment. He had arrived by train from South Carolina in 1927, at the age of eleven.

JONES: I don't remember. There's only one thing I can remember about that ride was the amount of people that crossed the street at Broad and Market. I had never seen that many people before.

BLOUNT: Were they African Americans or were they—
JONES: They were all people, mostly white I think. This was years ago, remember? I asked the taxi driver if there was a fire someplace. Where was all the people going!?

Subsequently, Jones apparently told Mrs. Blount, at a point when the tape recorder was off, that there was something he wanted to share on tape, a "significant incident." Toward the end of the interview, Mrs. Blount invited Jones to "go ahead" with the story. The incident in question concerned a fire Jones witnessed sometime around 1920, in Hartsville, South Carolina. Jones and his family lived three houses down from the "Oil Mill Houses." These were small company houses for the employees of the Hartsville Oil Mill, which produced cottonseed oil. Jones recalled hearing that the rent was $2.00 to $3.00 per month.

One night an Oil Mill House caught fire, and ultimately the whole row of homes burned down. "The only thing standing in those houses was a chimney," said Jones. His mother had warned him not to go down to that site, but the young boy snuck out anyway: "I must have been about four or five years old. I don't remember. Anyway, a lady got burned up in one of the houses, and she was still holding the baby to her bosom when she burned. She was layin' on those springs and the bed and everything and the mattress was all burned up. I'll never forget that. Never forget it. That's one of the worse things I guess I've ever seen."[18] One might imagine that when the 1967 uprising began, and fires were erupting, Mr. Jones may have been transported back to his childhood memory of that gruesome scene. And perhaps, thirty years later, his memory during the interview of the crowded Newark streets, , signaling disaster, also brought him back to his five-year-old self and the sight of the burned woman's remains.

Coyt Jones's childhood story, with its coinciding images, can symbolize the historic disposability of Black life in the United States—and of the lives of the poor more generally. The housing for these Southern mill workers was clearly subpar and the fire company, according to Jones, did not respond in any sort of timely manner. It took so long, in fact, that a little boy had time to run down the street and gaze upon the charred body of another human being.

Born in 1916, James "Chops" Jones recalled the days even before fire trucks. "The fire engines, they had the horses, three horses and the engine on it, you know, with the screen, smoke and stuff comin' up." As early as 1913, according to an unidentified newspaper photo published on the Old Newark website, three new "Palmer-Singer Roadsters" were purchased by the city to allow fire chiefs to "be able to reach fires more quickly." But for the ordinary firefighters, old-fashioned horse-drawn engines would be the norm for years to come.

Jones also remembered fires around Christmastime: "Oh, Christmas. Oh, let me tell you about Christmas. Christmas we used to have real Christmas trees. It used to have candles on them. And we used to light the candles on the tree. And they say that's a fire hazard now. But on the branches we had little dishes, you'd put the candle in like the birthday candle, you put the candles in and you light 'em. Never had no fires.... Never seen nobody else that had fires."[19] Chops Jones reported at the beginning of his interview that he was a retired fireman himself—as well as a musician. There was never any more discussion of the former vocation, nor is there evidence that he ever worked as a firefighter. Barbara Kukla, journalist and author of numerous books on Newark, was a good friend of the late Mr. Jones. Kukla reported to me that he never mentioned any time spent fighting fires.

So why would somebody want to remember themselves as a firefighter, so much so that he would be willing to perhaps lie about it? This was, after all, a statement that could have been easily confirmed, much like Sharpe James's claim of being a Newark Eagles baseball player. There are myriad reasons that we all, in one way or another, make up stories. This is in part because ordinary people tend to want to be seen as heroic, argues Sandy Polishuk in her introduction to *Sticking to the Union: An Oral History of the Life and Times of Julia Ruuttila*. Ruuttila was a union activist who was more than once called upon to testify in front of the FBI and other government agencies. Polishuk spent years interviewing Ruuttila and then more time comparing her interviews to various "official" transcripts. Often Ruuttila interviews turned out to be quite embellished, Polishuk observed. "I believe ... Julia wanted to have been more important, more effective, and more heroic than the actual facts might imply, but I also think it likely Julia believed what she told me, and that her memory of the events had changed to accommodate her desires over the years."[20] Perhaps at some point in Mr. Jones's life he adopted a memory of heroism "to accommodate his desires," one that provided him with an agency that was outside the realm of so many Black men of his time.

In her oral history interview, Senator Lipman did not indicate that her personal life had been marred by fire, but the element most certainly played a role in her childhood memories. The topic also motivated the senator's interviewer to interject her own memories. Fortuitously, a dialogue ensued between Mrs. Brickus and Senator Lipman after the latter was asked if she knew anybody who used snuff or chewing tobacco. Sometimes memory's paths can be circuitous.

> LIPMAN: Oh, the snuff, yes. Snuff, the lady who helped us do the washing, at the wash pot outside, you know, where you boiled your clothes for washing over a fire. Oh, she was a snuff dipper I tell you. And my father chewed tobacco. Yes.
> BRICKUS: Oh yeah. Yeah, we had one of those wash pots in the backyard. And somebody had to go and build a fire on the wash day.
> LIPMAN: I remember killing pigs, too. And making crackling.
> BRICKUS: Oh really? Yeah, we did too, we did too.

LIPMAN: We had chickens, and all of that.
BRICKUS: We did too. We raised chickens and guineas, and there was, you know, you'd wait for special kinds of days as far as the weather to kill hogs. And then you may kill three or four or more at a time. And I can remember seeing them strung up. You know, they'd put up these special poles, with the poles across the top and hang them up there.
LIPMAN: We had a smoke house.
BRICKUS: We did too. They would first salt the meat down for so long, and then take it out and hang it up and smoke it. Keep the fire going day and night to smoke the meat. And it would never spoil.
LIPMAN: No.
BRICKUS: You could keep it indefinitely and it would never spoil.
LIPMAN: It was wonderful. We had a cow until the town made us get rid of it.

Senator Lipman concluded this conversation with an assertion that farming was a hard life, and Brickus ended this section of the interview saying, "Oh, we have more in common than we knew about." What the two had in common, among other things, was a rural upbringing in the South. Brickus's father was a bricklayer in Louisiana and Lipman grew up in LaGrange, Georgia, also the daughter of a bricklayer. And evidently, there were myriad chores entailing fire that were performed around a farm. Here it was a source of production instead of destruction.

Senator Lipman also had a strong memory, as an adult, of a fire-related experience. She was at the Essex County Jail Annex in North Caldwell, while in her position as freeholder director, sometime between 1968 and 1972. Her political focus included juvenile justice issues, so that she, along with a news reporter, was asked to visit the prisoners when a fire broke out in the jail. Lipman told Glen Marie Brickus, "We walked the floors of that hall while the place was burnin'. And the floors were so hot they seemed to burn right through my shoes. They were puttin' out the fire but we were tryin' to calm the inmates. That was a novel experience."[21] The multiple references to fire in these interviews seem to solidify its significance, offering a varied assortment of stories related to the subject.

Sharpe James has shared a story many times in public, as well as in his Krueger-Scott interview, of being a young boy when his mother fled with him and his brother from Jacksonville, Florida. Having suffered physical abuse at the hands of her husband, his mother made her way to Newark to live with her brother. "One morning she woke us up very early in the morning, took no belongings, went down to the train track, lit a fire to stop the train. I always remember how you stop trains in the South at the location, build a fire by the railroad. The train stopped. We got on it."[22] This was clearly a memory that has stayed close to James throughout his life.

Schoolteacher Marzell Swain had a different sort of fire memory. First she lamented in her interview that she did not have her school yearbooks to share with the Krueger-Scott project. "Heaven only knows where they are, they all got—we had fires and everything." Her casual reference to house fires implies a certain normality to their existence. At a later point in the interview, when Mrs. Swain is answering questions about shopping, she recollects how many stores were closed on Jewish holidays because most shop owners, at one time, were Jewish. She remembers this because it was an inconvenience not to be able to purchase certain items on Saturdays. As with others in the Krueger-Scott collection, Swain's interview illustrates a common knowledge of Jewish culture, knowledge gained both by necessity and proximity. "We used to mingle with each other," Mrs. Swain explained.

Swain continued, "on Sunday [sic] they couldn't light their stove. We had to go over there and light their stove. They would always give you—if they didn't have money they'd give you a piece of bread—or somethin' to show their appreciation for you comin' in." Swain was describing the religious law that prohibits observant Jews from lighting fires or doing any other kinds of work on the Sabbath, Saturday. Perhaps she said "Sunday" unconsciously, in keeping with the Christian idea of what day the Sabbath day is.

Swain explained that she and other non-Jews would go into the Jewish homes and light their candles, unlock their doors, and so on. In the Yiddish language, the people who perform these tasks are referred to as *shabbos goys*, and many orthodox Jews today still employ people outside the faith to circumvent the law against the lighting of fires—literal and figurative—on Shabbat. "You shall kindle no fire throughout your settlements on the sabbath day" (Exodus 35:3). Here fire was used as a sort of currency, one that African Americans had access to in this case.

Cooperation (1944–1961). Retired teacher Mary Roberts said that the "major events" in Newark since she arrived in 1961 included "the riots," a fire behind her house where "five little children were burned up," some young boys who went missing, and a terrible snowstorm that brought great community cooperation. "It showed a closeness I had not seen," said Roberts.[23]

While there was not a question specifically on how supportive African Americans were of each other in Newark during crises, there were questions that engendered that discourse, as noted previously. Whether asked about the relationships between new and old arrivals, interactions with Black communities in nearby towns, or to whom one turned in times of need, there were several lines of questioning regarding the ways African Americans related to each other during varied circumstances. In response, many of the Krueger-Scott narrators were eager to provide examples of ways that the Northern Black community rallied around itself, especially in the face of disaster—such as fire. For example, Reverend Alvin Conyers remembered a fire on Hillside Avenue that started on a Sunday morning and burned a whole block. He attested that his church, Bethsaida Baptist, came to the aid of the community during that time.[24]

Sometimes Newark's Black and white communities even joined forces, albeit not necessarily enthusiastically. James Churchman told a story of St. Philip's Church, a predominantly African American parish at High and Market Streets. It had a reputation as a strong center of Black community life, and was a site of NAACP meetings in the early 1960s. In 1964, the church was destroyed by fire. After much discussion, the St. Philip's congregation finally agreed to accept the offer to merge with the predominantly white congregation of Trinity Church, located downtown opposite Hahne's department store on Broad Street. It took two years for this union to occur because, according to Churchman and other Krueger-Scott narrators, there were some at St. Philip's who balked at the idea of merging with a church that carried a racist past. Mr. Churchman gave a brief background:

> Ironically, when we got ready to merge with Trinity, some of the families that could remember the history where the Blacks used to meet at Trinity and they were asked to sit upstairs.... And then when [African Americans] got to be so many, I think they finally went on Foster Street and somebody gave them a piece of land to build a church up on High Street.... And I think that though some of the people [were] a little hesitant about returning back—the way we were put out. [But] I think the assets that the cathedral [had] were too great to turn our backs on.[25]

Fire had created strange bedfellows in this case.

Fires were common enough in the city that community organizations were prepared for them, much in the same way they were prepared to feed the hungry and shelter the unhoused. In his memoir *Political Prisoner*, Sharpe James writes about his work with the United Community Corporation (UCC) Area Board 9. "We held food and clothing drives for people who became homeless as a result of fires. We offered them temporary shelter."[26] There were cooperative organizations like this throughout America's cities, ready to support those in need of the essentials once disaster hit.

The extreme proximity of so many people, in Newark as in other cities, caused dire circumstances, including house fires. Yet at the same time, this situating built powerful community. Retired law enforcement officer Edward Kerr explained in his interview that any cooperation the Black community enjoyed came from the fact that everyone was "in the same boat."

The Personal (1935–1977). Fires changed people's lives, blazing unexpected paths for some, and chasing others from house to house, or church to church. Around 1935, Willa Rawlins was a student at Warren Street School when her house on Academy Street caught fire. "There was a blind woman that lived on the first floor and somehow she started a fire. And we just got out with the skin of our teeth. No clothes, no nothin'." The family then moved to Rutgers Street, which Rawlins called "one of the worst streets in Newark."[27]

Sharpe James's first home in Newark was on the notorious Howard Street at Springfield Avenue. Nathan Heard wrote a novel in 1968 entitled *Howard Street* based upon his own experiences growing up in that neighborhood. The place must have looked much like the novel depicts when the James family first moved there in the 1940s; Heard and James were both born the same year, 1936. The neighborhood remained economically depressed for decades. James lived with his mother and brother in a one-room apartment with an outhouse in the back yard. (Not an unusual setup for African American—and other poor—families at the time.) They heated water for their baths on top of a potbelly stove and hung their clothes around the same stove to dry. One day there was a fire at the house, James told his interviewer. "The fire people came. We almost lost our lives in that fire." James added that he also almost died once again in another house fire on Wilbur Avenue. "I learned then about coal and kerosene and why so many houses—Newark's old houses—probably caught fire, because they had makeshift conditions. The heat—they use the top of the stove, but the top of the stove was kerosene, little burners, little round ones that would—the wind would blow over or something like that."[28]

Louise Epperson echoed James's reasoning behind numerous fires in Newark. "Yes. I remember fires. I've seen fires. I've read about fires that have caused great damage to families, especially poor people who had kerosene stoves, that had no other way of heating except that way. They lose everything. And they have nothing." As in Owen Wilkerson's interview, Mrs. Epperson also mentions the Red Cross. "And I have to say one thing. The Red Cross always comes through, no matter who, and I like that."[29]

Epperson was accurate in her correlation of poverty and the high probability of fire. Multiple studies support just such a conclusion. From a 1977 study: "Of the variables that explained a lot or some of the variation in fire rates among census tracts within cities, parental presence, good education, adequate income, and home ownership were negatively correlated with fire rates. That is, as values of these variables increased, such as income, the fire rate decreased. All the other variables, including housing vacancy and age of housing, were positively correlated with fire rates—as the percent of impoverished persons in a census tract increased, for example, so did fire rates."[30] Lest we think circumstances have improved, "Between 1940 and 1994, the proportion of black children living in two-parent families decreased by 33 percentage points, from 67 percent to 34 percent."[31] Apparently, at least some of the aforementioned "variables" that predict fire were still closely linked to the lives of urban African Americans as recently as the end of the twentieth century. And the fact remains that parents are at home less frequently if they are heading up a low-income family, often forced to work extra hours—or additional jobs altogether; education is often limited for those who are poor—for a host of reasons; and, of course, the poor tend to rent more often than own. Fire, it seems, is an almost inevitable part of being poor and Black in America.

Fears. Fire represents, in many African American lives, both an immediate danger and a symbolic historic reminder of vulnerability. Willie Bradwell said she witnessed firsthand just how fearful people were of fire. In her interview, she was asked about music in Newark, which eventually brought her to a discussion of fire. She began by describing Newark's famous entertainment venue, Laurel Gardens, whose halcyon days were in the mid-1940s. Bradwell's interviewer said, "I remember you telling a story about, uh, when the Blind Boys were there . . ."

Bradwell retold that story: "Somebody hollered fire. . . . Well, everybody started running. I mean, the manager—and the Blind Boys was on stage singing. And they were selling hot dogs over on the side, and somebody knocked the pot over and it was just steam went up and someone hollered fire. And the manager was the only one of the Blind Boys who could see, and he ran off and left them . . . he forgot 'em for a minute."[32] Urban fear of fire is, of course, not without cause. In her book *Family Properties*, Beryl Satter explains the complex system of discrimination, greed, and laziness that contributed to so many of Chicago's fires in the early to mid-twentieth century. Illegal conversions were common in the rooming houses, a popular if not especially inviting destination for new arrivals during the Great Migration. Locked doors and closed-off fire escapes may have been some of the more obvious reasons for the high number of deaths in inner-city fires, but the insidious practices of redlining and contract sales were the underlying culprits, Satter argues. Because of the hyper-segregation of city neighborhoods, African Americans had limited options. Consequently, whenever code violations were discovered—or apartments restored to their original layout—this would disproportionately affect African Americans, quite often rendering them homeless.

Satter's study also highlights the role of Chicago's news media as the first to voice concern over these issues, calling for stricter housing law enforcement. Dramatic editorials about people "crammed into unsafe, unhealthy cubicle flats, paying exorbitant rents for the privilege of dying like cattle caught in a barn," attempted to catch the attention of policy makers and fellow Chicagoans. Unfortunately, penalties against "white collar" instigators and perpetrators of housing crime would be a long time coming. Many Black Americans would suffer and die in the meantime.[33]

Back in Newark, retired teacher Ella Rainey echoed a correlation made by so many other Krueger-Scott narrators, one between the 1967 uprising and fire. After confirming that her interviewer indeed wanted to hear about "bad" events too, Rainey agreed that the riot "created a lot of problems here in Newark . . . and it was frightening, too." She added, "Because I 'member standing at my window and watching all these white fellows coming from that side of Bloomfield Avenue and we didn't know what they were gonna do, you know. But luckily we didn't have that burning and all that stuff that went with the other riot business across town. But it was a frightening time."[34] Rainey's neighborhood was not in the thick of the rebellion, yet clearly the possibility of fire loomed large.

Urban fires fuel fear outside their city limits, too. Lurline Byass recalled that people from surrounding areas became afraid to come to Newark even after the fire-studded riots were over; and Senator Lipman remembered that one could see fires burning all the way from the suburban town of Montclair, some ten miles north. One result of urban unrest is the fixation upon violence—which often includes fire—that becomes identified with that urban location. In the case of Newark, this fixed incendiary image has been all but impossible to extinguish. The long-lasting effects of this can vary—from diminished tourism to investment freezes—events that affect a city's tax base, commerce, and federal funding for years to come. This is the case for Newark, even more than fifty years later.

In their analysis of the "Economic Aftermath of the 1960s Riots," Collins and Margo write:

> After the wave of 1960s riots passed, we found no evidence of a bounce back during the 1970s in the city-level data, particularly among black-owned property values. This persistence could be an indication of slow re-adjustment of perceptions in the postriot period (without true changes in each city's economic fundamentals), or it could indicate that certain places experienced real and lasting declines in local amenities relative to other places.... In either case, a sustained negative shift in perceived local amenities would translate directly into lower property values, particularly in the context of housing markets where the downward adjustment of the stock is slow.[35]

Perception influences reputation. State Senator Ron Rice answered his interview question regarding the lowest point in the city's history, saying that it was the fires of riot, and the fear created behind the riot. Rice lamented that people were "burnin' the buildings and structures up" during the rebellion. He claimed that Newark would have been further along by the time of his 1997 interview if it were not for the fear instilled in so many people about the city. They "starved" Newark's residents and scared people away from visiting, Rice claimed. "Those fears ... eradicating the fears of what we did ... will be passed on for generations."[36]

Historian Carl Smith confirms the powerful effects of fire on a city's identity. In writing about the famous Chicago fire of 1871, he states: "The most important lesson of the unhappy accident in the barn was that urban order was so vulnerable that, in the words of a popular song, a cow could kick over Chicago, setting off a night of horrors locally and threatening to bring down the whole system of modernity in which the city had assumed so important a position. The public mood could be skittish and brittle, and any bad news, feeding on fear and anxiety, could have large consequences near and far."[37] Much scholarly work has been done around anxiety and urban space. From the earliest metropolises of France to modern-day Manhattan, fear is one lens that has been used to interrogate collective urban experience over the centuries. And that lens is being directed upon city centers all the more often of late. Jon Fyfe and Nick Bannister write in their introduction to the 2001 *Urban Studies* issue on "Fear and the City": "The urban studies literature is infused with the image of the city as a celebration of difference, as a medium through which the totality of modern living is co-joined and given meaning. However, this vision of the city, of its public places and streets providing an arena in which to experience and learn from diversity ... is under threat. Alternative images which depict the city as an unruly, unsettling and disorderly place are increasingly dominant. Difference is now seen as overwhelming and dangerous, to be excluded or segregated where possible—indeed, something to be afraid of."[38] Some longtime Newark residents may suggest that this "threat" against its modern metropolitan vision has been around for a long while. A number of Krueger-Scott narrators explain that the outsider's perception of Newark as a "slum" or "ghetto" has been in place since they could remember, certainly prior to the 1967 uprising. Franklin Banks said it most simply. He was asked, "The areas where Black folk—primarily Black folk lived—were they considered to be slums as opposed to other areas in the city of Newark?" Banks replied, "Yeah. It's always considered where the Blacks live as slum area."[39]

Newark has borne the label of "scary" for some time. Today, between the legacy of the rebellion, carjackings, and the much-publicized murder rate, there are many who live only miles away in towns such as Montclair, South Orange, or Maplewood who refuse to visit the city based upon imagined dangers. It is said that fear was behind the decision to build the elevated walkways between downtown's Gateway office buildings and Pennsylvania Station. These bridges of sorts allow commuting employees the ability to avoid ever setting foot on the mean streets of Newark, New Jersey.

Fires and other "disorders" of city life ultimately leave indelible marks upon the public imagination, whether the events are witnessed or learned of after the fact. Assumptions surrounding a city's—and its people's—"material poverty," brought on by disasters not necessarily of their own doing, also manifest a correlating assumption of aesthetic poverty. These assumptions can translate into conclusions of a city's irrelevance. Even worse, the final diagnosis might be that a certain city is just not worth saving.

Rebellion

Martin Luther King Jr. visited Newark just one week before his assassination, an event that would incite civil disturbances in cities around the country, but not in Newark. Several Krueger-Scott narrators recalled the day that Dr. King visited South Side High School. Some saw him from afar, while others were in attendance at the speech he gave in the school auditorium. It was auspicious timing, many noted.

Sharpe James was one who recalled King's visit: "How about Dr. Martin Luther King who came to Newark one week before his death, March 27th, 1968. Who came to my high school, South Side High School, stood on that stage with a capacity crowd, saying he was tired. And Dr. King looked at a capacity student body and said, 'Learn, baby, learn, so you can earn, baby, earn.' He had that phrase before another person came with his chain and medallion."[40] King's full quote appears to be, "It's not burn baby burn, but learn, baby, learn, so that you can earn, baby, earn." King's mention of "burn, baby, burn" is probably a reference to a poem by the same name written by Marvin X following the 1965 Watts Riots in Los Angeles. King may well have even been imagining the fires of Newark's uprising too.

Burning cities capture the public imagination. Carl Smith's writing on the time surrounding Chicago's Great Fire of 1871 echoes much that was written about Newark's uprising almost one hundred years later:

> As powerful and even as justified as was the booster dream [of resurrection, purification, revival, and renewal], it could not dispel this fear, which the fire literature imagined as the fair city in distress at the hands of incendiaries and demons who would defame, defile, and destroy her unless good citizens were vigilant and forceful. All too soon the ritualized hanging of the enemy of the people would move from dark fantasy to real event and occupy center stage in the public imagination. The most terrible reality of the fire was that the unspeakable and the indescribable had happened, furnishing a vocabulary and a conceptual framework for a troubled future.[41]

In a 1968 essay entitled "A Testament of Hope," Dr. King argued that the Newark rebellion could have been avoided. King used language that those unfamiliar with his work outside the "I have a dream" speech may find surprising. The essay was published posthumously in *Playboy* in 1969. It reads in part:

> The Newark riots, for example, could certainly have been prevented by a more aggressive political involvement on the part of that city's Negroes. There is utterly no reason Addonizio should be the mayor of Newark, with the Negro majority that exists in that city. I'm sure that most whites felt that with the passage of the 1964 Civil Rights Act, all race problems were automatically solved. Because most white people are so far removed from the life of the average Negro, there has been little to challenge this assumption.
>
> Unfortunately, many white people think that we merely "reward" a rioter by taking positive action to better his situation. What these white people do

not realize is that the Negroes who riot have given up on America. When nothing is done to alleviate their plight, this merely confirms the Negroes' conviction that America is a hopelessly decadent society. When something positive is done, however, when constructive action follows a riot, a rioter's despair is allayed and he is forced to re-evaluate America and to consider whether some good might eventually come from our society after all.[42]

The July 1967 Newark uprising involves almost as many stories as there are people to tell them. It was not until sometime after the event that the words of those who actually experienced it were finally heard. And yet even today there persists a dominant narrative or "conceptual framework" surrounding Newark's rebellion, put forward by some who are less than knowledgeable of the circumstances. That narrative includes Black people "going wild" for inexplicable reasons. From the uprising came a particular vocabulary, used so consistently that even today Newark carries the identity of eternal fires to some.

Yet there may well have been more upsides to the protests than even those mentioned in the oral history collection. While some of the narrators believed that circumstances did improve after the uprising, they could not have known the ways in which that moment of Newark history would inform political protest right into the twenty-first century. But it did, as evidenced by the constant consideration of that moment juxtaposed with subsequent protests over the decades, including those surrounding the murder of Mr. George Floyd.

One of the biggest differences between the Newark uprising of 1967 and the spate of marches and protests in 2020, for example, was the validation of the anger emanating from the crowd. Instead of the people being told that everything was fine, or that change takes time, or in other ways having their demands dismissed by the powers that be, those participating in the 2020 marches—across the country—saw at least as much support as rejection. In Newark, Mayor Ras Baraka himself said that people had a right to be angry, having witnessed a police officer killing a man in plain sight. Of course, the mayor was well versed in what had transpired during that summer of '67, as his father, Amiri Baraka, had been deeply involved in that rebellion.

In a June 2020 *New York Times* article, Newark historian Junius Williams commented, "The mayor has kept touch with the people so they don't see him as an obstacle to their righteous anger. They know he's angry, too."[43] Memories of the urban uprisings of the 1960s, however unstable at times, brought a kind of intentionality from some leaders and law enforcement that many credit for the relative peace surrounding yet another "hot summer" in 2020.

For example, initially at least, the police did not sport riot gear in cities like Newark. This optic was a far cry from the police officers who streamed from the precinct building on July 12, 1967, in full riot gear. Many of the Krueger-Scott narrators vividly remembered the sight of all those police wearing helmets and vests, holding billy clubs in their white-gloved hands, lined up in front of the police station. Some say that was what set off the violence in the crowd, that antagonistic stance of majority-white law enforcement staring down a crowd of predominantly African American residents who had suffered humiliation and worse at the hands of so many of those men.

Is it possible that Newark actually benefited from the upheaval that was the 1967 rebellion? Is that why while cities like New York and Philadelphia saw violence in the summer of 2020, Newark was held up as an example of peaceful protest? Many believe so. One factor cited as contributing to the relative calm in Newark was the organization of the events, many organized by the longtime local activist organization People's Organization for Progress, led by Larry Hamm. As with many urban spaces, Newarkers trust those who show up for their city consistently. Contrarily, it was reported that throughout that summer of 2020 across the country some acts of violence were traced to outsiders, people who often appeared in the crowds of protesters, wreaking havoc, and then quickly disappearing. There will be references to this kind of thing happening in the stories of the Krueger-Scott narrators regarding the 1967 rebellion, too.

In a June 2020 PBS interview with Mayor Ras Baraka, the mayor attributed the lack of violence in part to the behavior of the police department. Back in 2016, due to the continuing tense relationship between the community and the NPD, a federal consent decree was issued demanding major reforms throughout the department. Baraka called that an "atoning" by the department, and by the city writ large. More than fifty years have gone by since the uprising, but there are still wounds to be healed and reparations to be made. Part of this attempted restoration will come in the form of the 17th Avenue police building being turned into a museum. This is the building in front of which stood the army of police in riot gear in 1967. And it was the site in 2020 of many of the protests against police brutality. Baraka along with many others in the city feel that space will always represent violence and animosity. So instead, it will be converted into a site of explanation and preservation.[44]

However, lest it seem that all are content with how things went during the summer of 2020, that is not the case. For example, as reported by several news agencies, direct surveillance of Black Lives Matter activists was ordered by law enforcement agencies across the country. According to an October 2021 article in the *New Jersey Monitor*, three different New Jersey law enforcement agencies asked the federal government to provide surveillance teams during the Black Lives Matter protests of 2020. One of those agencies was the Newark Police Department. According to the article, the June 2, 2020, NPD request read, "The purpose of this request is to identify people, identify protest leaders, agitators, and the individuals who are inciting violence or destruction of property."[45]

As well, there is also disappointment among many activists and civic leaders that reforms around policing continue to be weak to nonexistent. There was certainly an upsurge in law enforcement changes following that summer of protests. Some cities, like Camden, in New Jersey, actually fired every police officer and started over with new training programs and job requirements. Yet at the same time, many other police departments settled right back into the same routine once the attention had lessened. Each death at the hands of a police officer post–George Floyd has felt to many like the most blatant disregard for all that had supposedly been negotiated and accomplished—one step forward, but two steps back. And all that feels a bit too familiar to the residents of Newark who were there during the summer of 1967.

"*The Riots.*" Henry Robinson was a corrections officer at the Essex County Jail during the uprising. Located at New and Newark Streets, the prison closed in 1970. It has been named a historic landmark but, like the Krueger-Scott Mansion, it will take more than that to preserve the structure and its history. The building remains standing, empty, and crumbling.

Mr. Robinson recalled during his Krueger-Scott interview how his mother did not want him walking to work in his officer's uniform during the rebellion, fearing that people might assault him. Robinson reminded his mother that he had a gun, and "the Lord on my side." He described to his interviewer how he and his co-worker, Charlie Black, had been stationed on the roof of the jail, tasked with protecting inmates from anyone who might decide to storm the building. He expressed anger that "most killing of Black folk" was performed by the National Guard. They just did not "do right" by the Black citizens, he explained. His interviewer, Glen Marie Brickus, quickly interjected, "Right, do you remember any fires of any significance ever happening in Newark?" and then shared her own memory of the Avon Avenue fire as an example. Robinson answered, "I don't know too much about it." Brickus continued, "What about what we refer to as natural disasters?"[46]

Mrs. Brickus seemed to be finished with the discussion of the rebellion, even if Robinson was not. Perhaps Mrs. Brickus was uncomfortable with the critique of law enforcement, although she could simply have been focused on covering each question. For whatever reason, this may be a lost opportunity to hear more about those historically important days from one of the few African American law enforcement officers involved.

Reverend Robert Woods remarked on the level of frustration that existed in Newark preceding the rebellion. He and fellow community leaders had predicted that something was going to happen in Newark. Those who were knowledgeable of the scope of racial injustice, who were involved in the organizations that battled against it, saw civil unrest as inevitable. They were not alone. In 1969, sociologist Robert L. Allen wrote in *Black Awakening*: "Newark, New Jersey, is a drab city located on the Passaic River. Like many other municipalities hit by riots, Newark was a city in crisis. This was no secret, although public officials

Figure 4.3. "Rev. Ralph T. Grant at his recent fall affair at Quality Inn awards Louise Epperson of College Hospital," n.d. Courtesy Newark Public Library

may have done their utmost to conceal and obscure the facts. Conditions were bad and were known to be bad. This is why *Life* magazine would call the Newark rebellion 'the predictable insurrection.'"[47] Civil rights leaders, scholars, and activists saw the riots on the horizon through an early warning system of systemic injustice and racial bigotry. Yet most politicians and law enforcement, immediately after the rebellion, insisted that the people had simply decided to up and riot—and for no good reason. In his interview, Reverend Woods references the accusations against Blacks regarding the plotting of the uprising. "No way we would have planned to get that many of our people killed—murdered. I call it murder." Louise Epperson alluded to this same thinking when she shared stories of the politicians who begged her, as a local activist, to "call off" those who were rebelling. She explained to those men in question that she had never called anybody on.

Reverend Woods added that all those thirty years later his memories were still fresh when it came to the rebellion. He hadn't "gotten over it." He recalled walking alongside other community leaders wearing black armbands signifying their peacekeeping roles. His job was to talk to "his people." The armband was meant as a kind of shield against arrest—or worse—by law enforcement. Woods and other community leaders were also tasked with encouraging fellow Newarkers to follow the newly mandated curfews. But these men were deemed "traitors" by some, accused of working for "the man." Woods remembers a clothing store being "turned upside down in two minutes" and how he admonished those absconding with the merchandise. In response they called him an "Uncle Tom" and continued their activities. Woods was clear about the terminology, however, no matter his personal experience. "I don't think it was a riot."[48]

Another member of Black law enforcement, retired police Sergeant Edward Kerr said he believed the riots were planned, but not in the way others implied. Edward Kerr had previously referenced the rebellion and fire concurrently, when it came to the question regarding the "five most important events." He began, "I just mentioned the riots and the fires in the same breath. And that's my personal involvement. . . . And I don't want to get too deep in that because as I say I'm still paranoid about that doggone riot."

His interviewer, Mrs. Brickus, pushed, apparently wanting to pursue the subject this time. "Well, I want to ask you one specific question about the riot because we heard so much and so many different versions as to why the riot got started. What do you think was the cause of the riot?"

KERR: You're sure you want my opinion?
BRICKUS: Yeah.
KERR: Well, I think the CIA and the federal government had a lot to do with it. Okay. Because I was working as a street boss, a sergeant at the time. I was working out of the Third Precinct . . . my job was to be the sergeant of arms at the council meetings, every time they had a meeting. Okay? And I go down there, and I couldn't believe what was going on. There'd been people I'd never seen before. I don't know who they were. They're like rabble rousers. . . . You go out in the street, you'll find them. Okay. Rabble rousers. They disappeared the night the riots started. I haven't seen any of them since then. Okay? But I will never, as long as I live will believe otherwise: the government wanted to find out something. They had a lot of technology over in 'Nam at the time, and they wanted to know how it would work against civil uprisings. Okay.

Now, specifically in Newark, one of the major causes of the riot was— the people over here in this sector over here, the Weequahic section, they had just built all them houses along Fabyan Place. People had just bought them. They had bought a lot of that property along that section where 78 is comin'—came through, see. Number one.

Number two: City Hospital—University Hospital, whatever the hell you want to call it, where it is now. Historically, Black folks owned their own properties over there. Now they're gonna make a farm out of that too, for the university there. Rutgers University come in here. The same thing. Took. At the last count was 25 million dollars of ratables they got tax free. Not tax exempt see. . . .

Somebody told Addonizio when the riot was going to start. And they told me what Addonizio said. You know what he said? "I got fifteen hundred men between me and all them rioters. Let them go ahead and riot." You know what my answer was? I'm one of them fifteen hundred. Alright? [Nervous laughter.][49]

James Churchman confirmed that while the riots were a tragedy, the problems were there before—especially when it came to the public housing situation. Mr. Churchman also appeared to echo Sergeant Kerr's theory of outside agitators when he told a story to his interviewer: "the night before the riots started I was out walkin' my dog, past Bergen, Springfield Avenue, and it must have been twenty, twenty-five men standin' outside. And I didn't know [them]—but for somebody born and raised in the city, somebody's supposed to say, Hello Churchman or Junior or somethin'. And I went home and I told my mother, I said, you know, somethin's about to happen around here and it's not good. And I don't know whether these people were all from out of town or what, but it did not look well."[50] Churchman's voice sounds heavy in this segment; we can almost hear him visualizing the quiet streets and then coming upon that collection of strange men. The race of these "outsiders" is not specified, but it is a fair assumption that they were of color in both stories as the narrators were surprised that they did not recognize them. After Mr. Churchman tells Mrs. Brickus that "it did not look well," a few seconds of silence ensue in the interview. She then picks back up with the questionnaire, asking Mr. Churchman if he ever met Madam Louise Scott.

Reverend Conyers agreed in his interview that the causes of the uprising were many, and that they had been cropping up for some time. The subject arose when answering a question regarding racial discrimination in Newark. "I remember the riot," he said. Mrs. Brickus pushed: "Could you say that the riots, though, were an incidence of racial discrimination?" Conyers answered, "I think the riot in Newark was the result of a spinoff of a national problem that triggered down through the major cities of our country. To make people aware of the fact that all men were equal." Brickus interjected that in this case she believed the intent of the question she asked had more to do with relationships between "Blacks and whites and their attitudes and interactions. Did you know of any conflicts growing out of those kinds of relationships?" Conyers answered again regarding the rebellion: "I remember, and this could be somewhat of a hearsay, the thing that triggered the riots in Newark was the fact that some cab driver had gotten stopped by policemen, taken down to the station house and somehow another they had harmed him. And it just began to mushroom and they say, you know, it just built up—I guess—animosity to the extent that it exploded." Reverend Conyers clearly saw the uprising as a conflict that grew out of a dysfunctional relationship between the races in Newark, and in urban areas more generally. Brickus finally gave up her line of questioning, said "mmm huh," and went on to question #73, "What do you remember about the 'Mayor of Springfield Avenue'?"[51]

George Branch recounted the first night of the uprising, July 12, 1967, at the fourth police precinct. At the time he was employed by the Hayes Homes public housing development located directly across the street from the police station where the incarceration of taxi driver John Smith occurred. (Branch was probably at the housing project in his capacity as a community leader for youth athletics. He would not become a councilman until 1982.) Branch told his interviewer, Pauline Blount:

> And so I made it my business to come on up there to join with all of them to find out what was goin' on at the time. At that time, they had a young man by the name of Tim Still, and Dr. Odom, um, Oliver Lofton, and some of the others.[52] We had gathered all the folks who had came to the precinct as a result of the news saying that the cab driver was tailgating the police officer. And they arrested him and they drug him in like he was some dirt or pig or something. And the folks in the area, the project at that time where I worked at, right in Hayes Homes. And it was in the afternoon. And they all gathered around the precinct because of what was happenin'. People was tired of, um, listenin' to police brutality on Blacks in they community. . . . And that night when all this here took place, all I could think about [was] that long, hot summer—because it happened in the summer months when it was hot—is that the young people was just fed up—brothers in the community—of police brutality. And all they saw was a Black man, like you and I, was being beaten by policemen and drug into the precinct.[53]

"Oh my goodness," responded Mrs. Blount. Branch went on to describe what has become a universally entrenched image: a community leader standing on a car with a megaphone, and the crowd assembled beneath him. There have been a variety of people placed upon the hood of that vehicle, depending upon the storyteller. There is an iconic photo of Robert Curvin that is most often circulated, standing atop a car, speaking into a megaphone. At a Newark History Society panel a few years back, Oliver Lofton claimed to have been the one on the car, even as Bob Curvin sat in the audience raising his eyebrows. In other Krueger-Scott interviews we hear that George Branch was the one atop that automobile, as well as Tim Still and Edna Thomas. There are no corroborating images for these other claims.

The photograph of Bob Curvin was shared in numerous publications at the time of the uprising, and it is certainly possible that people simply began remembering the picture. In a study on the creation of memory through photographs, psychology professor Linda Henkel found, "In general, we remember the photographs. It's like the family stories we tell. There's the original experience, and then the story everyone tells every Thanksgiving. The story becomes exaggerated, a schema of the original event. The physical photo doesn't change over time, but the photo becomes the memory."[54] In this case the photo has seemed to become a memory but the person within that photo is apparently interchangeable.

In continuing his description of that first day, George Branch explained that arguments between onlookers and the police captain ensued—even as various community leaders attempted to steer the crowd into a peaceful march to City Hall. And then out came all the officers, the decision that many feel tipped the scales toward violence. "The captain sent the policemen out of the precinct with their white helmets on, with their white gloves, and their night stick in their hands. Like if they were coming after the Blacks," said Branch. And then "Molly cocktails" were thrown off the roofs of the housing project, and bricks started flying, according to Branch. He said he ran for cover at that moment, but did attempt to be a "part of the solution" in the ensuing days: "Every day and every night I was out there with the armband on—on my arm. Federal government—and the Prudential—gave money to the UCC, [Imamu] Baraka and them to be leaders in the community—tried to quiet the people down so they didn't finish burning up the community and the stores and whatever. They was turnin' over cars on the corner of Springfield Avenue and Morris Avenue. Pullin' the whites out of the cars, beating them up. I mean it was awful."[55] The reference to white people being pulled out of cars was not made by any of the other interviewees, nor has it been described in other sources used for this research. That does not mean it did not happen, but it is also possible that Mr. Branch was conflating the 1992 Los Angeles riots with Newark's 1967 rebellion. Only four years prior to his interview, the city of Los Angeles erupted after four police officers involved in the beating of Rodney King were acquitted. Another well-played image, that of white Reginald Oliver Denny being pulled from his truck by Black men, saturated the media. That story, and corresponding footage, continue to reappear in publications today.

George Branch's tale about the rebellion was one of equal culpability between citizens and law enforcement when it came to violence and property damage. He did not rationalize the behavior of those who threw firebombs or attacked innocent people, even as he explained that their behavior emanated from a high level of frustration with longtime injustice.

When it came down to the telling of this story, the people of the Krueger-Scott community tended to speak about the rebellion in terms of personal experience. This contrasts with the way many nonresidents recount the uprising. The locals' memories often took shape in bits of scenes or images; one could almost hear the flood of memories in their voices as they spoke. Allesandro Portelli writes in *The Death of Luigi Trastulli: Form and Meaning in Oral History*: "The discrepancy between fact and memory ultimately enhances the value of the oral sources as historical documents. It is not caused by faulty recollections . . . but actively and creatively generated by memory and imagination in an effort to make sense of crucial events and of history in general.

Indeed, if oral sources had given us 'accurate,' 'reliable,' factual reconstructions of the death of Luigi Trastulli, we would know much less about it."[56]

Memory and the Event. In her interview, Clara Little tried to "make sense" of the events she experienced through an anecdote about a dentist who watched looters from his office window. She was answering an interview question about popular stores and businesses. That led her to the memory of a dentist's office on Lyons Avenue where she said most every child she knew went. After that dentist moved, Little explained, people went to a Dr. Price on Bergen Street. "He was there when the riot came. And could stand at his window—because, you know, he was upstairs—and watch them take his sister's stuff. His sister owned that shop [Gertrude's] and they were takin' her stuff out, like the whole rack of clothes."[57]

Zaundria Mapson May remembered that the riots occurred on her younger brother's birthday. She was a college student, working as a junior librarian at the Springfield branch of the Newark Public Library. But before they got to the rebellion in the interview, a charming exchange ensued, as Mrs. May was being interviewed by her son, Bill May. (Mrs. May's husband, Bill Sr., was the portrait photographer for the Krueger-Scott Oral History Project, as well as many other valuable photographic collections.)[58] The interviewer first asked Mrs. May who she was married to and who her son was—perfunctory questions to start the interview. There were smiles in both of their voices as May enumerated her family members. But then she hesitated when asked her son's date of birth and the tape was shut off. (One might imagine the two perhaps laughing together as her son affectionately admonishes his mother for forgetting his birthday.) The tape resumes and the two begin speaking about 1967.

Mrs. May explains that they closed the library early that day so employees could get home. It is important to remember that for many Newarkers the rebellion started on the 13th and not the 12th. Some were not even aware of the events that occurred the day before at the police precinct; the rebellion had not yet spread. During Mrs. May's ride home on July 13th, provided by a fellow church member, May remembered seeing the National Guard and hearing gunshots as the car made its way through the streets to her home on Osbourne Terrace. "That was a scary time for me," said May. The riot was centered between the library and her house. Had she relied on her usual mode of transportation, the bus, she felt she may not have made it home that evening.[59]

Veronice Horne was living on 15th Avenue when the riots erupted. There were rumors that something was going to happen, but no one really believed them, said Mrs. Horne. On that Friday she recalled how she and her friends were at the Hayes Homes, how the place was "teeming with people—children out playin'." Then they heard gunshots right there in the middle of the day, around one o'clock she thought. They started running. Someone shouted that a riot was starting. By the time the group of women had crossed several streets on their way back to their 15th Avenue home, people were everywhere, running and screaming. "And we ran and got our children and we ran upstairs with them. And lockin' our doors and the only thing you could hear was bullets. You could hear shots. Oh, it was so frightening. Tellin' the children, 'Get on the floor, stay on the floor.' And this went on and it was so awful."

Horne recounted the sounds of cars speeding and glass breaking. That night the National Guard appeared, and she remembered the sound their boots made walking in the street, a sound others reported as well. The affective experience of this woman is starkly portrayed in a way that makes it clear that, along with the senses of sight and touch, the sense of hearing is another powerful tool in the recollection of memory. And these sense memories can evoke powerful emotions in the storyteller, as well as the listener.

Mrs. Horne described men carrying appliances down the street. A furniture store in her neighborhood was broken into and people were stealing the goods. "You were afraid to even move," said Horne. For the next few days buses were not running, so nearby residents hesitantly walked to the Mulberry Street markets to get food. It was a traumatic time for Black people, Horne explained. The community had been demolished, "like a hurricane had come through."[60]

Willie Bradwell told her interviewer, "I had no participation in the riots because when it started I was out of town." She then went on to tell the following story:

> BRADWELL: And I came back into town in the middle of it. And I know I had to walk right through all those soldiers and shootin' over my head, all the way from, I believe it was Renner Avenue at the time. All the way from Bergen Street to Renner and Audubon Terrace 'cause I couldn't get a cab into that area.
> INTERVIEWER: So how did you get home?
> BRADWELL: I got a cab from Penn Station, but the closest they could get me home was Winans Avenue, and I got off at Winans Avenue and Bergen Street and walked.
> INTERVIEWER: With your suitcases?
> BRADWELL: With my bags. And I was told later, I was lucky I didn't get shot 'cause I had these bags. But the troopers just shot over my head.
> INTERVIEWER: Deliberately, or you were just in the line of fire?
> BRADWELL: Deliberately. Because I was walkin' the street, there was other people walkin' the street, and I guess they were scare tactics or whatever—all along Bergen Street. But when I got to Renner Avenue and turned up they didn't follow me.[61]

What Mrs. Bradwell considers "no participation," others might name differently. But perhaps she simply wanted to make clear that she had nothing to do with the violence or destruction associated with the rebellion.

Figure 4.4. Armored car stands guard at Academy and University Street, 1967. Courtesy Newark Public Library.

Community activist Edna Thomas related a bit of her 1967 experience as a resident of the Hayes Homes:

> That was one part that I guess I left out because it's very painful. Very painful for me, '67. I took my children over my mother's house and left them. And actually left them because that's what I wanted to do, where I wanted them to be. And that's where they could go outside and play and feel at peace. When my son woke up that morning in 1967 and drew a picture of a plane, and said, "Mommy, they're coming to get us," that hurt me so bad. I said, let me get my kids out of here before they get scarred for life. And I went downstairs and all the soldiers were outside. And I saw a longshoreman that worked with my father. And we called him Big Apple. I said, "Take my kids over my father." And he did. I said, "Tell my father I'll come and get them when things are safe." Thank God I did. Because I couldn't take it.[62]

This mention of the little boy's fear speaks to a more general experience of so many of the Krueger-Scott interviewees growing up Black in America. Whether it was Sharpe James's description of the fear he knew at age nine of the Florida police, or the way whites "put the fear" in Blacks according to George Branch, or Owen Wilkerson's fear as he rode his bike past his neighborhood's unofficial border into "a whole new world," young African Americans lived, as they still do today, in a constant state of stress. The 1967 rebellion and its effects were simply an affirmation of that fear.

Fear and urban spaces, as noted before, are inextricably linked—whether by those living within a city's boundaries or by those on the outside. Krueger-Scott narrator Edna Thomas, years after the rebellion, was featured in a *Philadelphia Enquirer* article about the 1992 Rodney King verdict in Los Angeles that resulted in a civil disturbance. The thrust of the article was that Thomas was observing the events from a police precinct in Newark because there was fear of another riot in her own city. The article reads in part: "And she was unobtrusively monitoring the rat-tat voices that rasped across a police scanner, while the glistening skyscrapers in the heart of downtown Newark disgorged thousands of terrified suburban commuters who thronged the city's PATH railroad station, and jammed the mid-afternoon streets with their fleeing cars. . . . And Thomas, a lifelong Newark activist—a woman who stood on a car calling for peace outside the city's West District police station on the night that Newark erupted twenty-five years ago—was absorbed by the events taking place in her home city."[63] The image of someone standing atop a car is one of many used to paint the narrative of the Newark uprising, as previously mentioned. In this case, the journalist Ellen O'Brien seems to have inserted her subject into that iconic image. O'Brien further diminishes her authority by referencing a "West District police station" in the article; that station is typically referred to as the Fourth Precinct. This kind of poetic license is often taken with regard to Newark and other city centers unfamiliar to those reporting on them. This is one of the many reasons for the suspicion that is placed upon outsiders by longtime urban residents.

Katheryn Bethea shared with her interviewer that "an extended family member" was killed by a policeman during the 1967 uprising. She also took issue with the way the question was posed, as she did not feel it appropriate to call the riots "important." On the other hand, she acknowledged, perhaps they could be considered as such in terms of how people came to see Newark afterwards. Bethea observed that with the help of the media, it appeared as if the whole city was consumed by the rebellion: "And one of the things—they gave the impression—you were askin' before about people's impression of Newark. . . . [The media] gave the people the impression that every Black person in every part of Newark was on fire. Part of that was because of the way they showed usually the pictures of the same area pretending it was—not really stating that—pretending it was another part of Newark. All of Newark was not burnin' down, you know that."[64] The media replayed images of the same small portion of Newark, Bethea explained, while implying that these were different areas of the city under siege. The protracted optics made the riots seem all the more dramatic and widespread to those watching outside the community, Bethea argued, and were incredibly damaging to the reputation of her city. Those who suffered most from this narrative construction—both at the time, and for decades to come—would be the African American residents. "White flight," capital flight, ongoing associations between Blacks and violence, and diminished state and federal funding are just a few of the burdens that were borne most heavily by Newark's African American and working-class residents.

Bethea's assessment of the media coverage of Newark those many years back has also been leveled at the reporting done on contemporary urban uprisings, such as those in Baltimore surrounding the 2015 death of Freddie Gray. News stations repeatedly televised one particular image of a neighborhood CVS pharmacy in flames. From afar it did seem that all of Baltimore was on fire. In a critique following the not-guilty verdict surrounding the death of Mr. Gray, Jack Shafer of *Politico* magazine wrote:

> Riots are particularly complicated for the media to cover. TV's preferred presentation of any riot is the live shot, and who can object to that? But its next favorite is montage, the stacking of ghastly image upon ghastly image, of looted pharmacy upon burning senior center upon flaming automobile, which it can run in a loop. Not to diminish the horrors of the Baltimore riots, but looping of the Baltimore news makes it look as if the entire city is ablaze and scores have died, even though—praise be to glory—damage is localized and a human life has yet to be taken.[65]

Owen Wilkerson told his Krueger-Scott interviewer about his experience as a journalist covering the events of July 1967 for the *Afro-American*:[66]

> The city was under occupation. It was devastating to see. I think it was Sunday morning, walking along Spruce Street and everything—Bob Queen and myself. Bob Queen at that particular time was the editor of the *Afro-American* newspaper. And we were walking along Spruce Street and here the stores burned to the ground and what not, and people wandering around in bewilderment, and the National Guard was giving out—National Guardsmen were giving out food and containers of milk to people. And you could just see the expression on the people's faces. They were just humiliated. The people lost as much as the merchants in the community because I'm sure a lot of those merchants had fire insurance. . . . What the people lost was the services and what not. You know what I mean? Food was scarce then and what not. The city was just in a devastated situation.

"I don't want to get emotional," finished Wilkerson. At that moment he seemed torn between a journalist's analysis of the rebellion, and the personal experience of walking down Spruce Street, seeing "the blood in the streets." The listener can practically hear the visceral memories taking shape: the heads "cracked" by state troopers, sounds of gunfire, smells of burning stores. As a man—and a journalist—Wilkerson may have wanted to resist an affective response, but as a human he struggled with witnessing the human suffering.

By July 22 the *New Jersey Afro American* had images of the aftermath of the Newark rebellion, including broken shop windows and National Guardsmen instructing suspected looters to lie on the ground. The headline reads, "In Newark/Nothing Left but the Tears and Hope."[67] Of course, more of the city was untouched than was affected by the uprising, but that did not stop the hyperbolic headlines.

Aftermath of Words (1967–2007). In a 2015 television interview with talk-show host and Newark native Steve Adubato, Kevin McLaughlin recounts his experience as director, producer, writer, and editor of the 2007 film *Riot: One City's 50-Year Struggle to Leave Behind Its Worst Week Ever*. The film's website reads in part, "Today, it's hard to believe that an event that few people remember or know anything about could have had such a huge impact on millions of people. That's the story that this film attempts to tell."[68] Ironically, the event in question actually appears to be one of the few things people remember when it comes to the city, thanks in part to ongoing projects like this film that center the uprising in Newark's identity. Public memory is a powerful thing, and sometimes it is intentionally fostered.

In *Flammable Cities: Urban Conflagration and the Making of the Modern World*, historian Daniel Kerr writes on Cleveland's "forgotten fires" of the 1970s. His study intersects with Beryl Satter's work on urban housing while echoing the experience of many Newarkers around urban renewal as well. Journalist Emily Badger reviewed Kerr's book:

> The city [of Cleveland] experienced a spate of riots in the 1960s by blacks who sought more control over their own communities. Less well remembered is what happened next: In the '70s, some 24,000 housing units in some of these same neighborhoods were set on fire by arsonists—usually the property owners themselves—with the tacit approval of the city government. . . . Landlords no longer found it profitable to keep up basic maintenance and repair. Many simply abandoned their properties, pushing the final costs associated with them—their demolition—onto taxpayers. . . . In the end, whole tracts of land were cleared by fire to rebuild the types of housing that officials had long hoped would lure middle- and upper-class families back into the city. But today, few people in Cleveland remember the history of these neighborhoods this way. Rather, public memory has coalesced around the story that these communities were once destroyed by riots in the 1960s. Those thousands of cases of arson, Kerr writes, are Cleveland's "forgotten fires."[69]

Riot, the film, perpetuates public memories of fire and guns and looting, while implying that the blame for the rebellion rests most heavily upon Newark's citizenry. These are the "social scapegoats," as Badger identifies them, the marginalized groups regularly deemed culpable for all that has gone wrong in their cities. It could be argued that Newark itself is a scapegoat for urban crisis, while other cities such as Chicago—and even Cleveland—seem to have salvaged reputations less fraught with darkness and danger. Oral histories can be, once again, invaluable in challenging such well-worn tropes.

Senator Wynona Lipman tried to explain some of what Newark was facing—and why—at the time of her interview. "There are so many people in Newark who have dropped out of school, who didn't get an education, who remain unemployed for that reason. Just can't get jobs, just can't get—they need to go back to school to get educated. That's why we have all the crime we have. Because it seems that anybody can sell drugs." According to Lipman, all this dysfunction is not a result of the 1967 uprising. The senator identifies easy access to drugs as a major factor in her people's problems—problems that were present nationwide in the late 1990s.[70]

Meanwhile, Reverend Woods notes in his interview that the city's schools were declining around the same time as the rebellion, and that it was not the rebellion itself that was responsible for the educational "nosedive." These remarks are consistent with numerous studies of urban crises, concluding that uprisings are more often the result—not the cause—of deeper systemic maladies.[71] And we continue to wrestle with these same issues today.

In the interview with director Kevin McLaughlin, a dramatic clip from the *Riot* film is shared. It includes statistics of the dead and injured scrolling across the screen as giant flames of fire crackle loudly in the background. McLaughlin, born in Newark, tells Adubato that in making the movie he came to realize the value of speaking to ordinary people. "I wanted regular people, just citizens—those who remembered. And that was a little harder to dig up, but I did—"

Adubato interrupts: "What did your dad tell you?" (The director's father was a Newark firefighter at the time of the rebellion.)

"It was a bizarre thing for him," said McLaughlin. "Dad had not planned on being shot at when he signed up to be a fireman."

Adubato then explains to the viewers that he would like "to put things in perspective" regarding the rebellion. He introduces the narrative around "snipers in buildings," shooting at people who were there simply to protect them. McLaughlin interjects that this is a story that has been contested. Adubato expresses shock.[72] Although Mr. Adubato is from a long line of Newarkers, as well as a journalist, apparently he never came across any challenges whatsoever to the original reports surrounding the rebellion. Yet there are so many.

Owen Wilkerson, the journalist who covered the rebellion on the ground, said in his 1997 interview, "you had state troopers who just came in and started beating up on people, shooting people."[73] And yet unverified images of Black men lying in wait for their unsuspecting saviors quickly became locked into the national imagination, repeated often and in a variety of ways, thanks in large part to the media. The famous cover of the July 28, 1967, edition of *Life* magazine features the image of a wounded twelve-year-old boy, blood pooling under his left arm. It reads, "Shooting War in the Streets/Newark: The Predictable Insurrection." The boy looks to be dead in the photograph, but is in fact not. In the issue's editor's note, entitled "Our Men on the Streets of Newark," Bud Lee writes, "The gripping photographs and eyewitness reports which make up our lead story attest to the courage of the people who covered the Newark uprising for us. They faced danger and death in the riot-torn city, ducking sniper fire, skirting angry mobs."

Later in the magazine, a feature by Russell Sackett reports on his "secret meeting with the snipers." Next to the article is an image of a Black man holding a weapon, crouching in the corner of an apartment, a scarf obscuring his face. The man is identified as one of the "Negro snipers . . . who holed up in apartments and on roofs and carried on sporadic rifle exchanges with Guardsmen, state troopers and city police."[74] The coverage of the rebellion, incidentally, was the only section of this magazine issue containing images of African Americans.

The reference to citizen snipers is made regularly in the telling of the Newark rebellion. It was only sometime later that varied journalists, such as longtime New Jersey reporter Ron Porambo in his 1971 book *No Cause for Indictment*, questioned the veracity of these reports. Porambo writes regarding the sniper fire referenced in *Life*, "What was at most a meager and disorganized response to wild gunfire on the part of the occupation forces was subsequently blown out of proportion. The image of a black man, his head wrapped in a scarf, peering down the barrel of a Mauser [rifle] from a tenement window is based on colorful imagination rather than truth." Porambo goes on to say that the *Life* article and accompanying photograph were "fabrications."[75]

Director Spina of the Newark Police Department testified to the Commission on Civil Disorder after the rebellion, "I think a lot of the reports of snipers was due to the, I hate to use the word, trigger-happy guardsmen, who were firing at noises and firing indiscriminately sometimes, it appeared to me, and I was out in the field at all times."[76] Some Newark residents were simply trying to protect their families, because fifty plus years ago—and often still today—African Americans are regularly the victims of "trigger happy" law enforcement "firing indiscriminately."

When listening to the Krueger-Scott interviews, a group of "ordinary people" to whom the director of *Riot* might have turned, we hear no mention of snipers. And this is not due to any kind of consistent support for the rebellion, as many of them expressed quite adamantly that their neighbors had ruined the city. Yet snipers remain at the forefront of the 1967 rebellion's textual and visual lore. This situation is emblematic of what scholar Hazel Carby argues is the longtime depiction of the urban landscape as a battlefield of Black versus white. Carby cites the Hollywood film industry in particular as exoticizing Black communities, highlighting "the potential for violent masculine confrontations" within these communities. She argues that "the commercial marketability" in all of this is irresistible to the industry.[77]

At one point during the Adubato interview, the discussion of nomenclature arises, as it does so often around this event and others like it. Adubato reminds the audience that local historian (and leader of the oral history project) Clement Price always insisted it be called a *rebellion* as opposed to a *riot*.[78] McLaughlin, asserting that most whites called it a *riot* while "Black folk" preferred the term *uprising*, then relates an analogy surrounding the Boston Tea Party, which Dr. Price had made in the film: it was an *uprising* to the patriots, but a *riot* to the British. McLaughlin finally offers his own summary, claiming that "legitimate complaints" turned into a riot when people "took the opportunity to get a free television."[79]

There were certainly those in the oral history interviews, such as attorney Eugene Thompson, who refused the word *riot*. He called the 1967 event a "civil disturbance." And Reverend Woods said it was more of a "rebellion" than a "riot." Councilwoman Mildred Crump referred to it as a "racial disturbance." But, as has been clear, many others interviewed used the word *riot*. The point being that word choice in this case is not necessarily racially differentiated.

One more piece of this director's interview is useful in illustrating the familiar lack of understanding on the part of so many who report, write, and speak on Newark—and on majority African American cities more generally. The conversation between Adubato and McLaughlin moves to the production team, which is all white save for the narrator, who is the African American actor Andre Braugher. "He contributed more than his voice," McLaughlin remarks, "because he was the first Black person to see the whole thing [the film] and offer that perspective. So he kinda helped shape the narration based on his perspective."[80] That "perspective" Braugher contributed apparently came from simply being a Black person, as he had no experience with the rebellion itself.

I offer this film as a microcosm of what happens when those who have not experienced an event—and have then paid attention to other inexperienced people—tell stories of said event. Of course, this is not to say that there is a rule stating that one must never write or report about anything that has not been personally experienced; it would be unreasonable to limit historiography in that way. But the varied assortment of narratives surrounding the Newark rebellion is full of cautionary tales of what happens when one decides they are representing "the people," while "the people" themselves have been minimally engaged in the process. This has been Newark's plight more often than not, and yet one more reason why outsiders will find themselves under suspicion when launching any kind of project in, of, or about the city.

At the end of *Riot*, Senator Cory Booker gets the final word, waxing optimistic about the ways Newark is turning itself around. "It will go ablaze again," he says. "We will be on fire. And it's not gonna be an inferno of riot and rage and bigotry and hate, but I think it's going to be a different type of fire. It'll be the blaze of hope, the blaze of opportunity, the very torch of the American Dream."[81] It seems Booker is attempting to counter the blazing images depicted in the film with hopeful images of resurrection. In keeping with Booker's oratory, many Krueger-Scott narrators expressed the same kind of optimism for their city. Senator Lipman exclaimed, "I love the way that Newark is responding in the years that I have been here."[82] Twenty years after Lipman's interview, Booker was still envisioning a Newark on its way back. However, a full return arguably will have to include a major counterattack against the 1967 rebellion's "master narrative."

Some have asked what has proven most unexpected in listening to this trove of oral histories. My answer would be concerning the uprising. Many of the people interviewed for the Krueger-Scott collection believed that this civil disturbance brought positive changes to their city. I was surprised at the number of people willing to say so. From conservative ministers to progressive activists, more than a few of those interviewed shared the view that times were better for the city, and/or for urban African Americans in general, after that long hot summer of urban "race riots." Several narrators emphatically noted that this period was not "the low point" in Newark's history by any means—one reason why the naming of this event is so important to so many. For those who saw those five days as a catalyst for change, *riot* does not reflect what they witnessed. In fact, the post-rebellion moment was a time of elevated hope and optimism for many African Americans and their allies. There was a feeling that change was really going to come. Fast forward to the summer of 2020, rife with protests against racism in its many forms, and that same feeling of hope was expressed once again.

It should also be noted that there were Krueger-Scott narrators who were not all that engaged with the subject of the rebellion. The event did not seem to mean much to them, and they expressed their inability to answer certain questions surrounding it. Katheryn Bethea, for one, told her interviewer, "if I had been less occupied with earning a living and getting an education I might have been more aware."[83]

Lasting Perceptions (1967–1997). Question #68 asks, "How was Black Newark perceived? Was the community seen as a slum?" Mrs. Brickus posed this question to Mrs. Bethea. Bethea asked, "You mean like white people thinkin' of us?"

"Right," answered Brickus.

"Since I never really asked them I really can't say," responded Bethea.[84]

Perception—one's interpretation of a person, place, or thing—naturally plays a large role in the discourse surrounding Newark's 1967 events. As is evident, the Krueger-Scott narrators have varying perceptions surrounding the state of the city at the time of their interviews some thirty years later, as well as what role the rebellion played in that state of being.

As far as Mrs. Bethea was concerned, when it was all over the Newark rebellion did not seem to accomplish much of anything. Whatever it was they wanted, she said, all the people did was "destroy their own neighborhood." However, there were still some improvements she deemed worth noting. "I think one of the positive things that came out of it is that . . . that whole area—with the exception of the housing over there [at the center of the rebellion]—has been rejuvenated more or less to the credit of the New Community Corporation [sic]." Reverend Conyers concurred with the statement on improved development: "While we lost some houses in the riot situation, yet we have done some great things in reestablishing ourselves—our housing situation—and I think it has had a great impact on our city."[85] Yet in the end, Katheryn Bethea concluded, the event was disastrous, and that was why she would not call it "important."[86]

Danita Henderson told her interviewer, Mrs. Brickus, that thirty years later people still perceived the city as a war zone. "Anywhere you go if you say you're from Newark they'll say, 'ohhhh.' . . . You say 'Newark, New Jersey,' and they think of that, um, riot that they had thirty years ago—that it's still like that. That's all you have there is that one particular area just torn down and what not. Unfortunately." Henderson moved to Newark from New York City in 1974. The riot was something that "they" had, not her.

Glen Marie Brickus interjects in this interview with a story of her own, to confirm Mrs. Henderson's assertion. "I was in Ireland. And people asked me negative questions about . . . why was it that children in Newark don't like to go to school. . . . All the way over— . . . I don't know where they got it but they had it."

Henderson replies, "It's the media" who "promote slums. . . . And when you have people who come here they're surprised." The riots should no longer be at the center of Newark's identity, argued Mrs. Henderson, and it was partly the fault of the city, she claimed; so many years later something should have been done with the decimated landscape, specifically around the epicenter of the protests at Springfield Avenue. Henderson's perception of Newark's progress did not align with those of Bethea or Conyers, although she did add that she held high hopes for the New Jersey Performing Arts Center (NJPAC) being built downtown.[87]

Owen Wilkerson's perception of the rebellion's outcome was that it "energized the community," leading directly to the convening of the Black and Puerto Rican Convention, and ultimately to the election of Mayor Ken Gibson.[88] (The convention was planned prior to the uprising.) The economy of the city, however, was clearly devastated post-rebellion, Wilkerson conceded. Reverend James Scott described the uprising as a "turning point," as did Mildred Crump, although not in quite the same way. Crump felt that at the time of her interview, 1996, Newark was at its lowest point. "The unfortunate aspect of it all is that as we were climbing, our ascent was cut off by the 1967 civil disobedience. And we've just not been able to grapple with the comeback after that."[89] Matthew Little observed that before the riots the city was on an upward trajectory, but that it became derailed and was still trying to regain that momentum at the time of his interview. He, too, cited NJPAC as a hopeful sign of renewal. Beverly Scott countered in her interview that the peak of Black life in the city occurred after the riots, when both hope and federal funding were on the rise.

Retired municipal administrator Isaac Thomas repeated Scott's observation regarding federal subsidies, that the money provided a sense of uplift in numerous cities, including Newark. "Although you sound liberal when you say this, during the Johnson administration when he talked about the Great Society. During the Model Cities, monies that came down through HUD [Housing and Urban Development] and DOL [Department of Labor].... All these funds that came in.... You had people who was starting to move... in an upward mobility." The low point, as far as Mr. Thomas was concerned, was at the time of his interview, 1997.[90]

Willa Coleman said that Newark was most definitely at its lowest during the riots, and Mageline Little agreed. They were "like a bad dream," said Little.[91] Marzell Swain blamed the rebellion for an overall decline in Black life, but Owen Wilkerson said that positives came from the rebellion, bringing the city to a peak, and it was actually something else entirely that was negatively affecting urban centers nationwide. "The Reagan administration. I think that set things back, during the Reagan administration. That to me was the lowest peak in the city. The city is now being revitalized and what not."[92] Harvey Slaten said that after the rebellion things went downhill, but that the perception of it as a "black eye" for Newark was unfair. After all, he pointed out, a lot of cities had riots, all fighting against the same things: poverty and discrimination. Yet somehow these other cities managed to wriggle out of the straitjacket of riot identity.

What becomes clear is that the stories of those who were there have been overshadowed by those told from a distance. The narrative of destruction that so largely places blame upon Newark's African American population has muted the importance of the eyewitness story. Clearly the Black community shouldered the weight of the hardships that came as a result of the 1967 uprising, even as they were assigned an oversized responsibility for bringing it on. In the end, even as tragic stories were shared during these oral history interviews, there were still a good many of the Krueger-Scott narrators who claimed that progress had been made, due in large part to those five heated days in July 1967.

Conclusion

City living is not easy. Many of the Krueger-Scott participants had left quiet Southern rural lives for the crowded spaces and demanding schedules of urban living. Most enjoyed the benefits of these compromises, exposed as they were to experiences and opportunities they could not have imagined in their hometowns.

Parades and festivals filled city streets, and race pride progressed rapidly in the North, as African Americans rejected in myriad ways the unjust policies and behaviors of the past. Black Newarkers even began seeing people who looked like them working in municipal offices, something that would take much longer in the Southern towns of their youth.

Their opinions mattered in Newark, claimed Jessie Johnson, who moved to the city from Mariana, Florida. And Senator Lipman, originally from LaGrange, Georgia, said she loved the way that Newark had become a "buzzing metropolis." Even as Edward Kerr, also born in Georgia, observed that the city's education and economy had declined, he told his interviewer that he missed Newark when he was away. James Scott summed it up by saying that Newark was an "exciting but frustrating" place to live.

The Krueger-Scott narrators suffered—and challenged—notions of disposability placed upon them by those inside and outside the city. Fires destroyed homes, livelihoods, and lives. The rebellion did much the same. These events were seen through multiple lenses by the interviewees, but in the end they were events to be transcended, and sometimes even benefited from. Outsider tales of Newark might be filled with devastation, violence, and hopelessness, but even as some of the narrators and their families suffered great losses, the Krueger-Scott oral histories remind us there are numerous sides to any story. Within this discourse on urban fire and uprising, the historical significance of these Newarkers, their experiences, and the city within which they lived are illuminated. It is my hope that the next article, book, or public exhibit foregrounding Newark's 1967 uprising—or any other urban uprisings around the country—will privilege the voices of those who lived the event, leaving for the background the perspectives of those who were not there.

Afterword

Questions as to why one historical commemoration project is completed while another one stalls provide structure within which to build historical knowledge and understanding of the surrounding community. There are numerous queries to make of successful museums; from who was sitting in government, to whether there was competition for restoration dollars, to the mission of the museum itself. A comparative study of a handful of sites, such as Washington, DC's African American Civil War Memorial and Museum, New York City's African Burial Ground Monument and Visitor Center, and the Harvey B. Gantt Center for African-American Arts + Culture in Charlotte would offer lessons in the preservation of Black history, the navigation of bureaucracy, and the ongoing national issues of race.

The Krueger-Scott Oral History Project was a sort of phoenix, rising from the ashes of a doomed African-American Cultural Center. The collection alone has informed numerous works of art and scholarship since its reintroduction; glass artworks, library exhibits, and multimedia productions are just a few of these related projects. There are an infinite number of ways in which these oral histories—and the Krueger-Scott Mansion's story itself—can continue to contribute to a better understanding of so very many subjects going forward.

Is there still hope for a Black cultural center in Newark today? At this moment a new development project is underway. Those of us affiliated with African American history always carry hope when it comes to furthering the Black historical narrative, and it is a hopeful time in Newark right now. The city's mayor since 2014, Ras Baraka, is a proud African American with a Newark family lineage that positions him as a trusted insider. In 2016, Newark celebrated its 350th anniversary, and history was front and center at lectures, festivals, parades, and art exhibits. The momentum for historical commemoration has picked up.

As noted previously, the latest development plan for the Mansion property is a "makers space," a site for local merchants and artists to both reside and sell their wares. The Mansion itself is slated to act as a community center for the development, providing business courses and financial advice to the resident entrepreneurs. There is also a library dedicated to Madam Louise Scott and her mission of entrepreneurship and uplift in Newark.[1]

Newarkers are a hopeful bunch even in their skepticism, as is evidenced by the stories in the Krueger-Scott collection. The word on the street is that the Mansion is getting another chance at representing the city's past, while also contributing to its future. If this project remains firmly in the hands of locals, the city's vast historical significance might finally be recognized.

Appendix

Krueger-Scott African-American Oral History Project Questionnaire

CITY OF NEWARK, NEW JERSEY

MUNICIPAL COUNCIL

and the

KRUEGER-SCOTT MANSION CULTURAL CENTER

African American Oral History Project

Questionnaire

A. PERSONAL INFORMATION

1. Name?

2. Age?

3. Place of birth?

4. Occupation(s)?

Did you have a primary occupation? What about a secondary occupation? Did your occupation change over time?

5. Education

How far did you go in school?

6. Marriage

What person did you marry? When? Where? How did you meet your husband/wife? How long did you know each other before you married?

What kind of work did your husband/wife do?

What are the names of your children? When were they born? Where were they born?

Did you have a "primary relationship" other than marriage? If so, with whom? What was the nature of this relationship? (Apply preceding questions under #6 where appropriate.)

B. FAMILY BACKGROUND

7. Father's name? Place of birth?

APPENDIX

8. Mother's name? Place of birth?

9. Names of brothers and sisters (in order of birth)? Birthplace of each?

10. Father's occupation?

11. Mother's occupation?

12. Have you changed your name? If so, why did you change your name (e.g., membership in a religious faith, membership in a political organization)? Did others in your family change their names? If so, why?

C. MIGRATION TO NEWARK

13. If you migrated to Newark, when did you first decide to leave home? Why did you want to leave? Was your trip planned well in advance? How did you prepare to leave? What year did you leave? What time of the year did you leave? Were attempts made to prevent you from leaving? If so, by whom? Why? Was this your first trip of some distance?

14. Where did you go first after leaving home? Why? How long did you stay there?

15. Were you brought to Newark by others? If so, by whom? Why did they come to Newark?

16. Did you or your family know anyone in Newark before coming here? If so, who?

17. Did anyone tell you about Newark before you came? If so, who? What did they say? Did you have a well-formed image of Newark before you came here?

18. How did you travel in leaving the South (e.g., by boat, train, car, bus)? Who made the travel arrangements? How much did it cost?

19. Do you know anyone who came by boat? Who? What year? What route did they take?

20. What was your journey like? Where did you leave from? What routes did you take? How long did the trip take? Who came with you? What were the conditions like? How much money did you bring with you? Do you have any particular story or anecdote to tell about your trip to Newark?

Train/Bus

What segregated facilities were there (e.g., waiting room)? Where did you sit on the train/bus?

Was it clean? Crowded? Was food available? If not what kind of food did you bring? Why this kind of food? What kind of container?

Car

What segregated facilities did you encounter enroute (e.g., gas stations, hotels/motels, restaurants)? How did you manage?

21. What happened when you arrived in Newark? Who met you?

22. What personal effects did you bring with you? What was your luggage like? What personal effects did you send? What else did you bring/send?

23. Did you plan to return to the South? If so, why?

24. Did you know anyone who came to Newark around this time, stayed briefly, and returned to the South to live? If so, who? Why did they return?

25. Did you know anyone around this time who moved back and forth between the South and Newark periodically? (seasonally, intervals of several years)

26. Did you help anyone leave the South to come to Newark? If so, who? Why?

27. How would you describe your fellow migrants, those who left the South for Newark around the time you did? (e.g., young/old? single/married? educated/uneducated?)

28. What materials (e.g., photographs, travel tickets, luggage, trunks) do you have that pertain to your migration to Newark?

29. How many times have you returned to your home in the South? Why did you return? Do you see your southern birthplace as your "home"? If so, do you plan to return permanently? If so, why?

D. SETTLEMENT IN NEWARK

30. Where did you first live in Newark? Why? How long did you stay in this place?

31. What was your first impression of this place? Was it what you had expected?

32. What was your housing like (e.g., boarding house, apartment, single or multi-family unit)? How did you get it? What did it cost?

APPENDIX

33. What was your neighborhood like? Was it a commercial area (shops, businesses, factories) or a residential area? What other kinds of people lived there? Did people from your home live there?

34. Why did you settle in this neighborhood?

35. Where next did you live in Newark? Why did you settle in this place? What was your housing like? What was your neighborhood like? (Repeat questions #27-#31 for succeeding residences in Newark.)

36. Where did you do your shopping? On what basis (e.g., race of the owner, location, how you were treated as a customer) did you decide to patronize businesses and shops?

37. What was the ethnicity/race of merchants in your neighborhood? If they were not black, did they employ blacks? Was there any resentment against stores in your neighborhood not owned by blacks? If so, why? How was this resentment shown?

38. Did local stores offer you credit? If yes, did this influence your decision to shop at these stores?

39. How would you compare your experiences in the South with your new experiences in Newark with respect to the following:

> eating habits: When you came to Newark, were you able to purchase dry goods and foods that were familiar to you in the South? If so, what dry goods and foods? From what stores? What do you know about the appearance of "soul food" in Newark?
>
> dress: In what ways, if any, did people in Newark dress differently from people in your southern home?
>
> contact with relatives/existence of an "extended family:" Were relatives and friends as helpful and supportive here in Newark as they had been in your southern home? Were you part of an "extended family" in Newark?
>
> designation of "fictive kin:" Did you call people "Aunt" and "cousin" here in Newark when they were not really a relative? If so, why?
>
> marking of special events: Were events such as births, weddings, and funerals observed differently here in Newark than in your southern

home? If so, in what ways were they different?

celebration of holidays: Were holidays like Christmas, Easter, Fourth of July, and Thanksgiving celebrated differently in Newark than in your southern home? If so, how did the celebrations differ?

use of intoxicants and other substances: How did the use of items like liquor, drugs, tobacco (e.g., pipes, cigars, cigarettes, snuff, chewing tobacco) in Newark compare with their use in your southern home? What about substances like clay/dirt and starch?

traditional medical practices: How did the use of such as home remedies, patent medicines, and midwives in Newark compare with the use of such in your southern home?

belief in "fixing:" How did the belief in and practice of such as "conjure," "voodoo," "hoodoo," and "roots" in Newark compare with such in your southern home?

pets: How were pets regarded in Newark in comparison with your southern home?

crime/"juvenile delinquency:" How did the incidence of crime in Newark compare with that in your southern home? What about crimes involving juveniles?

self-help: What was your perception of blacks helping each other in Newark? Did it compare favorably with blacks helping each other in your southern home?

race relations: How would overall relations with whites in Newark compare to relations with whites in your southern home?

40. What major customs and traditions from the South do you recall surviving in Newark? What about "cookouts" and "barbecues"?

41. What things (e.g., hunting, fishing, trapping, gathering berries) do you recall doing in the South that you did not do once you came to Newark?

42. How were you received or treated by African Americans who had lived in Newark for a long time?

43. Do you know of any part of Newark where black people

APPENDIX

from a particular part of the South (e.g., state, town) have settled together? If so, give details.

E. WORK

44. What kind of work did you do in the South before coming to Newark? What was your wage? What skills did you have? How did you get them?

45. What was your first job in Newark? How did you get it? What did you do? How long did you have this job? How did you regard this job? Based on your work experiences in the South, what major adjustments did you have to make regarding this job?

46. How far was the job from your home? How did you get to work?

47. What were your work conditions like (e.g., wage, hours, work week, regularity)?

48. Did you work with people from your own southern home? Did you get along well with other workers?

49. What groups did you work with? Did their racial attitudes differ? Did you learn to speak the language of any particular group?

50. How were you treated by your supervisor? Were you treated the same as others? Were certain tasks reserved for certain groups? If so, what groups and what tasks?

51. Was there a union? Did you join the union? Were you active in the union?

52. Were there any strikes? If so, how long did they last? What were the issues? Did you join these strikes? If so, how did you manage during them?

53. What was your next job (repeat questions #38-#45)?

54. Did you ever do any casual or part-time work? If so, what kind? For how long?

55. Were you ever unemployed? If so, for how long? How did you manage during this period?

56. What were the common occupations for black men/women in Newark when you came? Did blacks enter new occupations during your residence in Newark? If so, what occupations? When?

57. What materials (e.g., photographs, pay stubs, uniforms) do you have that pertain to your work experiences in Newark?

F. INSTITUTIONAL ACTIVITIES

58. What church do you belong to? (Where appropriate, substitute mosque, temple, synagogue, etc., for "church.") How active has your religious life been? When did you begin being active? What positions do/did you hold in your church? What roles do/did you play in your church? What do you know about the history of your church? Who are/were its outstanding ministers/members? What do you consider to be its major accomplishments? What materials (e.g., photographs, records) do you have that pertain to your religious activities?

59. How much have you participated in social and cultural activities in Newark? What social and cultural clubs/organizations (e.g., Elks, Masons, Eastern Star, bridge clubs, literary societies, choral ensembles, benevolent associations) do/did you belong to? When did you first join them? What positions do/did you hold in them? What roles have you played in them? What do you know about the history of these clubs/organizations? Who are/were their outstanding leaders/members? What do you consider to be their major accomplishments? What materials (e.g., photographs, programs, uniforms) do you have that pertain to your social and cultural activities?

60. How much have you participated in political activities in Newark? What political organizations (e.g., political parties, protest groups) do/did you belong to? When did you first join them? What positions do/did you hold in them? What roles have you played in them? What do you know about the history of these organizations? Who are/were their outstanding leaders/members? What do you consider to be their major accomplishments? What materials (e.g., photographs, records, posters, banners) do you have that pertain to your political activities?

61. How much have you participated in community activities? What community organizations (e.g., neighborhood groups, civic organizations) do/did you belong to? When did you first join them? What positions do/did you hold in them? What roles have you played in them? What do you know about the history of these organizations? Who are/were their outstanding leaders/members? What do you consider to be their major accomplishments? What materials (e.g., photographs, charters, plaques, awards, flyers) do you have that pertain to your community activities?

62. Aside from being a consumer of regular goods and services, in what ways did you participate in the economic life of the community? Did you ever

APPENDIX   179

>   own/operate your own business? If so, why? What kind of
>   a business? Size? Location? Is it still functioning?
>   What is/was the significance of your business? Did you
>   purchase stock in any black-owned business or
>   enterprise? If so, which one(s)? What materials (e.g.,
>   photographs, business records) do you have that pertain
>   to your economic activities?

G. COMMUNITY LIFE

63. How did you get information on the news and events of the community? Did you read a black newspaper? If so, which one? Did you listen to a black-oriented radio station? If so, which one?

64. What was the relationship between black Newark and other black communities in New Jersey? Did you visit other black communities in the state? If yes, which one(s)? Why?

65. What outstanding blacks did you meet or hear in Newark?

66. What do you remember about such public servants as the police, firefighters, social workers, etc.?

67. When you or others in your neighborhood got in "trouble" or needed help to solve a problem, to whom in Newark did you turn? Why? How effective were they in helping you or others?

68. How was black Newark perceived? Was the community seen as a slum?

69. Did all classes of African Americans live close to you? If so, how did they get along with each other?

70. Other than white store owners and other whites with a vested economic interest, do you recall any other whites having an interest in the black community?

71. Did you shop downtown? If so, at which stores? Why? What do you consider to have been Newark's best stores?

72. What incidents involving racial discrimination in Newark have you experienced? Give details.

73. What do you remember about the "Mayor of Springfield Avenue"?

74. What do you remember regarding such local personalities as William Ashby (early black social worker), Meyer Ellenstein (Newark's first Jewish mayor), Prosper Brewer (Newark's first black policeman), Irvine Turner (Newark's first black elected official)?

75. What do you remember regarding black institutions like hospitals, hotels, and banks? Where were they located? How important were they to the black community? Were you served by such institutions? What individuals do you remember being associated with such institutions?

76. What do you recall regarding the kinds of music that one heard in black Newark? Do you remember listening to and/or seeing musicians perform jazz, gospel, or the blues? At what places? What musicians?

77. In what leisure-time activities (e.g., singing, storytelling, quilting, basket weaving, gardening, movies, playing sports) did you engage? What materials (e.g., photographs, quilts, baskets, bats and gloves) do you have that pertain to these activities?

78. What can you tell us about the Newark Eagles? Did you attend any of their games? Were there other black athletic/sports events you attended? What materials (e.g., score cards, pennants) do you have that pertain to such events?

79. What do you recall regarding the seamy side of black Newark life? What places/locations were involved? Do you recall any black gangsters? In what activities did they engage? What, if any, positive contributions did they make to the life of the community? How were they perceived by the community?

80. What do you recall regarding public education in Newark? How well academically did black students seem to perform? How were they treated by white teachers/students? Were black students involved in intramural sports and/or extracurricula activities? What black teachers do you recall?

81. What would you consider to be the five most important events/developments that have occurred in Newark during your residence here (e.g., strike, election, riot, fire, natural disaster, black in-migration)? Why? What was your personal involvement in these events/developments? What do you know about them? What materials (e.g., photographs, documents, placards) do you have that pertain to them?

82. In what major ways has Newark changed since you first arrived here? How do you view the changes that have occurred?

83. What traditions/celebrations/events in Newark that you witnessed in the past no longer exist? What happened to them? How do you feel about their disappearance?

APPENDIX

84. When do you feel black life in Newark reached its highest peak? What was so great about this particular time? When you do feel black life in Newark reached its lowest point? What was so bad about this particular time?

H. LOUISE SCOTT/KRUEGER-SCOTT MANSION

85. What do you recall regarding Louise Scott? Did you know her? Did you ever meet her? What was the community's perception of her? Did you ever visit her home on High Street?

86. What do you know about the High Street area in which the Krueger-Scott Mansion is found? Did you or anyone you know work for any the families in the High Street area?

87. What do you know about the occupants of the Mansion who preceded Louise Scott? Did you or anyone you know work at any of the city's breweries?

I. OTHER

88. How would you sum up your experience of living in Newark?

89. If you had your life to live over, would you live in Newark? Give reasons for your answer.

Acknowledgments

This book reflects the work of so very many people, both directly and indirectly. Initially a dissertation, I must acknowledge my dissertation committee—chair Robert W. Snyder, Sterling L. Bland, and Mark Krasovic, who contributed with commentary, historical knowledge, and consistent correspondence. I am also very grateful to my "fourth reader," oral historian extraordinaire Linda Shopes, for lending her time and expertise to the initial project. As well, if it were not for Dr. Maurice Lee, I never would have started an academic career in the first place; he is forever responsible—and culpable.

I must thank profusely my colleague Dr. Samantha Boardman, who has got to be the most generous scholar I know. In time, talent, and resources she has given me much that allows this manuscript to exist. I want to also shout out Rutgers University–Newark for being the place that it is. And I want to tell the city of Newark that I will always love it. Speaking of Newark, the Newark Public Library is a jewel in the city's crown. (Support your public library!) Thanks to Beth Zak-Cohen and Tom Ankner for their infinite help and support.

Speaking of loving forever, my children, Kayla and Jake, are the best children any parent could have. They have been supportive, informative, and most of all restorative throughout this process that their mother embarked upon. They will never totally understand what that has meant. I also happen to have a whole lot of wonderful friends who have had my back and poured me wine during these past years. Suzanne got me through an especially tricky moment in academia, and for that I will be forever grateful. I also have to thank my First Baptist Church family in Madison, New Jersey, for being a true site of sanctuary for so many years.

Libraries of all kinds are a sanctuary for writers, and for so many others. And they would be so much less if it were not for the undervalued librarians who do everything from showing senior community members how to use the internet to tracking down rights to an image. I want to thank them all, but especially Natalie Borisovets at Rutgers University's John Cotton Dana Library in Newark. She not only helped with this book in its many iterations but has put together an exhaustive research guide surrounding Newark history. It is invaluable, and yet some powers that be would like to pare it down, and change it up. All I can say is, you never know what you got till it's gone.

And finally, there is the late Dr. Clement A. Price. I am indebted to my friend and neighbor, the late Dr. Julia Miller, for introducing me to Dr. Price. As with so many others whose paths intersected with the city of Newark, and Rutgers University–Newark, Dr. Price was my mentor, friend, prophet, and role model. When he passed, we all lost a little something in us, never to return. I wrote every word of this imagining Dr. Price's thoughtful gaze upon the page. I hope you like it, Clem.

Notes

PROLOGUE

1. Leah Dickerman and Elsa Smithgall, eds., *Jacob Lawrence: The Migration Series* (New York: Artbook, 2014), https://www.moma.org/interactives/exhibitions/2015/onewayticket/panel/1/intro/

2. There are stories told that some Southerners, intending to disembark at New York's Pennsylvania Station instead got off too soon when they heard the conductor call, "Newark, Penn Station!"

3. James N. Gregory, *The Southern Diaspora: How the Great Migrations of Black and White Southerners Transformed America* (Chapel Hill: University of North Carolina Press, 2005), 15.

4. Davarian L. Baldwin, *Chicago's New Negroes: Modernity, the Great Migration, and Black Urban Life* (Chapel Hill: University of North Carolina Press, 2007).

5. Baldwin, *Chicago's New Negroes*.

6. Amiri Baraka, *Blues People: Negro Music in White America* (New York: Perennial, 2002), 108.

CHAPTER 1 — THE KRUEGER-SCOTT MANSION PROJECT

1. Sue G. Neal and Harold L. Bunce, "Socioeconomic Changes in Distressed Cities during the 1980s," *Cityscape: A Journal of Policy Development and Research* 1, no. 1 (1994): 123–152.

2. Mabel Wilson, *Negro Building: Black Americans in the World of Fairs and Museums* (Berkeley: University of California Press, 2012), 2.

3. "History," *Association of African American Museums*, http://www.blackmuseums.org/missionandhistory.

4. Karen Miller, "Whose History, Whose Culture? The Museum of African American History, The Detroit Institute of Arts, and Urban Politics at the End of the Twentieth Century," *Michigan Quarterly Review* 41, no. 1 (2002): 1, 4.

5. Gertrude Fraser and Reginald Butler, "Anatomy of Disinterment: The Unmaking of Afro-American History," in *Presenting the Past: Essays on History and the Public*,

ed. Susan Porter Benson, Steven Brier, and Roy Rosenzweig (Philadelphia: Temple University Press, 1986), 130–131.

6. "Charter Member News," *National Museum of African American History and Culture* (Washington, DC: Smithsonian Institution, 2016).

7. A wonderful documentary made by Dr. Samantha Boardman showcases the mansion's physical attributes as well as its history. *Castle Newark: The Krueger-Scott Mansion*, Clementine Productions, 2009, https://www.youtube.com/watch?v=g8W9nY1OUfk.

8. Newark was known for its breweries, taking advantage of the city's proximity to what was then considered some of the best water available. Other famous Newark brewers included the Feigenspans, the Ballantines, and the Henlsers. See John T. Cunningham, *Newark* (Newark: New Jersey Historical Society, 1988), for brief historical information and several photographs regarding the industry.

9. High Street's name was changed to Dr. Martin Luther King Jr. Boulevard in 1983.

10. James S. Allen, "Act 1: The Ocean Smell (1624–1938)," November 2010, http://opensiuc.lib.siu.edu/cgi/viewcontent.cgi?article=1001&context=histcw_pp.

11. "Freemasonry," wikipedia.org, and "History," scottishrite.org; "Frequently Asked Questions," *Scottish Rite of Freemasonry, The Supreme Council, 33°*, Washington, DC, https://scottishrite.org/about/questions/.

12. "New Home for Northern New Jersey," *Northern Light*, September 1977, "Castle Newark" Krueger-Scott Project Mansion File.

13. Eric Arnesen, *Black Protest and the Great Migration: A Brief History with Documents* (Boston: Bedford/St. Martin's, 2003), 4.

14. Madam C. J. Walker, born in 1867, was said to have been the first African American female millionaire in the country and became an icon to many African Americans. Walker made her money in "beauty culture," a popular means of income for African American women throughout the twentieth century. Scott, like Walker, gained her wealth in the beauty business and was said to have been the first African American female millionaire in Newark.

15. As opposed to being a live-in domestic, day workers went home at the end of what was usually an exceptionally long day. The name of Scott's hometown has been reported differently depending upon the source. Most likely she was born in Florence, SC.

16. *WPA Negro Case Histories—Newark* (New Jersey: Work Progress Administration, 1941). 1–5, bergen.org.

17. John P. Davis, *A Survey of the Problems of the Negro Under the New Deal* (Washington, DC: Howard University, Bureau of Educational Research, 1936).

18. Cunningham, *Newark*, 285.

19. Some information from The Krueger-Scott Mansion Cultural Center, "Castle Newark" Krueger-Scott Mansion Media File. Published by the City of Newark, this is a 1997 brochure giving a brief overview of the planned Mansion restoration.

20. "Case Predicts Caste System Destruction in Newark Talk," *Newark Evening News*, October 8, 1957, "Castle Newark" Krueger-Scott Mansion Media File. Progressive New Jersey Republican Senator Clifford P. Case spoke that night of "racial progress" while also lamenting the weakness of the newly adopted Civil Rights Act and the "caste system" still present in the U.S.

21. Louise Scott-Rountree, phone conversation with author, March 28, 2016.

22. Robert W. Kirschbaum, "Turns Mansion Into Haven," *Newark Evening News*, September 23, 1958, "Castle Newark" Krueger-Scott Mansion Media File.

23. There are rumors that the hotel may have been used as a place of ill repute at times. Some interviews imply that there were illegal occurrences there, but they also mention that prostitution was the norm in hotels during this period of time. The police allegedly raided the Scott Hotel, overlooking—say some—the white-owned hotels that participated in the same business practices.

24. Leah P. Boustan and Robert A. Margo, "A Silver Lining to White Flight? White Suburbanization and African-American Homeownership, 1940–1980," *Journal of Urban Economics* 78 (November 2013): 71–80.

25. "The 81 city blocks that made up Newark's old Third Ward ceased to exist as a unique neighborhood of Newark in 1954 when the City of Newark erased the old Third Ward lines and made the neighborhood a part of a larger, current Central Ward." Nat Bodian, "Books about the Third Ward Written by Former Neighborhood Dwellers," *Old Newark Memories*, http://www.virtualnewarknj.com/memories/thirdward/bodian books.htm

26. Mary Roberts, interview by Glen Marie Brickus, *Krueger-Scott Oral History Collection*, October 26, 1997.

27. Indenture, Louise Scott, Range's Temple, May 31, 1966, Newark City Archives. No further information on Range's Temple could be found. The author is making an assumption that it is an African American organization.

28. Beryl Satter, *Family Properties: Race, Real Estate, and the Exploitation of Black Urban America* (New York: Metropolitan Books, 2009), 92.

29. Elizabeth McFadden, "Aesthetic vs. the Practical on Fate of Krueger House," *Newark Evening News*, November 3, 1966, "Castle Newark" Krueger-Scott Mansion Media File.

30. Edna Thomas, interview by E. Alma Flagg, *Krueger-Scott Oral History Project*, October 7, 1996. Mrs. Thomas used "it" to refer to the property of one particular family she had mentioned earlier in the interview. Thomas probably directed the owners to dress down as they were well-off and might have given the impression that relocation would not be a hardship.

31. "Martin Luther King and Wisconsin," *Wisconsin Historical Society*, 1996–2021, https://www.wisconsinhistory.org/Records/Article/CS253

32. In 1968, Madam Scott, under the aegis of Scott's College of Beauty Culture and the Good Neighbor Cathedral, announced a fundraiser to open "a free school of music and art for underprivileged Newark young people." The school was to be housed at the Mansion. A lavish dinner to honor Scott was held at the Robert Treat Hotel ballroom with approximately 1,000 people in attendance. There is no further evidence of that proposed school. It is somewhat surprising that such an event occurred at the Robert Treat at this time. According to a number of oral histories in the Krueger-Scott collection it was still a segregated hotel—if only unofficially—through the 1960s. "Mrs. Scott to Be Feted," *Newark Sunday News*, March 10, 1968, "Castle Newark" Krueger-Scott Mansion Media File.

33. "History," *Newark Preservation and Landmarks Committee*, newarklandmarks .org.

34. This building is still preserved through memory, however, as is witnessed in the final section when Edward Kerr tells a story of guarding it during the rebellion.

35. Edna Bailey, "Once and Future Glory," *Sunday Star-Ledger*, March 1, 1981, "Castle Newark" Krueger-Scott Mansion Media File. This article also reported that the Scott

Beauty School was "temporarily closed" at that point. The Ballantine House ended up faring much better than Krueger-Scott, ultimately taken under the wing of the Newark Museum. See http://www.newarkmuseum.org/ballantine-house for a brief history of the house.

36. Bob Queen, "Funeral Services for Louise Scott, a Legend," *New Jersey Afro-American*, April 30, 1983, "Castle Newark" Krueger-Scott Mansion Media File. According to the article, Krueger had been laid out in the Mansion, yet the Krueger family had sold the Mansion years before his death.

37. Frederick W. Byrd, "Newark Seizes Landmark Mansion, Ousts 20 amid Family Feud," *Star-Ledger*, March 29, 1984, "Castle Newark" Krueger-Scott Mansion Media File.

38. Frederick W. Byrd, "Newark Red Tape Knots Historic Mansion Repair," *Star-Ledger*, July 26, 1984, "Castle Newark" Krueger-Scott Mansion Media File.

39. Robert C. Holmes and Richard W. Roper, *A Mayor for All the People: Kenneth Gibson's Newark* (New Brunswick, NJ: Rutgers University Press, 2020).

40. Frederick W. Byrd, "Community Groups Still Work to Resurrect Dilapidated Krueger Mansion," *Star-Ledger*, February 4, 1985, "Castle Newark" Krueger-Scott Mansion Media File.

41. Mary Jo Patterson, "Historical Headache: Mansion at Financial Crossroads," *Star-Ledger*, December 15, 1997, "Castle Newark" Krueger-Scott Mansion Media File.

42. Central Ward Coalition of Youth Agencies, "A Plan to Restore the Krueger-Scott Mansion into the Newark Library and Museum of Black Culture," August 1984, Newark City Archives. A copy of the original document shows a handwritten circle around the date with the annotation, "5½ years old." It is difficult to ascertain when or if the proposal was seriously considered. There is much research that supports the theory put forward in this proposal; see Joy DeGruy, *Post Traumatic Slave Syndrome: America's Legacy of Enduring Injury and Healing* (Portland, OR: Joy DeGruy, 2005).

43. Frederick W. Byrd, "Official Vows Fast Action on Repairs for Vandalized Krueger Mansion," *Star-Ledger*, May 22, 1985, 25, "Castle Newark" Krueger-Scott Mansion Media File.

44. Byrd, "Community Groups Still Work to Resurrect Dilapidated Krueger Mansion."

45. Grad Partnership, "Krueger Mansion," 1986, "Castle Newark" Krueger-Scott Mansion Media File.

46. Catherine Lenix-Hooker, memorandum to William A. DuPont, preservation architect, August 16, 1991, "Castle Newark" Krueger-Scott Mansion Media File.

47. Frederick W. Byrd, "Hope Is Crumbling for Victorian Castle," *Star-Ledger*, October 22, 1989, "Castle Newark" Krueger-Scott Mansion Media File.

48. Frank D'Ascensio to Elton Hill, Alvin Zach, May 28, 1986, Newark City Archives.

49. Frederick W. Byrd, "Krueger Cleanup Continues . . . as Does Dispute over Mansion's Future," *Star-Ledger*, August 23, 1986, "Castle Newark" Krueger-Scott Mansion Media File.

50. "Proposal for Renovation and Reuse of the Krueger Mansion," St. James Social Development Corporation, May 1988, Newark City Archives.

51. Kastl Associates, PC, Architects, *Krueger Mansion Report*, February 24, 1989, "Castle Newark" Krueger-Scott Mansion Media File. It is assumed that the "1987 report" they are referring to is actually the 1986 Grad Partnership report.

NOTES TO PAGES 19–24

52. Byrd, "Hope Is Crumbling for Victorian Castle." "Investigation into Housing and Urban Development Scandal Continues," in *CQ Almanac 1990*, 46th ed. (Washington, DC: Congressional Quarterly, 1991), 666–668, http://library.cqpress.com/cqalmanac/cqa l90-1113631.

53. Byrd, "Hope Is Crumbling for Victorian Castle."

54. George E. Curry, "Newark Finally Gets Some Respect," *Chicago Tribune*, October 30, 1991, http://articles.chicagotribune.com/1991-10-30/news/9104070671_1_mayor-sharpe-james-national-civic-league-livability-award.

55. Catherine Lenix-Hooker, interview with author, April 18, 2016.

56. Kastl Associates, PC, Architects, *Supplimental [sic] Report*, June 5, 1990, "Castle Newark" Krueger-Scott Project File. That same year Hanscomb Associates, Inc. came in with yet another project estimate of approximately $3.5 million. It is not clear who solicited this particular report and how Hanscomb was associated, if at all, with past architectural groups such as Kastl and Grad.

57. Anthony DePalma, "About New Jersey." *New York Times*, October 28, 1990, "Castle Newark" Krueger-Scott Mansion Project Media File.

58. "Grandeur in the Central Ward," *Newark Arts* 1, no. 3 (November/December 1990): 22, "Castle Newark" Krueger-Scott Project File.

59. Pam Goldstein, "Director Named for Krueger-Scott Mansion," Office of the Mayor of the City of Newark, October 4, 1990, "Castle Newark" Krueger-Scott Project File.

60. Lenix-Hooker, interview with author.

61. Damien Cave and Josh Benson, "Newark Mayoral Candidate Tries to Escape Shadows," *New York Times*, May 5, 2006.

62. Clifford J. Levy, "Newark Council Head among 3 Indicted," *New York Times*, February 24, 1994.

63. Lenix-Hooker, interview with author.

64. Cunningham, *Newark*, 365.

65. Scott-Rountree, phone interview with author.

66. City Architect, "Krueger/Scott Redevelopment Plan," *City of Newark*, 1990, Newark City Archives.

67. Carol DeSenne, "Newark High Street Mansion Receives Maximum Award from Historic Trust," *Krueger-Scott Mansion Cultural Center*, media release, 1996, "Castle Newark" Krueger-Scott Project File.

68. Sharpe James, email to author, March 15, 2017.

69. Departments of Veterans Affairs and Housing and Urban Development, and Independent Agencies, *Appropriation Bill, 1991*, 101st Cong., 2nd sess. (Washington, DC: U.S. Government Printing Office, 1991), Newark City Archives.

70. Catherine Lenix-Hooker, "Proposed Program for Space Use," *Krueger-Scott Mansion Cultural Center*, February 1991, "Castle Newark" Krueger-Scott Mansion Media File.

71. Robert M. Schwartz, letter to Alvin Zach, April 15, 1991, Newark City Archives.

72. Glenn Boornazian Architectural Conservators, *Krueger-Scott Mansion: Brownstone Testing, Conditions Assessment and Recommendations*, July 27, 1991, Newark City Archives.

73. Grad Associates, "Conference Report #6," August 12, 1991, "Castle Newark" Krueger-Scott Mansion Media File.

74. Sharpe James, *Political Prisoner: You Can Be Indicted, Arrested, Convicted and Sent to Prison without Committing a Crime: A Memoir* (Newark, NJ: Nutany, 2013), 137.
75. Curry, "Newark Finally Gets Some Respect."
76. Joan Berkey, "Preserving the Past," *NJCM Conference Quarterly*, 1991, 8, "Castle Newark" Krueger-Scott Mansion Project Media File.
77. Steven T. Walker, "Barrier-Free Step to History," *Star-Ledger*, November 13, 1991, "Castle Newark" Krueger-Scott Mansion Media File.
78. "Community Development Block Grant Program," U.S. Department of Housing and Urban Development, March 1991.
79. Lenix-Hooker, interview with author.
80. Towanda Underdue, "Krueger-Scott Restoration," *Star-Ledger*, n.d. [1992], "Castle Newark" Krueger-Scott Mansion Media File.
81. Lenix-Hooker, interview with author. See "Newark: A Brief History," *POV: Street Fight*, July 5, 2005, http://www.pbs.org/pov/streetfight/newark-a-brief-history/.
82. William A. Dupont, letter to Catherine J. Lenix-Hooker, May 21, 1993, Newark City Archives.
83. Catherine Lenix-Hooker, email to author, March 16, 2017.
84. Herbert A. Wiener Consulting Engineers, *Review of Structural Elements: Krueger Mansion*, January 20, 1993, 2, Newark City Archives.
85. "Krueger Mansion Gets Funds for Renovation," *Star-Ledger*, February 23, 1993, "Castle Newark" Krueger-Scott Mansion Media File.
86. Catherine Lenix-Hooker, memo to Glenn Grant, July 22, 1993, "Castle Newark" Krueger-Scott Mansion Project File.
87. Lenix-Hooker, memo to Grant.
88. Although decades earlier, the protests of Barringer High School's construction hiring practices in 1963 continue to be held up as an example of blatant discrimination in the building trades and a lesson in organization going forward. See riseupnewark.com for a piece on this event.
89. George F. Will, "A Racist Vestige of the Past That Progressives Are Happy to Leave in Place," *Washington Post*, June 19, 2017, https://www.washingtonpost.com/opinions/a-racist-vestige-of-the-past-that-progressives-are-happy-to-leave-in-place/2017/06/16/6d5cbbba-51f3-11e7-91eb-9611861a988f_story.html.
90. Amiri Baraka repeated his frustrations with the downtown-centricity of City Hall for decades at most any public venue available. His views often elicited loud agreement from the crowd. Mageline Little, director of the Krueger-Scott oral history project, claimed that Baraka was supportive of the project, but that it was hard to get him to stay in one place long enough to talk about it. Mageline Little, interview with author, May 31, 2016.
91. Evelin Nieves, "Joy Ride Turns Deadly in New Jersey," *New York Times*, September 21, 1993.
92. Clifford J. Levy, "4 High-Rises Torn Down by Newark," *New York Times*, March 7, 1994. "Krueger-Scott Mansion Cultural Center Planning Meeting," June 30, 1998, Minutes, Newark City Archives.
93. Reggie Garrett, "A Home for African-American History," *Star-Ledger*, May 9, 1994, "Castle Newark" Krueger-Scott Mansion Media File.
94. Robert Curvin, *Inside Newark: Decline, Rebellion, and the Search for Transformation* (New Brunswick, NJ: Rutgers University Press, 2014), 212.

NOTES TO PAGES 30–35

95. Barry Carter, "Mansion Restoration Costs Called into Question," *Star-Ledger*, September 14, 1994, "Castle Newark" Krueger-Scott Mansion Media File. The council minutes on file for this special budget amendment meeting have no details about the funding in question nor any record of the conversation or presence of Lenix-Hooker.

96. "Newark Mansion the Recipient of $1.1 Million Restoration Grant," *Star-Ledger*, March 30, 1995, "Castle Newark" Krueger-Scott Mansion Media File.

97. Virginia Morton, interview by Kitty Taylor, *Krueger-Scott Oral History Project*, August 8, 1995.

98. Camilo J. Vergara, "Krueger's Mansion, Newark: Lost Cause," in *American Ruins* (New York: Monacelli Press, 1999), "Castle Newark" Krueger-Scott Project Media File, 170.

99. Curvin, *Inside Newark*, 202.

100. James, *Political Prisoner*, 233–238.

101. Catherine J. Lenix-Hooker, memo to Mayor Sharpe James, June 16, 1998, "Castle Newark" Krueger-Scott Mansion Project File.

102. Planning Meeting Minutes, June 30, 1998, Newark City Archives.

103. Donald E. Moore, letter to Catherine Lenix-Hooker, July 9, 1998, "Castle Newark" Krueger Scott Mansion Project File.

104. Catherine J. Lenix-Hooker, memo to Mayor Sharpe James, July 17, 1998, "Castle Newark" Krueger Scott Mansion Project File.

105. Vergara, "Krueger's Mansion, Newark," 171.

106. Lenix-Hooker, interview with author, April 18, 2016. Ms. Lenix-Hooker might have had the dates somewhat confused. Lucas left the position in 1998, and in 1999 the NHA acting executive director was Robert Graham. Also, she had indicated in a memo the year before that she knew Lucas would be leaving, but in her interview she described his departure as a badly timed surprise.

107. Dominique Hawkins, letter to Catherine Lenix-Hooker, August 17, 1999, "Castle Newark" Krueger-Scott Mansion Project File.

108. JoAnne Y. Watson, memo to Robert P. Marasco, March 9, 2000, Newark City Archives.

109. Mary Jo Patterson, "Newark Trying Anew to Repair 1888 Mansion," *Star-Ledger*, June 5, 2000, "Castle Newark" Krueger-Scott Mansion Media File.

110. "Profile of General Demographic Characteristics: 2000," Census 2000 Summary File 1, 100-Percent Data for Newark City, Essex County, New Jersey, U.S. Census Bureau.

111. City of Newark, "The Living Downtown Plan," May 23, 2008, ci.newark.nj.us.

112. James, *Political Prisoner*, 233.

113. "Legacy cities are older, industrial urban areas that have experienced significant population and job loss, resulting in high residential vacancy and diminished service capacity and resources." *Legacy City Initiatives*, legacycities.org.

114. Bruce Murphy, "22% of City Workers Live in Suburbs," *Urban Milwaukee*, December 14, 2017, https://urbanmilwaukee.com/2017/12/14/murphys-law-22-of-city-workers-live-in-suburbs/.

115. Lenix-Hooker, interview with author.

116. James, email to author.

117. Michael Podolsky, dir., *The Once and Future Newark* (Newark, NJ: Rutgers University, Newark Office of Communications, 2015), https://www.youtube.com/playlist?list=PLB2A475FCD4EBAAEE&feature=plcp.

118. Barry Carter, "Finally, a Viable Plan to Save Newark's Castle on the Hill," *NJ.com*, May 25, 2018.

119. "From Ruins to Riches: Newark to Construct Makerhood at Krueger-Scott Mansion," *The Vector*, October 15, 2018.

120. Lawrence Lerner, "A Newark Mansion's 100-Year History Comes to Life through Technology," *Rutgers School of Arts and Sciences–Newark*, Mar 13, 2019.

121. Minutes of the Municipal Council of the City of Newark, April 19, 1995, 23, Newark City Archives.

122. City of Newark's African American Oral History Project Meeting agenda, March 4, 1998, courtesy Mageline Little.

123. Oral History Project, Minutes of Volunteers Meeting, March 6, 1999, and Catherine Lenix-Hooker, Letter of Agreement with Margaret S. Montana, December 1999, courtesy Mageline Little.

124. Photographs of some of the participants can be seen alongside their recorded interviews at https://kruegerscott.libraries.rutgers.edu/.

125. The cassette tapes of the interviews were recovered by my colleague Dr. Samantha Boardman in 2010. Along with other members of the Rutgers community, I have helped with their annotation and summary in order to create a finding aid for research and public use. The collection has now been digitized and is available through Rutgers University Community Repository, http://kruegerscott.libraries.rutgers.edu/.

CHAPTER 2 — SUNDAYS

1. See Joe Clark, *Laying Down the Law: Joe Clark's Strategy for Saving Our Schools* (Washington, DC: Regnery Publishing, 1989).

2. Joe L. Clark, interview with Pauline Blount, July 8, 1996. Note that all transcriptions in this book are my work. Although a handful of transcriptions were completed prior to the Krueger-Scott project's cancellation, they tend to contain numerous errors.

3. L. H. Whelchel, *The History and Heritage of African-American Churches: A Way Out of No Way* (St. Paul, MN: Paragon House, 2011), xix.

4. Davarian L Baldwin, *Chicago's New Negroes: Modernity, the Great Migration, and Black Urban Life* (Chapel Hill: University of North Carolina Press, 2007), 19.

5. Karl Ellis Johnson, "'Trouble Won't Last': Black Church Activism in Postwar Philadelphia," in *African American Urban History since World War II*, ed. Kenneth L. Kusmer and Joe William Trotter (Chicago: University Chicago Press, 2009), 246.

6. Tim Neary, interview with Karen Johnson, "Crossing Parish Boundaries: An Interview with Tim Neary," *Religion in American History*, http://usreligion.blogspot.com/2017/04/crossing-parish-boundaries-interview.html.

7. Robert Woods, interview with Glen Marie Brickus, February 17, 1997. I am unable to find any corroborating evidence of this fire.

8. Allesandro Portelli, *They Say in Harlan County: An Oral History* (New York: Oxford University Press, 2011), 16.

9. Robert Woods, interview with Glen Marie Brickus, February 17, 1997.

10. Woods, interview with Brickus.

11. Sharpe James, interview with Glen Marie Brickus, February 3 and 17, 1996.

12. Franklin Banks, interview with Richard Cooke, August 19, 1997.
13. Mildred Crump, interview with Glen Marie Brickus, January 12, 1996.
14. Willie Belle Hooper, interview with Catherine Lenix-Hooker, April 12, 1996.
15. Zaundria Mapson May, interview with Bill May, August 11, 1996.
16. Carolyn Wallace, interview with Glen Marie Brickus (no date recorded).
17. Beverly Scott, interview with Glen Marie Brickus (no date recorded).
18. Scott, interview with Glen Marie Brickus.
19. Katheryn Bethea, interview with Glen Marie Brickus, August 7, 1997.
20. Bethea, interview with Brickus.
21. Isaac Thomas, interview with Pauline Blount, July 2, 1997.
22. Veronice Horne, interview with Katherine Bethea, June 3, 1997.
23. Elma Bateman, interview with Pauline Blount, April 29, 1999.
24. Willa Coleman, interview with Kitty Taylor, May 16, 1996.
25. James A. Scott, "Bethany Baptist Church: Growth through Planning and Social Action," in *Church and Synagogue Affiliation: Theory, Research, and Practice*, ed. Amy L. Sales and Gary A. Tobin (Westport, CT: Greenwood Press, 1995), 135.
26. "A Religious Portrait of African Americans," *Pew Research Center*, January 30, 2009; "5 Facts about the Religious Lives of African Americans," *Pew Research Center*, February 7, 2018.
27. Dr. James A. Scott, interview with Glen Marie Brickus (no date recorded).
28. Catherine Lenix-Hooker, interview with author, April 18, 2016.
29. "History," *Bethany Baptist Church*, http://www.bethany-newark.org/history.
30. Amorel E. O'Kelly-Cooke, *Faded Foliage and Fragrant Flowers from the Heart of Bethany* (Newark: Joseph Schreiner, 1922), 17, https://catalog.hathitrust.org/Record/101643354..
31. O'Kelly-Cooke, *Faded Foliage*, 22–25.
32. O'Kelly-Cooke, *Faded Foliage*, 8.
33. Ed Crawford, interview with Glen Marie Brickus, February 23, 1997
34. Franklin Banks, interview with Glen Marie Brickus, August 19, 1997.
35. Henry Robinson, interview with Glen Marie Brickus, January 17, 1997.
36. Crawford, interview with Brickus.
37. Edna Thomas, interview with E. Alma Flagg, October 7, 1996.
38. Willa Rawlins, interview with Katheryn Bethea, August 8, 1997.
39. "History," *Bethany Baptist Church*.
40. Beverly Scott, interview with Glen Marie Brickus (no date recorded).
41. "History," *Bethany Baptist Church*.
42. Crawford, interview with Brickus.
43. Dr. James A. Scott, interview with Brickus.
44. Paul Thompson, *The Voice of the Past: Oral History* (New York: Oxford University Press, 1978), 4.
45. Newark does pride itself on its churches, each its own page of Newark history. One can access brief information on many of them with very few clicks. Try, for example, http://newarkreligion.com/mainindex.php.
46. "The History of Queen of Angels Church," *Society of African Missions*, http://www.smafathers.org/about/our-history-2/queen-of-angels-church/. This link is now dead; I am assuming that the society finally removed the church from its website as the building no longer exists.

47. Bateman, interview with Blount.
48. A. Zachary Yamba, interview with E. Alma Flagg, April 26, 1999.
49. Nathaniel L. Potts, interview with E. Alma Flagg, December 12, 1997.
50. Hortense Williams Powell, interview with Annemarie Dickey-Kemp, July 2, 1998.
51. "The Black Church," *blackdemographics.com*, http://blackdemographics.com/culture/religion/.
52. Barry Carter, "Queen of Angels: Beloved Catholic Church in Newark Remains in Limbo," *Star-Ledger*, October 29, 2014.
53. Barry Carter, "Archdiocese to Demolish Newark's First African-American Catholic Church," November 10, 2015, https://www.nj.com/essex/2015/11/archdiocese_to_demolish_newarks_first_african-amer.html.
54. "Queen of Angels: When a Church Dies," Facebook, accessed February 9, 2017. For more on African Americans and the Catholic Church see Timothy B. Neary, *Crossing Parish Boundaries: Race, Sports, and Catholic Youth in Chicago, 1914–1954* (Chicago: University of Chicago Press, 2016). A subsequent interview with the author of the book does not reference any negative experiences Black Catholics may have had within the church, such as that of Krueger-Scott's Hortense Williams Powell. See Karen Johnson, "Crossing Parish Boundaries: An Interview with Tim Neary," *Religion in American History*, 2017, http://usreligion.blogspot.com/2017/04/crossing-parish-boundaries-interview.html.
55. Marzell Swain, interview with Annemarie Dickey Kemp, May 14, 1998.
56. Crawford, interview with Brickus.
57. Alvin Conyers, interview with Glen Marie Brickus, 1997 (no date recorded).
58. Hooper, interview with Lenix-Hooker.
59. Louise Epperson, interview with Glen Marie Brickus, February 25, 1997.
60. Owen Wilkerson, interview with Glen Marie Brickus, August 12, 1997.
61. Wilkerson, interview with Brickus.
62. Amiri Baraka, *Blues People: Negro Music in White America* (New York: Perennial, 2002), 108.
63. Wilkerson, interview with Brickus.
64. Epperson, interview with Brickus.
65. Wynona Lipman, interview with Glen Marie Brickus, April 5, 1997.
66. Erma McLurkin, interview with Giles Wright, July 22, 1995.
67. Ronald L. Rice, interview with Glen Marie Brickus, April 7, 1997.
68. Mildred Crump, interview with Glen Marie Brickus, November 12, 1996.
69. James is probably referencing a popular gospel song, "We've Come This Far by Faith," written by Albert Goodson in the mid-twentieth century.
70. Sharpe James, interview with Brickus. Irvine Turner Boulevard would have still been called Belmont Avenue at the time of the wedding as its name was not changed until 1977.
71. Sharpe James, interview with Brickus.
72. Crump, interview with Brickus.
73. Judith Weisenfeld, *New World a-Coming: Black Religion and Racial Identity during the Great Migration* (New York: New York University Press, 2017), https://doi.org/10.18574/9781479853687.
74. Cynthia S'thembile West, "Revisiting Female Activism in the 1960s: The Newark Branch Nation of Islam," *The Black Scholar* 26, nos. 3–4 (1996): 41–48, https://doi.org/10.1080/00064246.1996.11430812.

75. Crump, interview with Brickus.
76. Isabel Wilkerson, *The Warmth of Other Suns: The Epic Story of America's Great Migration* (New York: Random House, 2010), 89.
77. W.E.B. Du Bois, *The Education of Black People; Ten Critiques, 1906–1960* (Amherst: University of Massachusetts Press, 1973), 54.
78. Wilkerson, interview with Brickus.
79. Malcolm X, *The Autobiography of Malcolm X: As Told to Alex Haley* (New York: Ballantine Books, 1964), 48–52.
80. Wilkerson, interview with Brickus.
81. Matthew Little, interview with Pauline Blount, October 22, 1997.
82. Zaundria Mapson May, interview with Bill May, August 11, 1996.
83. Harvey Slaten, interview with Pauline Blount, January 6, 1997.
84. Mary Roberts, interview with Glen Marie Brickusober, October 26, 1997.
85. Andrew Washington, interview with Annemarie Dickey-Kemp, November 24, 1997.
86. Wilkerson, interview with Brickus.
87. Clara Watkins, interview with Glen Marie Brickus (no date recorded).
88. Bernice Johnson, interview with Annemarie Dickey-Kemp, July 8, 1997.
89. James Overmyer, *Queen of the Negro Leagues: Effa Manley and the Newark Eagles* (Lanham, MD: Scarecrow Press, 1993), 58.
90. James Churchman, interview with Glen Marie Brickus, October 11, 1996.
91. Hooper, interview with Lenix-Hooker.
92. Wallace, interview with Brickus.
93. Richard Cooke, interview with Glen Marie Brickus (no date recorded).
94. Coyt Jones, interview with Pauline Blount, January 25, 1996.
95. Sharpe James, interview with Brickus.
96. Sharpe James, interview with Brickus. An excellent documentary covering this issue is *Boss: The Black Experience in Business*, produced by PBS in 2019.
97. Overmyer, *Queen of the Negro Leagues*, 216.
98. Wilkerson, interview with Brickus.
99. Sharpe James, interview with Brickus.
100. Alessandro Portelli, "What Makes Oral History Different?" in *The Death of Luigi Trastulli, and Other Stories: Form and Meaning in Oral History* (Albany: State University of New York Press, 1991), 50.
101. Portelli, "What Makes Oral History Different?"
102. Overmyer, *Queen of the Negro Leagues*, 59. Effa Manley's own life was fascinating; born to a white mother who was married to an African American man but who had an affair with a white man who was presumably Effa's father, Manley lived most comfortably within the African American community. See Amy Ellis Nutt, "Baseball's 'Black' Trailblazer: The Peculiar Story of Effa Manley and Her Negro League Team," *Star-Ledger*, February 22, 2006, http://www.amynutt.com/starledgerPDF/EffaManley.pdf.
103. Dr. James A. Scott, interview with Brickus.
104. Lipman, interview with Brickus.
105. Epperson, interview with Brickus.
106. Sharpe James, interview with Brickus.
107. Mageline Little, interview with Pauline Blount, November 18, 1998. Sarah Vaughan was a Newark native, born in 1924.

108. Calvin West, interview with Pauline Blount, March 20, 1996.
109. Wilkerson, interview with Brickus.
110. Roberts, interview with Brickus.
111. Baldwin, *Chicago's New Negroes*, 30.
112. Wilkerson, interview with Brickus. In a list of 140 music venues that existed in Newark, none are named "Meyers" or anything similar. It does not come up in an internet search either. Barbara Kukla, "Newark Jazz Clubs, Theaters, Hangouts and Other Venues," in *Swing City: Newark Nightlife, 1925–1950* (Philadelphia: Temple University Press, 1991); Leo Johnson, "JJ's Theme: Newark Jazz Clubs of the 1960's and 70's" (Master's thesis, Rutgers University, 2005).
113. Willie Bradwell, interviewer unstated, December 8, 1997. In terms of oral history and the practice of transcription, it should be noted that Bradwell's transcript reads "Olive Garden." After much research I confirmed that indeed there was no such place and that Mrs. Bradwell was referring to the famous Laurel Gardens club at 457 Springfield Ave.
114. West, interview with Blount.
115. Dr. James A. Scott, interview with Brickus.
116. Queen James, interview with Glen Marie Brickus (no date recorded).
117. Churchman, interview with Brickus.
118. West, interview with Blount.
119. Queen James, interview with Brickus.
120. Coyt Jones, interview with Blount.
121. Rose Tucker, interview with E. Alma Flagg, September 29, 1997.
122. Pauline Mathis, interview with Glen Marie Brickus, October 7, 1997.
123. Ethel Richards, interview with Bertha Miller, April 16, 1999.
124. Marion Williams, interview with Pauline Blount, June 28, 1999.
125. "Father Divine Dates from 1876 Pertaining to the Work and Mission of Father Divine," *Word Press*, 2006, http://peacemission.info/father-divine/.
126. Mia De Graaf, "Inside the Secluded World of Father Divine," *Daily Mail*, January 30, 2015, https://www.dailymail.co.uk/news/article-2933996/Inside-secluded-world-Father-Divine-living-followers-Harlem-religious-leader-Philadelphia-mansion-live.html.
127. "Father Divine Nourished Souls," *Newark Public Library*, https://knowingnewark.npl.org/father-divine-nourished-souls-and-amassed-a-fortune/.
128. Eugene Thompson, interview with Annemarie Dickey-Kemp, October 1, 1997.
129. Kitty Taylor, interview with Virginia Morton, August 31, 1995.
130. Taylor, interview with Morton.
131. Epperson, interview with Brickus.
132. Bateman, interview with Blount.
133. Barbara Kukla, "Radio Personality Eulogized as Newark's Unsung Hero—The Fearless Bernice Bass Took Her Battles to Help the City's Ordinary People and Older Residents to the Airwaves," *Star-Ledger*, February 3, 2000.
134. George Branch, interview with Pauline Blount, August 28, 1996.
135. Mageline Little, interview with Blount.
136. Frank Hutchins, interview with Pauline Blount, June 29, 1998.
137. See *Star-Ledger* articles on this event at the Newark Public Library New Jersey Room's microfilm archives: July 24, 1968, "Negro Leaders Assail Dismissal by WNJR," and September 18, 1968, "Radio Personality Gets Her Job Back."

138. Joe L. Clark, interview with Pauline Blount, July 8, 1996.
139. James "Chops" Jones, interview with Pauline Blount, April 7, 1997.
140. Coyt Jones, interview with Blount.
141. Branch, interview with Blount.

CHAPTER 3 — WORKDAYS

1. "African Americans, Pt. 1 (Enslaved)," *Rise Up, North: Newark*, http://riseupnewark.com/chapters/chapter-1/african-americans/african-americans-part-1/.
2. Nell Irvin Painter, *Creating Black Americans: African-American History and Its Meanings, 1619 to the Present* (New York: Oxford University Press, 2007), 163.
3. W.E.B. Du Bois, *The Philadelphia Negro: A Social Study*, ed. Elijah Anderson and Isabel Eaton (Philadelphia: University of Pennsylvania Press, 1996 [1899]), 328.
4. Clement Alexander Price, *Freedom Not Far Distant: A Documentary History of Afro-Americans in New Jersey* (Newark: New Jersey Historical Society, 1980), 164–165.
5. Mandi Isaacs Jackson, *Model City Blues: Urban Space and Organized Resistance in New Haven* (Philadelphia: Temple University Press, 2008), 84. See also Robert Curvin's *Inside Newark: Decline, Rebellion, and the Search for Transformation* (New Brunswick, NJ: Rutgers University Press, 2014), for discussion of the SDS and the Clinton Hill Neighborhood Council, 87–90.
6. James Overmyer, *Queen of the Negro Leagues: Effa Manley and the Newark Eagles* (Lanham, MD: Scarecrow Press, 1941), 176.
7. *WPA Negro Case Histories—Newark* (New Jersey: Work Progress Administration, 1941), 1–5.
8. Joshua B. Freeman, "Labor during the American Century," in *A Companion to Post-1945 America*, ed. Jean-Christophe Agnew and Roy Rosenzweig (Malden, MA: Blackwell Publishing, 2002).
9. Louise Epperson, interview with Glen Marie Brickus, February 25, 1997.
10. Joe L. Clark, interview with Pauline Blount, July 8, 1996.
11. Wynona Lipman, interview with Glen Marie Brickus, April 5, 1997.
12. Olugbenga Ajilore, "On the Persistence of the Black-White Unemployment Gap," Center for American Progress, February 24, 2020, https://www.americanprogress.org/article/persistence-black-white-unemployment-gap/.
13. Robert Woods, interview with Glen Marie Brickus, February 17, 1997.
14. While a law was enacted in the 1950s that required employers to include domestic laborers in their tax returns, it was not until the mid-1990s that the "Nanny Tax" had its own section on the 1040 form. See Albert B. Crenshaw, "Simplified Nanny Tax Rules Can Still Create Headaches," *Washington Post*, December 10, 1995.
15. Marzell Swain, interview with Annemarie Dickey-Kemp, May 14, 1998.
16. Johnston is not her actual name. While deeds of gift were signed, these were specifically to the church. I believe it inappropriate to utilize in my own work much more than my experience, and some general anecdotes, with regard to this particular project that I undertook as a member of my church in honor of its 120th anniversary.
17. Elizabeth Clark-Lewis, *Living In, Living Out: African American Domestics and the Great Migration* (New York: Kodansha International, 1996), 160–161.
18. Donald A. Ritchie, *Doing Oral History*, 3rd ed. (New York: Oxford University Press, 2014), 225.

19. See, for example, Tera W. Hunter, *To 'Joy My Freedom: Southern Black Women's Lives and Labors after the Civil War* (Cambridge, MA: Harvard University Press, 1997).

20. Queenie James, interview with Glen Marie Brickus (no date recorded).

21. See, for example, Isabel Wilkerson's *The Warmth of Other Suns; African American Urban History* (New York: Random House, 2010), or Giles Wright's *Afro-Americans in New Jersey: A Short History* (Trenton: New Jersey Historical Commission, 1988).

22. Katheryn Bethea, interview with Glen Marie Brickus, August 7, 1997.

23. U.S. Federal Emergency Relief Administration, "Unemployment Relief Census, October 1933" (Washington, DC: U.S. Government Printing Office, 1934), 2, 215, https://babel.hathitrust.org/cgi/pt?id=mdp.39015016906987&view=1up&seq=3

24. Owen Wilkerson, interview with Glen Marie Brickus, August 12, 1997.

25. Hortense Williams Powell, interview with Ann Marie Dickey-Kemp, July 2, 1998.

26. Alvin Conyers, interview with Glen Marie Brickus, 1997 (no date recorded).

27. W.E.B. Du Bois, *Black Reconstruction in America 1860–1880* (New York: Free Press, 1998 [1935]), 80.

28. Willie Bradwell, interview with Cleta Bradwell, December 8, 1997.

29. Elma Bateman, interview with Pauline Blount, April 29, 1999.

30. John Cunningham, *Newark*, rev. and expanded ed. (Newark: New Jersey Historical Society, 1988), 215–216.

31. There are a number of pieces written on Montclair High School and the tracking issue, circa 2015.

32. Bateman, interview with Blount.

33. Sarah Ahmed, "Happy Objects," in *The Affect Theory Reader*, ed. Melissa Gregg and Gregory J. Seigworth (Durham, NC: Duke University Press, 2010), 39. See also Nicole Fleetwood's *Troubling Vision: Performance, Visuality, and Blackness* (Chicago: University of Chicago Press, 2011), for a discussion of the assumptions projected upon Black bodies.

34. Pauline Mathis, interview with Glen Marie Brickus, October 7, 1997.

35. *120 Years of American Education: A Statistical Portrait* (Washington, DC: U.S. Department of Education, National Center for Education Statistics, 1993), 8.

36. Mathis, interview with Brickus.

37. Woods, interview with Brickus.

38. Marion L. Courtney, *Employment Practices in Selected Retail Stores* (Trenton: New Jersey Department of Education, 1956), 7.

39. Pearl Beatty, interview with Geri Smith, December 12, 1997.

40. In a 1917 publication entitled *The American Stationer and Office Outfitter*, there is a section for tradespersons to place queries for goods and services. On page 14, No. 2777 reads, "Will you kindly give me the names of people who make Rubber Cushion Key Tops for typewriter keyboard?" The editors answer with the name of the Imperial Manufacturing Company of Newark.

41. Ed Crawford, interview with Glen Marie Brickus, February 23, 1997.

42. P. D'Antonio and J. C. Whelan, "Counting Nurses: The Power of Historical Census Data," *Journal of Clinical Nursing* 18, no. 19 (2009): 2719.

43. Darlene Clark Hine, "Mabel K. Staupers and the Integration of Black Nurses into the Armed Forces," in *Black Leaders of the Twentieth Century*, ed. John Hope Franklin and August Meier (Urbana: University of Illinois Press, 1982), 241–257.

44. Charles M. Payne and Adam Green, *Time Longer Than Rope: A Century of African American Activism, 1850–1950* (New York: New York University Press, 2003), 4–5.

45. "Historical Review," American Nurses Association, ANA Enterprise, n.d., https://www.nursingworld.org/~48de64/globalassets/docs/ana/historical-review2016.pdf.

46. Powell, interview with Dickey-Kemp.

47. D'Antonio and Whelan, "Counting Nurses," 1724.

48. Dr. James A. Scott, interview with Glen Marie Brickus (no date recorded).

49. Willie Bradwell, interview with Cleta Bradwell.

50. Executive Order 10925, Establishing the President's Committee on Equal Employment Opportunity, March 6, 1961.

51. Woods, interview with Brickus.

52. Payne and Green, *Time Longer Than Rope*, 1.

53. Kevin Gaines, "The Historiography of the Struggle for Black Equality Since 1945," in *A Companion to Post-1945 America*, eds Jean-Christophe Agnew and Roy Rosenzweig (Malden, MA: Blackwell Publishing, 2002), 217.

54. Payne and Green, *Time Longer Than Rope*, 1–4.

55. Langston Hughes's poem "Mother to Son" reads in part, "Well, son, I'll tell you: Life for me ain't been no crystal stair."

56. Robin D. G. Kelley, *Race Rebels: Culture, Politics, and the Black Working Class* (New York: Free Press, 1994), 9. Kelley received some criticism for his "tendency to politicize every aspect of African American life" instead of regarding some acts simply as "alternative forms of expression." See Bruce Nelson, "Review: *Race Rebels: Culture, Politics, and the Black Working Class* by Robin D. G. Kelley," *Journal of Southern History* 62, no. 1 (February 1996): 171–172. Yet Kelley has much support in his argument. Consider bell hooks's work on photography as an activist measure in the Black community. hooks, *Art on My Mind: Visual Politics* (New York: New Press, 1995).

57. Frances Lee, "Excommunicate Me from the Church of Social Justice," *Autostraddle*, July 13, 2017, https://www.autostraddle.com/kin-aesthetics-excommunicate-me-from-the-church-of-social-justice-386640/?fbclid=IwAR1f9wk4Std6MyqFbxkoHDBkLnixC1Yxa-oEj8YhsY1R8ihRVmoMWMSuPws.

58. Paul Ortiz, "'Eat Your Bread without Butter, but Pay Your Poll Tax': Roots of the African American Voter Registration Movement in Florida, 1919–1920," in Payne and Green, *Time Longer Than Rope*, 196–229.

59. E. Alma Flagg, interview with Catherine Lenix-Hooker, October 20, 1999.

60. Carolyn Wallace, interview with Glen Marie Brickus (no date recorded).

61. Ricky Bell, "International Youth Organization Celebrates 40 Years of Serving Newark Youth," *Star-Ledger*, June 18, 2010. As was the case with so many high-rise subsidized housing projects, Brick Towers—famous for its one-time resident Cory Booker—was demolished in 2008.

62. "Home," International Youth Organization, http://www.iyo-newark.org/about/; Wallace, interview with Brickus.

63. Mildred Crump, interview with Glen Marie Brickus, November 12, 1996. "Here again" is referring to her experience of first arriving in Newark with her husband, having been promised an apartment, and then being told it was unavailable once the landlord realized that the Crumps were African American. Her discussion of this situation appears in a later section.

64. District leaders were appointed to each election district within a ward. Their main job was to get voters to turn out on Election Day.

65. Vivian Berry, interview with Glen Marie Brickus, 1997 (no date recorded).

66. Mary Roberts, interview with Glen Marie Brickus, January 26, 1997.

67. The full questions read as follows: #60. How much have you participated in political activities in Newark? What political organizations (e.g., political parties, protest groups) do/did you belong to? When did you first join them? What positions do/did you hold in them? What roles have you played in them? What do you know about the history of these organizations? Who are/were their outstanding leaders/members? What do you consider to be their major accomplishments? What materials (e.g., photographs, records, posters, banners) do you have that pertain to your political activities? #61. How much have you participated in community activities? What community organizations (e.g., neighborhood groups, civic organizations) do/did you belong to? When did you first join them? What positions do/did you hold in them? What roles have you played in them? What do you know about the history of these organizations? Who are/were their outstanding leaders/members? What do you consider to be their major accomplishments? What materials (e.g., photographs, charters, plaques, awards, flyers) do you have that pertain to your community activities?

68. Crump, interview with Brickus.

69. Francesca Russello Ammon and John Hockenberry, *The Takeaway*, April 13, 2016.

70. Frank Hutchins, interview with Pauline Blount, June 28, 1998.

71. Jean-Paul Sartre, "Preface," *The Wretched of the Earth*, by Frantz Fanon (New York: Grove Press, 2004), 18.

72. Allesandro Portelli, *They Say in Harlan County: An Oral History* (New York: Oxford University Press, 2011), 174.

73. Hutchins, interview with Blount.

74. Willie Belle Hooper, interview with Catherine Lenix-Hooker, April 12, 1996.

75. Ronald Rice, interview with Glen Marie Brickus, April 7, 1997.

76. Max Pizarro, "Six All-Time Newark Ward Contests and Why They Mattered," *Observer*, July 14, 2015, http://observer.com/2015/07/six-all-time-newark-ward-contests-and-why-they-mattered/.

77. George Branch, interview with Pauline Blount, August 28, 1996.

78. Rice, interview with Brickus.

79. W.E.B. Du Bois, "The Negro Church," *The Crisis: A Record of the Darker Races*, May 1912, 24.

80. Paul Robeson, "'The Battleground Is Here,'" in *Freedomways Reader: Prophets in Their Own Country*, ed. Esther Cooper Jackson (Boulder, CO: Westview Press, 2000), 12–13.

81. "Races: Spreading Fire," *Time*, July 28, 1967.

82. L. H. Whelchel, *The History and Heritage of African-American Churches: A Way Out of No Way* (St. Paul, MN: Paragon House, 2011), 211–212.

83. Robert L. Allen, *Black Awakening in Capitalist America: An Analytic History* (Trenton, NJ: Africa World Press, 1990) 12.

84. Bateman, interview with Blount.

85. Hon. Donald M. Payne, "A Tribute to Reverend Henry Cade," June 6, 1996, *Congressional Record*.

86. Scott, interview with Brickus.

87. Woods, interview with Brickus.
88. "Statistical Abstract of the United States" (Washington, DC: U.S. Census Bureau, 1999).
89. Clark, interview with Blount.
90. Lipman, interview with Brickus.

CHAPTER 4 — HOT DAYS

1. Throughout this section, the term *riot* will be utilized when quoting or referencing those who employ that term. The author chooses to use the terms *rebellion, uprising,* and *disturbance.*
2. John Cunningham, *Newark,* rev. and expanded ed. (Newark: New Jersey Historical Society, 1988), 319, 327.
3. Philip Roth, *American Pastoral* (New York: Vintage Books, 1998), 268.
4. Thomas Allan McCabe, *Miracle on High Street: The Rise, Fall, and Resurrection of St. Benedict's Prep in Newark, N.J.* (New York: Fordham University Press, 2011), 157, 158.
5. Ida Clark, interview with Pauline Blount, December 9, 1996.
6. Vivian Berry, interview with Glen Marie Brickus, 1997 (no date provided).
7. Mary Roberts, interview with Glen Marie Brickus, October 26, 1997.
8. Marion Williams, interview with Pauline Blount, June 28, 1999.
9. James Churchman, interview with Glen Marie Brickus, October 11, 1996.
10. Beverly Scott, interview with Glen Marie Brickus (no date recorded).
11. "Hail to the Fire Chiefs!" *Ebony,* July 1988, 92–98.
12. David Margolick, "At the Bar; Falsely Accused: In a Humiliating Arrest, a Black Judge Finds Lessons of Law and Race Relations," *New York Times,* January 7, 1994.
13. Owen Wilkerson, interview with Glen Marie Brickus, August 12, 1997. Further research indicates that Wilkerson is referencing Eugene Campbell, who was superintendent of the Newark public schools from 1987 until they were taken over by the state in 1995. Google Maps shows a large building of orange brick across from the Central Ward Boys and Girls Club at 1 Avon Avenue. This may be the building in question.
14. Ed Crawford, interview with Glen Marie Brickus, February 23, 1997. The church in question appears to be the Canaan Baptist Church at 215–217 Avon Avenue, which established itself on that site in 1956.
15. Carl S. Smith, *Urban Disorder and the Shape of Belief: The Great Chicago Fire, the Haymarket Bomb, and the Model Town of Pullman* (Chicago: University of Chicago Press, 1995), 1.
16. Alessandro Portelli, "What Makes Oral History Different?" in *The Death of Luigi Trastulli, and Other Stories: Form and Meaning in Oral History* (Albany: State University of New York Press, 1991), 69.
17. Jacquelyn Dowd Hall, "'You Must Remember This': Autobiography as Social Critique," *Journal of American History* 85, no. 2 (1998): 440.
18. Coyt Jones, interview with Pauline Blount, January 25, 1996.
19. James "Chops" Jones, interview with Pauline Blount, April 7, 1997. It is out of the ordinary, in these oral histories, to hear someone say there were *no* fires.
20. Sandy Polishuk, *Sticking to the Union: An Oral History of the Life and Times of Julia Ruuttila* (New York: Palgrave Macmillan, 2003), 1–16.
21. Wynona Lipman, interview with Glen Marie Brickus, April 5, 1997. After her passing, there would be a halfway house built for "troubled boys in the senator's honor," the

Wynona M. Lipman Education and Training Center. According to a *New York Times* article, "It caters to children with severe emotional and behavioral problems, including sexual offenders and arsonists." Richard Lezin Jones, "New Jersey Suspends Youth Home Admissions after a Beating," *New York Times*, September 20, 2003.

22. Sharpe James, interview with Glen Marie Brickus, December 3 and 17, 1996.

23. Roberts, interview with Brickus.

24. It seems possible that this could have been the Avon Avenue fire that Ed Crawford, Owen Wilkerson, and others referenced; Hillside and Avon intersect.

25. Churchman, interview with Brickus.

26. Sharpe James, *Political Prisoner: You Can Be Indicted, Arrested, Convicted and Sent to Prison without Committing a Crime: A Memoir* (Newark: Nutany, 2013), 66.

27. Willa Rawlins, interview with Katheryn Bethea, August 8, 1997.

28. James, interview with Brickus.

29. Louise Epperson, interview with Glen Marie Brickus, February 25, 1997.

30. "Socioeconomic Factors and the Incidence of Fire," Federal Emergency Management Agency, U.S. Fire Administration National Fire Data Center, June 1997.

31. Donald J. Hernandez, "America's Children, Resources from Family, Government and the Economy," Russell Sage Foundation, New York, 1993, https://aspe.hhs.gov/sites/default/files/private/pdf/172181/pf2.pdf.

32. Willie Bradwell, interview with Cleta Bradwell, December 8, 1997. It is somewhat unclear as to whether Mrs. Bradwell was being interviewed by her daughter or not. There are those involved with the oral history project who say that indeed she was, yet others claim that was not the case. The discussions sound as if the two women are closely related at times, yet other questions and comments reflect a sense of unfamiliarity.

33. Beryl Satter, *Family Properties: Race, Real Estate, and the Exploitation of Black Urban America* (New York: Metropolitan Books, 2009), 60–61, quoting W. N. Sutherland, "4 Points Offered to Halt Slum Fires," *Chicago American*, January 29, 1958.

34. Ella Rainey, interview with Ann Marie Dickey-Kemp, April 16, 1998. Unfortunately, it is not stated exactly where Mrs. Rainey was living at the time, but if she was looking out on Bloomfield Avenue, then she was probably in the North Ward. Most of the damage occurred in the Central Ward, south of there.

35. W. Collins and R. Margo, "The Economic Aftermath of the 1960s Riots in American Cities: Evidence from Property Values," *Journal of Economic History* 67, no. 4 (2007): 849–883, doi: 10.1017/S0022050707000423

36. Ronald Rice, interview with Glen Marie Brickus, April 7, 1997.

37. Smith, *Urban Disorder and the Shape of Belief*, 4.

38. Jon Bannister and Nick Fyfe, "Introduction: Fear and the City," *Urban Studies* 38, nos. 5–6 (2001): 807–813.

39. Franklin Banks, interview with Richard Cooke, August 19, 1997.

40. James, interview with Brickus.

41. Smith, *Urban Disorder and the Shape of Belief*, 6.

42. Playboy Magazine, "'A Testament of Hope' by Dr. King," *Hef's Philosophy: Playboy and Revolution from 1965–1975*, https://forthearticles.omeka.net/items/show/37.

43. Junius Williams, quoted in Tracey Tully and Kevin Armstrong, "How a City Once Consumed by Civil Unrest Has Kept Protests Peaceful," *New York Times*, June 1, 2020, https://www.nytimes.com/2020/06/01/nyregion/newark-peaceful-protests-george-floyd.html.

44. Ras Baraka, interview with Hari Sreenivasan, "How Newark's Protest Preparations Have Helped Remain Calm," *PBS News Hour Weekend*, June 18, 2020, https://www.newarknj.gov/news/how-newarks-protest-preparations-have-helped-maintain-calm.

45. Sophie Nieto-Munoz, "Activists Troubled That N.J. Cities Sought DEA Surveillance of 2020 Protests," *New Jersey Monitor*, October 22, 2021, https://newjerseymonitor.com/briefs/activists-troubled-that-n-j-cities-sought-dea-surveillance-of-2020-protests/.

46. Henry Robinson, interview with Glen Marie Brickus, January 17, 1997.

47. Robert L. Allen, *Black Awakening in Capitalist America: An Analytic History* (Trenton, NJ: Africa World Press, 1990), 129. The magazine issue he refers to is that of July 28, 1967, whose cover features the image of a young boy lying in the street and the headline "Newark: The Predictable Insurrection."

48. Robert Woods, interview with Glen Marie Brickus, February 17 and 18, 1997.

49. Edward Kerr, interview with Glen Marie Brickus, September 24, 1997.

50. Churchman, interview with Brickus.

51. Alvin Conyers, interview with Glen Marie Brickus, 1997 (no date recorded).

52. Timothy Still, director, Newark Community Development Corporation; Dr. L. Sylvester Odom, executive director, United Community Corporation (UCC); Oliver Lofton, attorney with Newark Legal Services Project.

53. George Branch, interview with Pauline Blount, August 28, 1996.

54. Teddy Wayne, "Shutterbug Parents and Overexposed Lives," *New York Times*, February 20, 2015.

55. Branch, interview with Blount.

56. Portelli, "What Makes Oral History Different?" 26.

57. Clara Little, interview with Pauline Blount, October 6, 1997.

58. See the Krueger-Scott Oral History Collection website for several portraits and the "William M. May Collection" via Newark Public Library website for other photographs.

59. Zaundria Mapson May, interview with Bill May, August 11, 1996.

60. Veronice Horne, interview with Katheryn Bethea, June 3, 1997.

61. Willie Bradwell, interview with Cleta Bradwell.

62. Edna Thomas, interview with E. Alma Flagg, October 7, 1996.

63. Ellen O'Brien, "As LA Smoldered, Newark Remembered after 25 Years, the City Has Made Progress. But for Whom?" *Philadelphia Inquirer*, May 26, 1992.

64. Katheryn Bethea, interview with Glen Marie Brickus, August 7, 1997.

65. Jack Shafer, "CNN Feasts on Baltimore Riot Coverage," *Politico*, April 28, 2015.

66. Searching the microfilm of all *Afro-American* issues surrounding the time of the rebellion, Wilkerson's byline does not appear. However, there are a number of articles without bylines. Bob Queen's name appears most often as the reporter on these stories. Perhaps one or more of the anonymous articles was written by Wilkerson, or he collaborated with Queen, who is referenced a number of times by the interviewees when discussing common sources of news for the Black community.

67. *New Jersey Afro-American*, July 22, 1967, Newark Public Library, microfilm. It seems the *Afro* had some significant lag time between when articles were written and published; this explains the absence of news about the July 12 rebellion in a July 15 newspaper. For example, on July 22nd, there was a comparison of the Newark uprising to the recent Watts rebellion. Comparing the duration of the disturbances, the article reports that Newark was "Now in its fifth day," fifteen days after the rebellion had ended.

68. *Riot: One City's 50-Year Struggle to Leave Behind its Worst Week Ever* (Avon by the Sea, NJ: Stumpsfilm, 2015), http://riotthefilm.com/.

69. Emily Badger, "The Uncomfortable Politics behind the History of Urban Fires," *The Atlantic*, August 22, 2012; Greg Bankoff, Uwe Lübken, Jordan Sand, eds., *Flammable Cities: Urban Conflagration and the Making of the Modern World* (Madison: University of Wisconsin Press, 2012).

70. Lipman, interview with Brickus.

71. See, for example, Mark Krasovic, *The Struggle for Newark: Plotting Urban Crisis in the Great Society*, Thesis (Ph.D.), Yale University, 2008; and Thomas J. Sugrue, *The Origins of the Urban Crisis: Race and Inequality in Postwar Detroit* (Princeton, NJ: Princeton University Press, 2005).

72. Kevin McLaughlin, interview with Steve Adubato, *One on One with Steve Adubato*, September 22, 2015, 3:00 mark.

73. Wilkerson, interview with Brickus.

74. "Newark: The Predictable Insurrection," 16.

75. Porambo, *No Cause for Indictment*, 130.

76. Spina, *Report for Action*, 136.

77. Hazel V. Carby, *Race Men* (Cambridge, MA: Harvard University Press, 1998), 170.

78. This is not exactly accurate. For example, in Dr. Price's documentary, *The Once and Future Newark*, he employs the word, *riot* on several occasions.

79. McLaughlin, interview with Adubato, 6:00 mark.

80. McLaughlin, interview with Adubato, 8:00 mark.

81. McLaughlin, interview with Adubato, film clip with Cory Booker.

82. Lipman, interview with Brickus.

83. Bethea, interview with Brickus.

84. Bethea, interview with Brickus.

85. Conyers, interview with Brickus.

86. Bethea, interview with Brickus.

87. Danita Henderson, interview with Glen Marie Brickus, August 13, 1997.

88. "On November 14–16, 1969, the Committee for Unified Newark (CFUN) sponsored the Black and Puerto Rican Convention, which was designed to formally select the 'Community's Choice' for Mayor and City Council in the 1970 election," riseupnewark.com.

89. Mildred Crump, interview with Glen Marie Brickus, November 12, 1996.

90. Isaac Thomas, interview with Pauline Blount, July 2, 1997.

91. Mageline Little, interview with Pauline Blount, November 18, 1998.

92. Wilkerson, interview with Brickus.

AFTERWORD

1. Makerhoods is the name of the development company directing the project. See the website, https://www.makerhoods.com/kruegerscott-mansion. As of November 2021, the construction project was underway. There have, inevitably, been disputes regarding labor practices, historic accuracy, and the like. In April 2023, the Newark Makerhoods was offering "upscale one, two, and three-bedroom apartments, complemented by a prominent historic site."

Bibliography

Ahmed, Sarah. "Happy Objects." In *The Affect Theory Reader*, edited by Melissa Gregg and Gregory J. Seigworth. Durham, NC: Duke University Press, 2010.
Allen, Robert L. *Black Awakening in Capitalist America: An Analytic History*. Trenton, NJ: Africa World Press, 1990.
Arnesen, Eric. *Black Protest and the Great Migration: A Brief History with Documents*. Boston: Bedford/St. Martin's, 2003.
Baldwin, Davarian L. *Chicago's New Negroes: Modernity, the Great Migration, and Black Urban Life*. Chapel Hill: University of North Carolina Press, 2007.
Baraka, Amiri. *Blues People: Negro Music in White America*. New York: Perennial, 2002.
Boardman, Samantha. "Castle Newark: The Krueger-Scott Mansion." Clementine Productions, 2009. https://www.youtube.com/watch?v=g8W9nY1OUfk.
Boustan, Leah P., and Robert A. Margo. "A Silver Lining to White Flight? White Suburbanization and African-American Homeownership, 1940–1980." *Journal of Urban Economics* 78 (November 2013): 71–80.
Carby, Hazel V. *Race Men*. Cambridge, MA: Harvard University Press, 1998.
Clark, Joe. *Laying Down the Law: Joe Clark's Strategy for Saving Our Schools*. Washington, DC: Regnery Publishing, 1989.
Clark-Lewis, Elizabeth. *Living In, Living Out: African American Domestics and the Great Migration*. New York: Kodansha International, 1996.
Cunningham, John T. *Newark*, rev. and expanded ed. Newark: New Jersey Historical Society, 1988.
Curvin, Robert. *Inside Newark: Decline, Rebellion, and the Search for Transformation*. New Brunswick, NJ: Rutgers University Press, 2014.
D'Antonio, P., and J. C. Whelan. "Counting Nurses: The Power of Historical Census Data." *Journal of Clinical Nursing* 18, no. 19 (2009): 2717–2724.
Davis, John P. *A Survey of the Problems of the Negro Under the New Deal* (Washington, DC: Howard University, Bureau of Educational Research, 1936).
Dickerman, Leah, and Elsa Smithgall, eds. *Jacob Lawrence: The Migration Series*. New York: Artbook, 2014.

Du Bois, W.E.B. *Black Reconstruction in America 1860–1880.* New York: Free Press, 1998 (1935).

———. *The Education of Black People; Ten Critiques, 1906–1960.* Amherst: University of Massachusetts Press, 1973.

———. "The Negro Church." *The Crisis: A Record of the Darker Races* 4, no. 1 (1912): 24. https://books.google.com.

———. *The Philadelphia Negro: A Social Study.* Edited by Elijah Anderson and Isabel Eaton. Philadelphia: University of Pennsylvania Press, 1996 (1899).

Fleetwood, Nicole. *Troubling Vision: Performance, Visuality, and Blackness.* Chicago: University of Chicago Press, 2011.

Fraser, Gertrude, and Reginald Butler. "Anatomy of Disinterment: The Unmaking of Afro-American History." In *Presenting the Past: Essays on History and the Public. Critical Perspectives on the Past,* edited by Susan Porter Benson, Steven Brier, and Roy Rosenzweig. Philadelphia: Temple University Press, 1986.

Gaines, Kevin. "The Historiography of the Struggle for Black Equality Since 1945." In *A Companion to Post-1945 America,* edited by Jean-Christophe Agnew and Roy Rosenzweig. Malden, MA: Blackwell Publishing, 2002.

Governor's Select Commission on Civil Disorder. *Report for Action.* Trenton, NJ: Governor's Select Commission, 1968.

Gregory, James N. *The Southern Diaspora: How the Great Migrations of Black and White Southerners Transformed America.* Chapel Hill: University of North Carolina Press, 2005.

Holmes, Robert C., and Richard W. Roper. *A Mayor for All the People: Kenneth Gibson's Newark.* New Brunswick, NJ: Rutgers University Press, 2020.

Hunter, Tera W. *To 'Joy My Freedom: Southern Black Women's Lives and Labors after the Civil War.* Cambridge, MA: Harvard University Press, 1997. https://doi.org/10.2307/j.ctv287s9nb.

Jackson, Lee. "WPA Negro Case Histories—Newark, New Jersey." Works Progress Administration, version 2, chapter 3, 1941. http://sites.bergen.org/ourstory/resources/great_depression/PrimaryDocs/WPANegroNewark.pdf.

Jackson, Mandi Isaacs. *Model City Blues: Urban Space and Organized Resistance in New Haven.* Philadelphia: Temple University Press, 2008.

James, Sharpe. *Political Prisoner: You Can Be Indicted, Arrested, Convicted and Sent to Prison without Committing a Crime: A Memoir.* Newark, NJ: Nutany, 2013.

Johnson, Karl Ellis. "'Trouble Won't Last': Black Church Activism in Postwar Philadelphia." In *African American Urban History since World War II,* edited by Kenneth L. Kusmer and Joe William Trotter. Chicago: University of Chicago Press, 2009.

Kelley, Robin D. G. *Race Rebels: Culture, Politics, and the Black Working Class.* New York: Free Press, 1994.

Mark, Krasovic. *The Struggle for Newark: Plotting Urban Crisis in the Great Society.* Thesis (Ph.D.), Yale University, 2008.

McCabe, Thomas Allan. *Miracle on High Street: The Rise, Fall, and Resurrection of St. Benedict's Prep in Newark, N.J.* New York: Fordham University Press, 2011.

Miller, Karen R. "Whose History, Whose Culture? The Museum of African American History, The Detroit Institute of Arts, and Urban Politics at the End of the Twentieth Century." *Michigan Quarterly Review* 41, no. 1 (Winter 2002).

Neal, Sue G., and Harold L. Bunce. "Socioeconomic Changes in Distressed Cities during the 1980s." *Cityscape: A Journal of Policy Development and Research* 1, no. 1 (1994): 123–152.

Neary, Timothy B. *Crossing Parish Boundaries: Race, Sports, and Catholic Youth in Chicago, 1914–1954*. Chicago: University of Chicago Press, 2016.

O'Kelly-Cooke, Amorel E. *Faded Foliage and Fragrant Flowers from the Heart of Bethany*. Newark: Joseph Schreiner, 1922.

Overmyer, James. *Queen of the Negro Leagues: Effa Manley and the Newark Eagles*. Lanham, MD: Scarecrow Press, 1988.

Painter, Nell Irvin. *Creating Black Americans: African-American History and Its Meanings, 1619 to the Present*. New York: Oxford University Press, 2007.

Payne, Charles M., and Adam Green. *Time Longer Than Rope: A Century of African American Activism, 1850–1950*. New York: New York University Press, 2003.

Playboy Magazine. "'A Testament of Hope' by Dr. King." *Hef's Philosophy: Playboy and Revolution from 1965–1975*. https://forthearticles.omeka.net/items/show/37.

Podolski, Michael, dir. *The Once and Future Newark*. Newark, NJ: Rutgers University, Newark Office of Communications, 2015. https://www.youtube.com/playlist?list=PLB2A475FCD4EBAAEE&feature=plcp.

Polishuk, Sandy. *Sticking to the Union: An Oral History of the Life and Times of Julia Ruuttila*. New York: Palgrave Macmillan, 2003.

Porambo, Ronald. *No Cause for Indictment: An Autopsy of Newark*. Hoboken, NJ: Melville House, 1971.

Portelli, Alessandro. *The Death of Luigi Trastulli, and Other Stories: Form and Meaning in Oral History*. Albany: State University of New York Press, 1991.

———. *They Say in Harlan County: An Oral History*. New York: Oxford University Press, 2011.

Price, Clement Alexander. *Freedom Not Far Distant: A Documentary History of Afro-Americans in New Jersey*. Newark: New Jersey Historical Society, 1980.

"Races: Spreading Fire." *Time*, July 28, 1967, 15–16. https://content.time.com/time/subscriber/article/0,33009,837079,00.html.

Riot: One City's 50-Year Struggle to Leave Behind Its Worst Week Ever. Avon by the Sea, NJ: Stumpsfilm, 2015. http://riotthefilm.com/.

Ritchie, Donald A. *Doing Oral History*, 3rd ed. New York: Oxford University Press, 2014.

Roth, Philip. *American Pastoral*. New York: Vintage Books, 1998.

Sartre, Jean-Paul. "Preface." In *The Wretched of the Earth*, by Frantz Fanon. New York: Grove Press, 2004.

Satter, Beryl. *Family Properties: Race, Real Estate, and the Exploitation of Black Urban America*. New York: Metropolitan Books, 2009.

Scott, James A. "Bethany Baptist Church: Growth through Planning and Social Action." In *Church and Synagogue Affiliation: Theory, Research, and Practice*, edited by Amy L. Sales and Gary A. Tobin. Westport, CT: Greenwood Press, 1995.

Smith, Carl S. *Urban Disorder and the Shape of Belief: The Great Chicago Fire, the Haymarket Bomb, and the Model Town of Pullman*. Chicago: University of Chicago Press, 1995. http://press.uchicago.edu/Misc/Chicago/764176.html.

Sugrue, Thomas J. *The Origins of the Urban Crisis: Race and Inequality in Postwar Detroit*. Princeton, NJ: Princeton University Press, 2005.

Thompson, Paul. *The Voice of the Past: Oral History*. New York: Oxford University Press, 1978.

U.S. Federal Emergency Relief Administration. "United States Summary: Showing by Geographic Divisions, by States, and by Cities Detailed Data Concerning Color and Size of Relief Families, and the Age, Color, and Sex of Persons in Relief Families: Report Number One." In *Unemployment Relief Census: October 1933*. Washington, DC: U.S. Government Printing Office, 1934. https://fraser.stlouisfed.org/title/153/item/5332, accessed on April 13, 2023.

Weisenfeld, Judith. *New World a-Coming: Black Religion and Racial Identity during the Great Migration*. New York: New York University Press, 2017. https://doi.org/10.18574/9781479853687.

Whelchel, L. H. *The History and Heritage of African-American Churches: A Way Out of No Way*. St. Paul, MN: Paragon House, 2011.

Wilkerson, Isabel. *The Warmth of Other Suns: The Epic Story of America's Great Migration*. New York: Random House, 2010.

Williams, Rhonda Y. *The Politics of Public Housing: Black Women's Struggles against Urban Inequality*. Oxford: Oxford University Press, 2004.

Wilson, Mabel. *Negro Building: Black Americans in the World of Fairs and Museums*. Berkeley: University of California Press, 2012.

Wright, Giles R. *Afro-Americans in New Jersey: A Short History*. Trenton: New Jersey Historical Commission, 1988.

X, Malcolm. *The Autobiography of Malcolm X*. Edited by Alex Haley. New York: Ballantine Books, 1999.

Index

Italicized page numbers indicate images.

Abrams, Stacey, 121
activism. *See* civil rights movement; sociopolitical work
Addonizio, Hugh, 8, 123, 130, 136, 147, 152; administration of, 118, 125
Adkins-Jones, Timothy Levi, 53
Adubato, Steve, 161, 162, 164
affirmative action, 111, 135
African American Museums Association (AAMA), 2
Ahmed, Sarah, 101
Ali, Drew, 62
Allen, Robert L., 124, 150–151
Allen AME Church, 60
American Nurses Association (ANA), 108, 109
Ammon, Francesca Russello, 118
ANA. *See* American Nurses Association (ANA)
Apex Beauty School, 6
Arnesen, Eric, 5
arson. *See* fires, in Newark; Cleveland: forgotten fires in
Ashby, William, 12
Association of Community Organizations for Reform Now (ACORN), 117
Avon Avenue fire, 135, 136, 150

Badger, Emily, 161–162
Baker, George. *See* Father Divine
Baldwin, Davarian, xii–xiii, 40, 73
Baltimore, 34, 160, 169

Bamberger's department store, 77, 92, *93*, 103–104, 105
Banks, Franklin, 42, 50, 146
Bannister, Nick, 146
Baptists, 50, 54, 59, 61. *See also specific Baptist churches*
Baraka, Amiri: and baseball, 69; and collectivity vs. disunion in Newark, 119–120; frustrations of, with City Hall, 28, 190n90; and Lenix-Hooker, 22; on the old settler/new settler rift, xiii, 57; participation of in "informational meetings" on Newark's problems, 41; as a radio guest, 80; and the rebellion of 1967, 148, 155
Baraka, Ras, 28, 148, 149, 169
bars, taverns, and clubs, 71–73
baseball, 67–71, 84, 139
Bass, Bernice, 7, 80–83, *81*
Bateman, Elma, 45, 54, 80, 99–101, 124
Beatty, Pearl, 104–105
Berkey, Joan, 25
Berry, Vivian, 106, 116–117, 131, 134
Bethany Baptist Church, 46–53, *47*, 56, 59, 61, 83; clergy at, 33, 43, 46, 50–52, 60, 72, 124–125; and community collectivism, 43–44, 46; concerts at, 26; history of, 47–50; ministries of, 45
Bethea, Katheryn, 75, 89; on church's importance, 43–44, 52; employment history of, 92, 165; on racism in the workplace, 103; on the rebellion of 1967, 159–160, 165–166

209

INDEX

Bethsaida Baptist Church, 41, 142
Birmingham, 11, 123
Black, Charlie, 150
Black and Puerto Rican Convention, 16, 166, 204n88
Black Hebrews, 62
Black Lives Matter, 131, 149
Black Renaissance, xii
Blake, Rev. Eustace L., 61
Blind Boys. *See* Five Blind Boys of Alabama
Blount, Pauline, 65, 100, 120, 137–138, 154
Boardman, Samantha, 186n7, 192n125
Booker, Cory, 31, 71, 121, 164–165, 199n61
Booker, Vickie, 58
Bottone, Michael "Mickey," 121, 126
Boyd, Alex, 21
Bradwell, Cleta, 97–99
Bradwell, Willie, 73, 97–99, 111, 144, 157, 202n32
Branch, George: on Bernice Bass, 82; on church attendance, 84–85; employment history of, 64; on fear and stress from growing up Black, 158; investment of in Newark's youth, 121–122; on the Krueger-Scott Mansion, 15, 17, 19, 22, 29–30, 31; political career of, 122; on the rebellion of 1967, 154–155
Braugher, Andre, 164
Brickus, Glen Marie: animation of, as an interviewer, 59; as an interviewer, asking about church, 41, 57–58, 59, 63; as an interviewer, asking about domestic life, 139–140; as an interviewer, asking about domestic work, 88, 89; as an interviewer, asking about dress, 64–65; as an interviewer, asking about perceptions of Black Newark, 165–166; as an interviewer, asking about police and fire departments, 134; as an interviewer, asking about political activities, 125–126; as an interviewer, asking about the rebellion, 150, 152–153; as an interviewer, asking about shopping, 75; as an interviewer, asking about work, 103, 105, 117; and James's claim that he played for the Newark Eagles, 70–71; rural upbringing of, 140
Broad Street, shopping on, 75–76, 77, 142
Bunch, Lonnie, 3
Burgess, Ray, 122
Burroughs, Margaret and Charles, 2
Butler, Reginald, 3
Byass, Lurline, 106, 135, 145

Cade, Rev. Henry, 124
Campbell, Eugene, 120, 136, 201n13
Carby, Hazel, 163–164
Carey, Thomas, 54
Carrino, Anthony, 29, 117
Carter, Barry, 29
Case, Clifford P., 186n20
Catholics, 54–55, 194n54. *See also specific Catholic churches*
Central Presbyterian Church, 124
Central Ward (Newark), 131, 187n25; abandoned buildings and deteriorating housing in, 8, 12; and the building of a Black history/culture center, 2, 22, 28, 29, 50; Coalition of Youth Agencies in, 16, 18; and the rebellion of 1967, 202n34
Chicago: Black population of, 8, 10; conservation in, 9; DuSable Museum of African American History in, 2; fire in, including the Great Fire,137, 144, 145, 147; as a Great Migration destination, xi, xii; housing in, 9–10; reputation of, 162; uprisings in, 11; urban "blight" in, 78
Chicago Defender, x
children/youth: better lives for, in the North when compared to the South, ix; community work for, 115, 117; in the justice system, 128, 140; and self-esteem from exposure to Black cultural institutions, 16; and services provided by Black churches, 44
Chisholm, Shirley, 116
Christians/Christianity, 40, 46, 50, 59, 60, 61, 62, 141. *See also* church, Black
Christmas, 92, 138–139
church, Black, 39–41, 83–84, 106; and community, 41–46; individuals' experiences of, 56–59; and politicians, 59–62. *See also* work/employment: in the ministry; *and specific churches*
Churchman, James, 68, 74, 134, 142, 153
Civil Rights Act (of 1964), 147, 186n20
civil rights movement, 82, 87, 89, 111, 112, 122, 124, 151. *See also* sociopolitical work
Civil War, 137
Clark, Ida, 131
Clark, Joe, 39, 74–75, 83, 89, 105, 127
Clark-Lewis, Elizabeth, 90–91
clergy, 41, 42, 53, 122–126. *See also* church, Black; *specific clergypersons*
Cleveland, 1, 8, 92; "forgotten fires" of, 161–162
Coleman, Claude, 135–136
Coleman, Willa, 45–46, 52, 56, 167
Collington, Rev., 58

Collins, William J., 145
community organizing. *See* civil rights movement; sociopolitical work
Confederate monuments, 1, 17
Conyers, Rev. Alvin: on the importance of church, 56; on fire, 141–142; on political activity to fight discrimination, 126, 134, 153; on the rebellion of 1967, 166; work history of, 96
Cooke, Richard, 48, 69
Crawford, Ed: on church, 50, 51, 52, 53, 56; on important events in Newark history, 136, 202n24; working life, 105
crime, 60; and the Black body, 43; drop in rate of, in Newark, 34; high rates of, in Newark, and fears about, 4, 29, 146, 162; housing, 144; vandalism, 19, 27
Crump, Mildred, 199n63; on her career path, 115–116; on the church, 42, 52, 60, 63; on her family, 89; on the Krueger-Scott Mansion, 20, 29, 30, 36; on her politics and community activity, 117–118; on the rebellion of 1967, 164, 166
Cunningham, John T., 100, 130
Cuomo, Andrew, 33
Curvin, Robert, 154

Dandridge, Ray, 68
D'Antonio, Patricia, 106, 110
Danzig, Lou, 10
D'Ascensioto, Frank, 18
Davis-Bacon Act, 27–28
Del Tufo, Elizabeth, *13*, 17, 18, 19
Democratic Party, 60, 117, 121, 126
Denny, Reginald Oliver, 155
DePalma, Anthony, 20
Department of Housing and Urban Development (HUD), 19, 25, 33, 119, 167
desegregation, 69–70, 108. *See also* segregation
DeSenne, Carol, 26
Detroit, 63, 89, 115, 116, 118; changing demographics and effects on Black population of, 1, 8, 10; as destination for Great Migration migrants, xi; exodus of urban population from, 34; Museum of African American History in, 2; uprisings in, 11
Dickey-Kemp, Annemarie, 94, 96, 108, 110
Dietz, Ulysses Grant, *13*
discrimination. *See* racism/racial discrimination
district leaders, 9, 117, 126, 200n64
Divine, Father. *See* Father Divine
Doby, Larry, 68, 69

domestic work/workers, xi, 6, 43, 85, 87, 88–91, 96, 97
dress and fashion, 63–67
drugs, 162
Druid, Rev. Richard T., 60
Du Bois, W.E.B., 63, 86, 97, 123, 127
Dukakis, Michael, 60

Edmunds, Florence Jacob, 110
education: Baraka's emphasis on, 120; and Black teachers/administrators, 85, 112, 132, 134; and the church/clergy, 53, 124; community engagement in, 86; as a consciousness raiser, especially for Black women, 114; decline in, 168; and dropouts, 162; for immigrants, but not for Black residents, 100; among Krueger-Scott interview subjects, 102–103; in the North, xiii; and philanthropy, 12; racism in, 86; and the rebellion of 1967, 162; and school overcrowding, 9; and the teachers' strike of 1971, 132; among the variables for fire rates, 143, 144
Emmanuel Missionary Baptist Church, 45, 56
employment. *See* work/employment; unemployment/underemployment
Epperson, Louise, *151*; on Bernice Bass, 80; church experiences of, 57, 58–59, 72; on domestic work, 88–89; on fires in Newark, 143; political organizing of, 72, 117, 124, 151
Equal Employment Opportunity Commission (EEOC), 27–28

Faded Foliage and Fragrant Flowers from the Heart of Bethany, 48–50, *49*
Fanon, Frantz, 119
Father Divine, 62, 78–80, *79*
firefighters, Newark, 126, 134–136, 138–139, 162
fires, in Newark, 132–136, 141, 142–144, 168
Five Blind Boys of Alabama, 73, 144
Flagg, E. Alma, 12, 76, 113–114
Floyd, George, 148, 150
food: nostalgia about, 74–75; pantries, 44; and the rebellion of 1967, 157, 160
Franklin, Martha, 109
Fraser, Gertrude, 3
Freeman, Joshua, 88
Freeman, Richard, 134
Freemasons. *See* Scottish Rite Freemasons
Fyfe, Jon, 146

Gaines, Kevin, 112
Gibson, Ken: election of, 136, 166; as mayor of Newark, 12, 14, 16, 41, 119–120, 122
Good Neighbor Baptist Church, 7, 187n32
Gosser, Matt, 55
government aid/assistance, 6, 42, 67, 92–93, 96, 99
Grad Partnership architectural firm, 17, 18, 24, 189n56
Graham, Robert, 191n106
Grant, Glenn, 29
Grant, Harry, 22–23
Grant, Rev. Ralph T., 16, 41, *151*
Grant, Ulysses S., 129
Gray, Freddie, 160
Great Depression, 6–7, 44, 62, 66, 88
Great Migration, ix–xiv, 6; art and literature inspired by, 101; and job opportunities for migrants, 85, 87; as a labor action against white supremacy, 112; literature on, 92; and the old settler/new settler rift, 22, 41, 63, 119, 141; participants in, as a part of the Krueger-Scott Oral History Project, 5, 38; and religious practices of migrants, 62; stories of, and parallels to Kentucky coal mining community, 119
Great Society, 115, 167
Greater Abyssinian Baptist Church, 39, 45
Green, Adam, 108, 112
Gregory, James N., xii
Grossklauss, Richard, *13*

Hall, Jacquelyn Dowd, 137
Hamm, Larry, 149
Harvey B. Gantt Center for African-American Arts + Culture, 2, 169
Hatfield, Rev. Glenn, 53
Hayden, Tom, 87
Hayes Homes, 51, *51*, 154, 156, 158
Hayes, Rev. William P., 50–51, 52
Heard, Nathan, 143
Heater, Gabriel, 80
Henderson, Danita, 166
Henkel, Linda, 154
higher education, 102, 114
Hill, Elton, 17
Hill Manor, 28, 31, 32, 34, 115
Hines, Earl "Fatha," 12
homelessness, 124, 142, 144
homeownership. *See* housing
Homes, Robert, 16
hooks, bell, 199n56

Hooper, Willie Belle, 43, 56, 69, 120
Horne, Veronice, 45, 156–157
housing: and Black homeownership, 7–8; and fires, 132–133, 136–145; and housing law enforcement, 144; and lowered property values, 145; shortages of, during the Great Migration, xii; subsidized public projects, 28, 67, 122, 153, 161 (*see also* Hayes Homes; Hill Manor); vacancies, 34, 143; and youth, 121. *See also* homelessness
Howard, Bill, 50
HUD. *See* Department of Housing and Urban Development (HUD)
Hughes, Langston, 112
Hurdle, Rev. L. C., 52
Hutchins, Frank, 82, 119, 120

International Youth Organization (YO), 115
Irish community, Newark, 55, 121
Islam, 61, 62
Italian community, Newark, 2, 104, 121

Jackson, Mandi Isaacs, 87
James, Queen Elizabeth Wright ("Queenie"), 74, 75, 91
James, Sharpe: on Bernice Bass, 81; on Black churches, 60–61; on the Black community helping each other, 44; claim of, that he played for the Newark Eagles, 70–71, 139; on the club and bar scene, 72; and fear of police, 158; first home of, 143; as mayor, 18, 19, *21*, 23, 25, 26, 28, 31, 71, 121; memoir of, 25, 142; on MLK, 147; on people's reliance on government, 42; on segregation, 69–70; as South Ward councilman, 17
Jewish community, Newark, 90, 118; as doctors, 45; holidays and religious observances of, 90, 141; in Philip Roth's work, 131; neighborhoods of, 118, 135; stores owned by, 67, 141. *See also* Black Hebrews
Jim Crow, xi, 5, 135. *See also* racism/racial discrimination
jobs. *See* work/employment
Johnson, Bernice, 67, 135
Johnson, Jessie, 102–103, 168
Johnson, J. Stewart, 10
Johnson, Karl Ellis, 40
Johnson, Lyndon Baines, administration of, 167
Jones, Coyt, 69, 75–76, 83, 102, 137–138

INDEX

Jones, James "Chops," 83, 138
Jones, Johnny, 119
Jones, LeRoi. *See* Baraka, Amiri
Jones, Sadie, 91
justice system, 127–128; for juveniles, 128, 140

Kastl Associates Architects, 18, 20, 189n56
Kelley, David B., 130
Kelley, Robin D. G., 112–113, 199n56
Kennedy, John F., 111
Kerr, Daniel, 161
Kerr, Edward, 142, 152–153, 168, 187n34
King, Rodney, 155, 159
King, Rev. Martin Luther, Jr., 54, 84, 124, 146, 147
Krueger, Gottfried, 4, 12, 17, 188n36
Krueger Mansion. *See* Krueger-Scott Mansion
Krueger-Scott African-American cultural center (proposed), 3, 19, 31, 33, 38, 51, 105, 137; idea of, introduced, 16; James (mayor) on, 34–35; Lenix-Hooker on, 34; mission of, xiii, 2; and the oral history interviews, 96, 169
Krueger-Scott African-American Oral History Project, xiii–xiv, 2, 5, 31, 36, 37–38, 169; Bill May Sr. as portrait photographer for, 156; desire of, to attract nurses as participants, 106; Lenix-Hooker's supervision of, 34; publicity and recruitment for, 48; questionnaire for, 132, 172–181
Krueger-Scott Mansion: history of, 1–37, 5, 8, 13, 15, 24, 35
Kukla, Barbara, 80, 81–82, 139
Ku Klux Klan, xii

labor unions, xi, 97–98; African Americans in, xiii; and racism, 88; and strike breakers, xi, xii; and the teachers' strike of 1971, 132; women organizers and, 114
Latino community, Newark, 27, 46, 128
Lawrence, Jacob, ix, xii, 84, 101, 103
Lee, Frances, 113
legacy cities, 34, 38, 191n113
leisure activities, 71–78. *See also* baseball; radio
Lenix-Hooker, Catherine, 21; as a Bethany Baptist Church member, 46; as executive director of the Krueger-Scott Mansion restoration project, 19, 20, 22–35, 37, 48, 191n95, 191n106
Lewis, John, 3

Lipman, Wynona, 72; childhood memories of, 139–140; on domestics, 89; on drugs and crime, 162; on fires in Newark, 140, 145; halfway house named for, 201n21; on optimism in Newark, 165, 168; on the police and fire departments, 134; political career of, 59; on racism in the justice system, 127–128; on racism in the workplace, 106
Little, Clara, 156
Little, Mageline, 37, 72, 82, 106, 167, 190n90
Little, Matthew, 65, 134, 166–167
Lofton, Oliver, 154
Los Angeles "riots" of 1992, 155, 159
Louis, Joe, 83
Lucas, Harold, 31, 33, 191n106
lynchings, x

Madison, Mary, 61
Malcolm X, 64, 123
Mandhart, Margaret, 12
Manley, Abe, 68
Manley, Effa, 67–68, 70, 71, 195n102
Manning, Max, 68
Marasco, Robert P., 33
Margo, Robert A., 145
Margolick, David, 136
Martin, John, 132
Marvin X, 147
Masons. *See* Scottish Rite Freemasons
Mathis, Pauline Faison, 76, 101–102, 103, 114, 132
May, Bill, Jr., 66, 156
May, Bill, Sr., 156
May, Zaundria Mapson, 43, 66, 156
McCabe, Tom, 131
McCarroll, E. Mae, 65
McLaughlin, Kevin, 161, 162, 164
McLurkin, Erma, 59
McNeil, Wilbur, 118
Means, Lenora, 106
Means, Rev. Raphus Phillips, 39
media, Black, 69–70, 83. *See also* radio
media coverage of Newark, 123, 132–134, 159–160, 162–163, 166
Methodists, 54, 59. *See also specific Methodist churches*
Migration Series, The (Lawrence), ix, 84, 101, 103
military service, 94, 97, 107–108
Milwaukee, 11, 34
ministry. *See* church, Black; clergy
Minneapolis, 11
Mississippi, xi

Monteilh, Richard, 19
Morningstar Baptist Church, 41
Morton, Virginia, 30
Murrow, Edward R., 80
music: blues, 71; gospel, 50, 57, 71, 73, 80, 194n69; jazz, 12, 71, 72, 73
Muslim community, Newark, 61, 62, 112

NAACP, 123, 125, 136, 142
National Association of Colored Graduate Nurses (NACGN), 107, 109
National Black Nurses Association, 108
National Guard, 150, 156, 157, 160, 161
National Negro Labor Council, 123
National Union Radio Corporation, 94, 95
Neary, Timothy, 40
Negro Leagues, 67–71
New Jersey Afro American (newspaper), 12, 160, 161
New Jersey Board of Education, 114, 122
New Jersey Historic Trust (NJHT), 20, 23, 25, 26, 27, 30, 31, 33
New Jersey Institute of Technology, 36, 55
New Jersey Performing Arts Center (NJPAC), 25, 28, 166, 167
New Jersey Senate, 59, 121. *See also* Lipman, Wynona; Rice, Ronald
Newark Bears, 67, 69
Newark City Council, 41, 82,121, 122; first Black member of, 43; and the Krueger-Scott Mansion restoration project, 16–23, 27, 28–32, 36–38. *See also specific city council members*
Newark City Hospital School of Nursing, 111
Newark Eagles, 67–71, *68*, 75, 139
Newark Historical Society, xiv
Newark Housing Authority (NHA), 10, 31, 32, 33, 34, 191n106
Newark Museum, 10, 187n35
Newark Police Department, 27, 45, 135, 149, 187n23; Black police officers in, 134, 150, 152; and community policing, 73; and the rebellion of 1967, 129, 148–150, 153–156, 159, 163; in the summer of 2020, 148–149
Newark Preservation and Landmarks Committee (NPLC), 12, 17, 55
Newark Public Library, 22, 78, 156
Newark Public Schools, 114
Newark-Scott Cultural Center Foundation, 37
Newark *Star-Ledger*: Bernice Bass's obituary in, 81; on the Krueger-Scott Mansion, 14, 16, 17, 18, 19, 25, 26, 28–29, 30, 33, 34
"New Newark" era (1970s), 12, 22
News and Views, 7, 80–82
New York City: *News and Views* in, 81; nursing in, 109, 110; people from, looking for affordable housing in Newark, 121; shopping in, 61, 75; violence in, in 2020, 149
NHA. *See* Newark Housing Authority (NHA)
NJPAC. *See* New Jersey Performing Arts Center (NJPAC)
North Ward (Newark), 2, 29, 117, 202n34
Nurses Guilds, 106, *107*
nursing, 106–112

Obama, Barack, 16
O'Brien, Ellen, 159
Odom, L. Sylvester, 154
O'Kelly-Cooke, Amorel E., 48, 50
Ortiz, Paul, 113
Overmyer, James, 68

Paige, Satchel, 69
Patterson, Mary Jo, 33–34
Payne, Charles, 108, 112
Payne, Donald, 124
Peace Mission Movement, 62, 78
Peddie Memorial Church, 48, 53
Pennsylvania Station, Newark, 19, 137, 146, 185n2
Philadelphia, 1, 109, 149
Phillips, Vel, 11
Pittsburgh, xi, xiii, 8, 104
police. *See* Newark Police Department; police shootings/brutality
police shootings/brutality, 87, 149–150, 154
Polishuk, Sandy, 139
Porambo, Ron, 163
Portelli, Alessandro, 41, 70–71, 119, 137, 155
Potts, Nathaniel, 54
poverty, 1, 3, 92, 96, 135, 143, 146, 167
Powell, Hortense Williams: on bars and taverns, 72; on church, 54–55, 194n54; on government aid/assistance, 94; on work, including in nursing,105, 106, 108–110
Presbyterians, 54, 57, 61, 124. *See also specific churches*
Price, Clement A., 35–36, 38, 87–88, 129, 132, 164, 184
professions, x, 5, 46, 86, 96, 111, 127. *See also* work/employment

INDEX

Prohibition, 72
Prudential Insurance Company: building of, 19; donations by, after the 1967 rebellion, 155; as employer in Newark, 18, 78; expansion of, 8
Pullman Company, xiii

Queen, Bob, 160, 203n66
Queen of Angels Church, 45, 53–56, 118, 193n46

race relations, 41, 43, 45, 66–67, 86, 99, 115, 135, 142
"race riots," xii. *See also* rebellion of 1967 (Newark); Red Summer; Watts riots
racial justice protests of 2020, 131, 148, 149, 165
racism/racial discrimination, 86, 167; in Chicago, 144; as a contributing factor in the rebellion of 1967, 150–151, 153; and fires as a disproportionate burden for Black residents, 132, 143–144; in labor unions, 88; in lending policies, 7; in Newark's shopping district, 76; and the protests of 2020, 131, 148, 149, 165; in the South, x, xi–xii; in voting, 121; in the workplace, 96–97, 100–113, 126; and the WPA, 6–7. *See also* segregation
radio, 78–83
Rainey, Ella, 144–145, 202n34
Randolph, A. Philip, xiii
Rawlins, Willa, 52, 142–143
Reagan, Ronald, administration of, 167
rebellion of 1967 (Newark), 11, 45, 118, 129–134, 137, 138, 144–145, 146–168, 203n67; causes of, 150–156; and the "citizen snipers" story, 162, 163; job opportunities opened up by, 112; looting during, 131, 156, 160–162; media coverage of, 123, 133–134, 163
Red Cross, 108, 136, 143
Red Summer, xii
Rice, Ronald, 20–21, 121, 122, 145
Richards, Ethel, 76, 135
Riot: One City's 30-Year Struggle to Leave Behind Its Worst Week Ever (McLaughlin, 2007), 161–165
"riot" of 1967, Newark. *See* rebellion of 1967 (Newark)
Ritchie, Donald A., 91
Roberts, Mary, 9, 66, 73, 117,131, 141
Robert Treat Hotel, 26, 187n32
Robeson, Paul, 123

Robinson, Henry, 50, 150
Robinson, Jackie, 68–69
Robinson, Thelma B., 52
Roper, Richard, 16
Ross, Sylvia, 61
Roth, Philip, 131
Rountree, Bernice, 106
Rountree, Malachi, 11, 36
Rutgers University–Newark, xiv, 36, 58, 92, 152
Ruuttila, Julia, 139

Sackett, Russell, 163
Sartre, Jean Paul, 119
Satter, Beryl, 9, 78, 144, 161
Schmeling, Max, 83
Schomburg Center for Research in Black Culture, 20
schools. *See* education; Newark Public Schools
Scott, Beverly, 43, 52, 59,135, 167
Scott, Louise (also known as Madam Louise Scott), 2, 23, 37, 75, 80, 153, 186nn14,15, 187n32; biography of, 5–7; daughter of, 20; marriage and divorce of, 11; as a philanthropist, 7, 9, 11–12, 17, 40, 91, 170, 187n32
Scott, Rev. James, 33, 168; on Bethany Baptist, 50, 53; community engagement of, 124–125; on employing Black-owned businesses, 43; on food, 74; on jazz, 72; and the Krueger-Scott Oral History Project, 46; on occupations opening up to Black employees, 110–111, 112; as pastor of Bethany Baptist, 51, 52, 60; on the rebellion of 1967, 166; on the separation between church and state, 125
Scott Cultural and Civic Center, 7, 80
Scott Hotel, 7, 14, 80, 187n23
Scottish Rite Freemasons, 4–5, 7, 24
Scott-Rountree, Rev. Louise, 20, 36
Scott's College of Beauty Culture, 7, 8, 91, 187n32, 188n37
Scudder Homes Association, 10
Second World War. *See* World War II
segregation, xii, 46, 187n32; in churches, 55; in the military, 107–108; in Newark's shopping district, 76; in the North vs. in the South, 69. *See also* desegregation
sexism, 7, 88, 103
Shafer, Jack, 160
sharecropping, x, xi, 127
shoeshining, 64

Shuttlesworth, Fred, 123–124
Slaten, Harvey, 43, 66, 167
slavery and enslaved people, x, 11, 40, 43, 56, 85, 97, 119
Smith, Carl, 137, 145, 147
Smith, Geri, 104–105
Smith, John, 129, 133, 153, 154
Smithsonian's National Museum of African American History and Culture (NMAAHC), 3, 16
Social Security, 98, 99
sociopolitical work, 86, 87, 91, 96–97, 112; women doing, 113–122
South (American): and the Great Migration flight from, ix–xiii. *See also specific states*
South Carolina, xi, 4, 6, 65, 91, 137, 138
South Side High School, 147
South Ward (Newark), 9, 17
Spina, Dominick A., 163
Staupers, Mabel K., 107–108
St. Benedict's Prep, 54, 118, 131
Still, Tim, 154
St. James AME Church, 18, 44, 47, 57, 61, 83, 94
St. Louis, 1, 10; East, uprisings in, xii
St. Patrick's Church, 54
St. Peter's Church, 54
St. Philip's Church, 142
Students for a Democratic Society (SDS), 87
Sundays. *See* baseball; church, Black; dress and fashion; leisure activities; radio
Suttles, Mule, 68
Swain, Marzell, 56, 90, 141, 167
Sylvan, Shirley, 106

Taylor, Kitty, 80, 81
teachers/teaching. *See* education
Telyas, Avi, 36, 37
Third Ward (Newark), 7, 8, 187n25
Thomas, Clarence, 28
Thomas, Edna, 51–52, 154, 187n30; on the need for Black cultural centers/museums, 16, 17, 18; on the rebellion of 1967, 158, 159; on saving the High Street neighborhood, 10–11, 16
Thomas, Isaac, 44–45, 167
Thomas, William, Jr. (first Black Newark firefighter), 134
Thomas, Nancy, 48
Thompson, Eugene, 80, 89, 164
Thompson, Paul, 53

train porters, work as, xiii, 85, 96
Trastulli, Luigi, 156
Trinity Church, 142
Tucker, Donald, 28, 29, 37
Tucker, Rose, 76
Turner, Irvine, 43
Turner, Lewis, 132

UCC. *See* United Community Corporation (UCC)
unemployment/underemployment, 1, 89, 93, 99, 106, 162
unions. *See* labor unions
United Community Corporation (UCC), 117, 142, 155, 166
uprising in Newark. *See* rebellion of 1967 (Newark)
Urban League, 52, 125
urban preservation movement, 12, 14
urban renewal, 9, 78, 118, 161
US House of Representatives, 124

Vaughan, Sarah, 72, 73, 195n107
Vergara, Camilo Jose, 32
Villani, Marie, 22–23
Villani, Ralph, 22
vocational education/training. *See* work/employment: getting work, and vocational education
voting/voter registration, x, 113, 121, 200n64; claims of ballot fraud, 121

Walker, Madam C. J., 5, 7, 186n14
Wallace, Carolyn, 89; on church's importance, 43; on the Newark Eagles, 69; political activism of, 114–115; on the rebellion of 1967, 131; work of, as a nurse, 106; youth work of, 115, 117, 122
Washington, Andrew, 66
Washington, Booker T., 127
water safety, 9
Watkins, Clara, 67
Watson, Jackson, 48
Watson, JoAnne Y., 33
Watts Riots, 147, 203n67
WBHI, 78, 80
Weisenfeld, Judith, 62
welfare. *See* government aid/assistance
Wesley, Milton, 57–58
West Ward (Newark), 17, 20, 29, 121, 126
West, Calvin, 72–73, 74, 75, 118
West, Cynthia S'thembile, 62
Whelan, Jean C., 106, 110

Whelchel, L. H., Jr., 40, 123–124
white community, Newark: authority shifting away from, in urban centers, 8; churches for, 50; flight of from Newark and other urban centers, 4–5, 160; relations of, with Black community, 41, 43, 45, 66–67, 86, 99, 115, 135, 142; religiosity of, 46
Whitney Houston Foundation, 18
Wilkerson, Isabel, 63
Wilkerson, Owen, 75; on bars and taverns, 73; on the Black faith community, 57, 59, 60, 64–65; on dress, 64–65; on fear and stress from growing up Black, 158–159; on fires in Newark, 136, 143, 201n13, 202n24; on government assistance, 67; on the rebellion of 1967, 160–161, 162, 166, 167, 203n66; on segregation, 70; on white people offering material aid to Black families, 94
Williams, Junius, 41, 148
Williams, Marion, 77, 131–132
Williams, Ronnie, 73
WNJR, 78, 80, 82
women: and community activism, 87, 113–122; gendered rules for, 65; in the Great Migration, xi; inclusion of in oral histories, 53; lack of, in police and fire departments, 134; working for the first time as a result of the war, x
Woodruff, Connie, 80, *81*

Woods, Rev. Robert: on Black firemen, 135; career path of, 102, 103–104, 126; on the church's importance, 41–42; on clergy's importance, 125–126; on domestics, 89; on racism in the workplace, 103; on radio listening, 78; on the rebellion of 1967, 112, 150, 151–152, 162, 164
work/employment, ix–xiii, 85–88; domestic, for women, xi, 6, 43, 85, 87, 88–91, 96, 97; getting work, and vocational education, 99–106; in the military, 100,107–108; in the ministry, 122–126; non-domestic, for women, 91–99; nursing, 106–112. *See also* professions
Works Progress Administration (WPA), 6, 87
World War I, xii, 87
World War II, x, 78, 80, 97, 118; Black laborers and women lose jobs after, 87, 92, 94; and the economy, 7; and Newark's production of war material, 130; and segregation of Black military nurses, 107–108
Wright, Charles H., 2
Wright, Giles, 37, 38, 50, 59, 88, 132

Yamba, Zachary, 54
youth. *See* children/youth

Zach, Alvin, 19, 23, 24
Zion Hill Baptist Church, 44, 57–58, 65

About the Author

Katie Singer has a PhD in American studies from Rutgers University–Newark and an MFA in creative writing from Fairleigh Dickinson University. She recently completed cowriting a memoir centering on a friend's time in prison and is teaching college courses in history and writing in her new home of Los Angeles. She also coaches boxing twice a week at her local gym.

Her writing consists of articles, essays, short stories, poetry, and a blog. Dr. Singer has published in a number of journals, newspapers, and anthologies, from *New Jersey Studies*, the *Washington Post*, and *Food, Migration, and Diversity: The Many Flavors of the Short Story*.

Dr. Singer has presented at conferences, in the United States and abroad, upon topics that include preservation, oral history, racial justice, African American literature, and African American historical commemoration. Public scholarship projects include the creation of an oral history video archive for her church, as well as historical guidebooks for bus tours of Newark, New Jersey. She is presently volunteering at the Center for Restorative Justice in Pasadena, California.

Singer is currently working on a collection of linked short stories featuring women "of a certain age" and a memoir following her religious trajectory. She has two fabulous adult children and lives with her somewhat odd but endearing cat, Skittles.

Available titles in the Ceres: Rutgers Studies in History series

James M. Carter, *Rockin' in the Ivory Tower: Rock Music on Campus in the Sixties*
Thomas Gustafson, *American Anti-Pastoral: Brookside, New Jersey and the Garden State of Philip Roth*
Jordan P. Howell, *Garbage in the Garden State*
Maxine N. Lurie, *Taking Sides in Revolutionary New Jersey: Caught in the Crossfire*
Jean R. Soderlund, *Separate Paths: Lenapes and Colonists in West New Jersey*
Camilla Townsend and Nicky Kay Michael, eds., *On the Turtle's Back: Stories the Lenape Told Their Grandchildren*
Hettie V. Williams, *The Georgia of the North: Black Women and the Civil Rights Movement in New Jersey*